This book shares key lessons from a range of exceptional leaders who provide unique insights into the nature of change and navigating uncertainty. ADI IGNATIUS, EDITOR IN CHIEF, HARVARD BUSINESS REVIEW

Never has the importance of courage and empathy been more critical for navigating change in an uncertain world. AMY C. EDMONDSON, NOVARTIS PROFESSOR OF LEADERSHIP AND MANAGEMENT, HARVARD BUSINESS SCHOOL

To face the world's dramatic changes, *The Change Mindset* is both a fresh and indispensable book for leaders today. Vive la différence! MAURICE LEVY, CHAIRMAN OF THE SUPERVISORY BOARD, PUBLICIS GROUPE

This new research concerning transitions is inspiring and exciting. It gives us the opportunity to examine oneself, to walk in huge steps through our own life and consider our different stages, contrary forces and paradoxes. ANDREAS JUNG, CREATOR OF THE MUSEUM HOUSE, C.G. JUNG

The Change Mindset combines fascinating case studies with insightful stories on how leaders can embrace change. A must-read for entrepreneurs facing new challenges with courage and empathy in today's post-Covid-19 world. PASCAL CAGNI, FOUNDER AND CEO OF C4 VENTURES, VICE PRESIDENT OF APPLE EMEIA (2000–2012)

It's hard to figure out the right way forward in today's turbulent world. In this fascinating new book, Andy Craggs provides you with the playbook you need. Based on many years' experience as a coach and consultant, *The Change Mindset* takes you through the obstacles to progress and identifies the key things you need to do to navigate the difficult transitions many of us face today. JULIAN BIRKINSHAW, PROFESSOR STRATEGY AND ENTREPRENEURSHIP, LONDON BUSINESS SCHOOL

As we peer from the present into the future, uncertainty and change loom large. In *The Change Mindset*, Andy Craggs provides a framework and practical guidance for how you can navigate a path forward with control and confidence, and seek not just a transition but your transition. ANDREW SCOTT, PROFESSOR OF ECONOMICS, LONDON BUSINESS SCHOOL

Andy Craggs' new book draws on lessons from a wide range of notable leaders who share their own experiences of change in a unique collection of stories and insights. The resulting psychological framework and change toolkit that emerge are powerful, fresh, and practical, providing a new route to tackling the leadership challenges we all face today. The twin practices of Courage and Empathy stand out as the critical skills for navigating change in our uncertain world, while self-awareness and the value of deep reflection become evident as we discover and explore our inner change archetypes as dreamers, drivers, shapers and sherpas. Find out how to build your own Change Mindset and more successfully navigate your biggest challenges as a leader in your own field of practice. A relevant and timely book in today's ongoing unpredictable Covid-19 world. DR L. MEE YAN CHEUNG JUDGE, FOUNDER, QUALITY AND EQUALITY LTD AND ACADEMIC OD PRACTITIONER

The Change Mindset

*The psychology of leading and thriving
in an uncertain world*

Andy Craggs

Kogan Page
INSPIRE

First published in Great Britain and the United States in 2022 by Kogan Page Limited

2nd Floor, 45 Gee Street	8 W 38th Street, Suite 902	4737/23 Ansari Road
London	New York, NY 10018	Daryaganj
EC1V 3RS	USA	New Delhi 110002
United Kingdom		India

www.koganpage.com

Kogan Page books are printed on paper from sustainable forests.

© Andy Craggs, 2022

ISBNs

Hardback	978 1 3986 0494 0
Paperback	978 1 3986 0492 6
Ebook	978 1 3986 0493 3

British Library Cataloguing-in-Publication Data
A CIP record for this book is available from the British Library.

Library of Congress Cataloging-in-Publication Data
Names: Craggs, Andy, author.
Title: The change mindset : the psychology of leading and thriving in an uncertain world / Andy Craggs.
Description: London, United Kingdom ; New York, NY : Kogan Page, 2022. | Includes bibliographical references and index. | Summary: "In The Change Mindset, leadership development expert Andy Craggs unpicks the main reasons why teams fail when it comes to dealing with change and navigating uncertainty. He defines the common traps that lead to failure; from not allowing yourself to reimagine the possible, mimicking the behaviour that your competition has shown when dealing with change, to doubting yourself and your team. Leading through change requires business leaders to be courageous and to show empathy, both for themselves and their people. With those attributes, this book, which is steeped in behavioural and organizational psychology analysis, catapults you to developing meaningful and long-lasting adaptability and resilience in the face of uncertainty"– Provided by publisher.
Identifiers: LCCN 2022012707 (print) | LCCN 2022012708 (ebook) | ISBN 9781398604940 (hardback) | ISBN 9781398604926 (paperback) | ISBN 9781398604933 (ebook)
Subjects: LCSH: Organizational change. | Leadership. | Change (Psychology)
Classification: LCC HD58.8 .C6953 2022 (print) | LCC HD58.8 (ebook) | DDC 658.4/06–dc23/eng/20220314
LC record available at https://lccn.loc.gov/2022012707
LC ebook record available at https://lccn.loc.gov/2022012708

Typeset by Integra Software Services, Pondicherry
Print production managed by Jellyfish
Printed and bound by CPI Group (UK) Ltd, Croydon CR0 4YY

To Charles Handy, who first asked me the question,
'Do you have a book in you?'

Contents

List of figures and tables

Acknowledgements

Three distinct moments that each occurred about five years apart sowed the seeds for this book.

The first happened when my friend and mentor, Charles Handy, invited my wife and me to lunch at his country home in Norfolk, England with his wife Liz. After a tour of the property, which included a visit to his extensive library, writing room, the croquet lawn, and a view of the surrounding countryside, we settled down to a home-cooked meal on an unusually sunny English afternoon overlooking the rippling wheat fields of East Anglia.

Over coffee Charles looked at me and asked, 'Andy, do you think you have a book in you?' I was slightly intimidated by this question coming from someone who had written over 20 bestselling management books during his 30-year career, with multiple nominations to the Thinkers 50 list of recognized global management experts. I said, 'Well Charles, I would love to, but I have no idea what it would be about, and I'm not sure I could say anything worthwhile.' He smiled, took a sip of his coffee and left it at that.

Charles is a wonderful teacher and mentor because, of course, that question stayed lodged in the back of my mind from that moment on.

The second moment occurred a few years later when I was running an executive education programme for London Business School with a group of senior leaders from a global retail organization. During a coffee break I was having a conversation with Lisa Robinson-Davis, an American executive at the company who in her role was sharing her time between the US and the UK. I had also spent 15 years working in America, and the conversation turned to the various challenges the world seemed to be facing, particularly the alarming polarization we were both witnessing across society in our respective countries. I said something like, 'I wish there were a platform to put these questions onto a bigger stage so we could make better progress navigating change.' It seemed to me we were stagnating as a society, not only in America but also in other countries, unable to successfully manage change around a wide range of social problems that appeared to be multiplying.

Lisa looked at me very wisely – reminding me of Maya Angelou in her tone – and said simply, 'Andy, I believe when the time is right, your voice will be heard.' Those words also stayed with me and along with Charles' question came back into my mind in the third moment, in early 2020, when it was clear the world was experiencing an event unprecedented in modern times when the global Covid-19 pandemic first began to hit.

In those early days, the most startling change for me was the impact of the Covid-19 pandemic on people's personal and professional lives beyond the immediate health crisis and the havoc it was wreaking on lives and families around the world. Nationwide lockdowns, arrested economic activity, supply chain shortages and widespread job losses were all new and unintended consequences of this seismic shift, in addition to the physical and mental health effects of the disease for millions around the world. It was inflicting extraordinary changes on life as we knew it.

As we were hit by subsequent waves of the pandemic during 2020, what I also noticed was a depressingly consistent pattern of response from global leaders and institutions to this new and unanticipated threat. We were seeing the kinds of management traps that Charles Handy had been writing about for decades: the dangers of poor communication during uncertainty, our tendency to ignore collaboration when tackling big problems, and the importance of engaging and listening to others rather than distancing ourselves and assigning blame. These messages are abundantly clear in his work and the work of other management experts as keys to effective leadership during change and uncertainty, but they seemed entirely absent in those early days and months of the crisis.

The private sector fared no better, as most businesses continued to chase profits and cut costs in response to lowered demand while holding onto their cash hoards that could have been put to better common use. Big Pharma and Big Tech might have helped significantly in the early days by sharing IP to accelerate research and vaccine production, or by donating idle billions – most of which sit in dormant offshore tax havens – to systems such as track-and-trace or data analytics about global infection rates.

There were some inspiring highlights with brilliant scientists like Chemistry Nobel Laureate Jennifer Doudna creating new Covid-19 detection technology, along with Oxford's Professor Sarah Gilbert and Professor Uğur Sahin, and Dr. Özlem Türeci of BioNTech as they developed a clutch of highly effective new Covid-19 vaccines in record time. It seemed they were among the few displaying the courage, commitment and collaboration needed to respond to this very real and very new threat to global human wellbeing.

But the varied and mostly dismal responses to change in early 2020 as we went deeper into the Covid-19 crisis rekindled those two moments with Charles and Lisa.

Was there something new we could learn about navigating change, especially in a crisis? Could I find a way to discover this and could I share it in a way so it could be useful to other leaders?

I floated this question to a few trusted colleagues and hit on the idea of investigating how other leaders had experienced their own moments of crisis and transitional change, and trying to extract lessons learned. What had made them fail or succeed in such moments, and could there be some new insights or solutions about how to navigate the new 'Black Swan' events we were witnessing?

Over the next 18 months I continued to pose this question to several dozen leaders from business, academia, social enterprises, the arts, conservation, journalism, politics and medicine. I approached entrepreneurs in small start-ups as well as executives in large corporates. I deliberately sought leaders across sectors, professions, countries, cultures and disciplines to gather diverse and inclusive views about navigating change. Together, these remarkable leaders have helped me uncover some powerful new insights into dealing with the increased pace of change and the inevitable transitions they cause for us as leaders and human beings in our 'never normal' world.

It has become clear to me that being more skilled at navigating major transitions is now a daily requirement for all of us, whether we are actively leading others in an organizational context or simply leading ourselves through personal and professional endeavours against a backdrop of increasing uncertainty.

On this journey of discovery, I have been extremely fortunate to be guided by superb friends and mentors. Professor Jules Goddard from the London Business School, himself a recognized author on business and the philosophy of leadership, has greatly shaped my thinking. Adi Ignatius, Editor in Chief of the Harvard Business Review and a former colleague from The Wall Street Journal, helped me shape the narrative with his unparalleled journalistic instincts and storytelling skills. Finally, Sir Andrew Likierman, the previous Dean at the London Business School and now a Professor of Management researching the intriguing question of judgement in an age of AI, has generously shared his wisdom and his keen eye for detail as I formulated the ideas for this book.

To these people, and to all my interviewees who generously offered their time and personal stories, I say thank you. You planted the early seeds of this work and helped them to germinate into a clear idea.

My hope is that the result of this work will contribute new ideas and insights about change as we confront one of the biggest transitional challenges the world has faced in the new millennium.

I must also extend my thanks to those others who helped me think through the book's main premise, provided invaluable feedback, or shared their own stories of change: Pascal Cagni, Géraldine Collard, Andreas Jung, Penny Lawrence, Maurice Lévy, Ed Marsh, John McMahon, Laure de Panafieu, Maria Papadopoulos, and Gabriele Reuter.

Introduction

The road to Shigatse

Almost exactly twenty years ago I was travelling along the Freedom Highway across the Tibetan plateau between Lhasa, the spiritual home of Tibetan Buddhism, and Tashi Lhunpo, one of the oldest monasteries in Tibet. Since it was founded in the 15th Century, it has been a place of worship and rest for pilgrims on the long road to Lhasa. At the time of our visit, the monastery was still active, with a small coterie of saffron-robed monks sweeping the dusty courtyard and tending to one of the oldest libraries of ancient Tibetan scripts in the world. When we arrived, we found a group of them reading from linen-wrapped wooden prayer tablets in the flickering light of yak-butter candles. As they chanted the Tibetan mantras, the low hum of their voices seemed to pass gently through the billowing curtains to echo into the surrounding Himalayan valleys.

I had been inspired to take this voyage by the photographs of environmentalist Yann Arthus-Bertrand and the films of anthropologist Éric Valli, and had set off from Los Angeles with a dream to learn about and document the fast-disappearing monasteries and cultures of Tibetan Buddhism. I had received a 3-week travel permit from the Chinese government to venture as far as I could along the road that connected the Tibetan capital of Lhasa to the Nepalese and Chinese borders, and we were accompanied on the journey by a government-approved Tibetan guide and a driver. We made our way in a very old Jeep that rattled along at about 30 miles an hour on the corrugated dirt road that stretched like a thin brown ribbon across the 5,000-metre plateau surrounded by towering Himalayan peaks. Our two travel companions were wonderful company with enough rudimentary English to explain the local landscape and history.

One morning about a week into the journey as we bumped along the road, a lone bicycle appeared over the horizon. Its movement kicked up a thin trail of dust rising behind the cyclist from the unpaved road that was swept away in a thin veil by the wind. As it came closer the small figure that had been silhouetted against the piercing blue sky emerged more clearly into view and I could see that it was not a Tibetan traveller but a young Westerner who appeared to be cycling alone on this remote 500-mile-long unmarked road. The explorer turned out to be a young American from Oregon, Tad Beckwith. He was in the middle of a 20-country solo cycling tour for a non-profit organization he had created. As he told me with great energy and enthusiasm, his goal was 'to increase cross-cultural empathy and under-standing between students around the world'.

As one does when travelling in faraway places, we exchanged notes on the route and what we had seen and scribbled down our addresses and landline phone numbers back home. This was well before contact-sharing on iPhones or the convenience of the internet and Google Maps. We prom-ised to reconnect back in America when we had returned from our adventures and went our separate ways. I remember watching him recede between the rocky hillsides that flanked the road until I could no longer read the small tattered flag snapping in the cold wind that read 'PeaceBike'.

Twenty years later as I began this book on change and transitions, Tad was one of the first people I thought of. After some fairly exhaustive research on the Internet and LinkedIn I eventually found out that what had started as a one-man NGO had eventually connected over 15,000 students globally as a result of his epic bike ride and subsequent volunteer work. All that had been created by one 20-year-old kid with a bike and a big idea to provoke change – an idea compelling him to leave Oregon and launch his dream on a bigger world stage.

Today, the question I wanted to ask him was: what were the attributes and mindset that allowed you to set off from a medium-sized town on the West Coast of America to pedal your way halfway across Asia on two small wheels and one big idea? His decision to launch that project seemed to capture the spirit of navigating transitional change – which to him was seeing something in the world that urgently needed change, feeling compelled to take it on, and then executing a plan with courage and clarity to make a difference. I wanted to find out more about people like him and what they might teach us about navigating the huge changes being forced on us by the global Covid-19 pandemic.

I began my research by approaching other entrepreneurs, leaders, and academics on the subject of their own transitions. I again thought of Charles Handy and he became the first name on my interview list. Our conversation took me to his lovely home in Putney near London, where over the years he had been fond of receiving guests for 'breakfast chats'. With characteristic humour and humility, he refers to these as the way he keeps himself educated about the world, by listening to stories and ideas from guests around his kitchen table over tea and biscuits. It is a deliberately informal and therefore thought-provoking setting.

As I began to speak to Charles about his own remarkable life and managing moments of transitional change, I found him recounting some analogous stories to those of my friend from Oregon. While less physically adventurous, Handy's own journey to seek the bigger stage, explore the world and provoke change on a large scale was really the same psychological journey as Tad and PeaceBike. Like Tad, Handy's writings have created global impact by challenging traditional management practices and triggering permanent changes in how leaders create and run their organizations. His early shamrock organization theory presaged today's virtual and hybrid working practices, while books like *The Empty Raincoat* foresaw the rise of the portfolio career and the gig economy.

What was it that gave him such foresight, and how did he use this to change our fundamental understanding of organizations?

The answers emerged during our conversation in Putney. As the stirring leaves of the centenary maple trees surrounding the house threw dappled shadows across his study floor, Charles reminisced about how he grew up in modest surroundings in a small town in County Kildare, Ireland, the son of the local archdeacon. It was very far away from the world of global business that he would later inhabit. Our conversation turned to the question of what makes us choose between staying where we are – literally or figuratively – as 'a big person on a small stage', the choice made by his father in his small Irish parish for example, or embracing change in an attempt to become a 'small person on a big stage'. Charles himself chose the latter path and left Ireland as a young man to build a career that has spanned business, academia, writing, consulting and philosophy. Today he is a recipient of that curiously British distinction, *The Most Excellent Order of the British Empire*, or OBE.

In his case he did rather well in the end as a 'big person on a big stage' and when I asked how he had successfully managed these transitions it was clearly his courage to act and constant curiosity that allowed him to achieve them. It was also clear that his energy for further change and new ideas remains undiminished even in his mid-80s. As I walked back through the quiet suburb towards the tube station, it struck me that Handy's courage and determination were also paired with openness towards others, no matter their background or rank, and a good dose of self-inquiry. Together these attributes have allowed him to successfully navigate his many personal and professional transitions.

After Handy, my next goal was to seek perspectives and insights from an equally successful female leader about transitional change. For this, Gillian Tett was first on my list. She is the US Editor at Large for the *Financial Times* and a multiple award-winning author on economics and anthropology. She is a regular presence at global forums on business and finance where she challenges world leaders with her insights and analysis. She broadly predicted – and then explained – the 2007 Financial Crisis in her book *Fool's Gold* (Tett, 2009) and her subsequent bestseller *The Silo Effect* (Tett, 2015) that provided further insight into the dangers of excessive specialization, assumed expertise and groupthink that often lead to similar organizational and leadership blind spots. I was fortunate enough to meet Tett at an FT event a few years earlier through some mutual connections in journalism and publishing, and a few months after tea with Charles she was speaking to me via Zoom from her home in New York.

Yet despite her undeniable success as a world recognized expert, like Handy she recounted a similar story about finding courage in the face of uncertainty as she pursued a bigger stage despite a host of challenges. She described to me first her 'safe' upbringing in England 'where girls were really not supposed to do anything at all'. Her insatiable curiosity and 'desire to travel to weird places' led her to volunteer work in Pakistan, followed by anthropology studies and field work in Tajikistan. Her exploratory mindset served her well on the FT news desk during her internship in the summer of 1991. As the Soviet Union was collapsing she was the only person in the building who spoke Russian, so without hesitation, and at a very young age, she volunteered to go back to the Soviet Union for the unique opportunity to cover the momentous events of that time from the front line. Her advice for navigating such moments of transition successfully is simply, 'Give yourself permission to roam and collide with the unexpected.' This maverick mindset created her own road to Shigatse, and set her up for a long and successful career of bold and provocative ventures such as the think tank Moral Money that challenges leaders about the social and human consequences of their financial decisions, and her new book *Anthro-Vision* that yet again challenges our assumptions about the human dynamics of business and leadership (Tett, 2021).

We will encounter these leaders again later in the book, but for me these three encounters encapsulate some of the early insights into what it takes to successfully embrace and navigate significant transitions and moments of change in life and as leaders. I decided to call this rare ability the Change Mindset.

In my research on the subject of building the Change Mindset it was also clear to me that the leaders I had chosen to interview were the exceptions in a more general world of people struggling to cope with change and uncertainty. My experience suggests that, more often than not, while most of us have a desire to change ourselves, our organizations or the world for the better, we often fail in action and in execution. Maybe we lack the insight or the requisite characteristics to navigate new pathways towards a bigger stage. Perhaps we are discouraged by the difficulty of the process, or put off by the likelihood of failure. Indeed many 'successful' leaders I have worked with and coached do in fact seek the 'larger stage', be it for themselves or to help those they lead, yet will remain undecided and often fail when it comes to real action. In some cases, the more senior and experienced these leaders are, the more they can become trapped by their rigid assumptions or learned routines – which are often invisible to them but that pull them away from realizing their potential or achieving their ambitions as powerful change agents.

But as we saw from Tad, Charles and Gillian, there are others who do manage to navigate transitions with energy and conviction despite the associated uncertainty and risks. These people become role models and the inspiration for others in times of change and disruption, and my question as I started to interview more leaders about this was: what is it that you do differently?

Finding answers to this important question is the aim of this book, and translating them into a set of principles, frameworks and practical tools for leaders to improve their own success rates when faced with transitional moments is what I hope to offer the reader.

How this book is organized

This book explores how to build a Change Mindset and the process of navigating transitions in three ways:

1 Defining transitional change, explaining how it is distinct from other change situations, why it is challenging, and what we can learn from connecting the psychology of change to our natural developmental journeys as human beings.
2 Sharing insights and experiences from other leaders across a spectrum of professions, and analyzing their lessons learned from their own change challenges and transitions, including successes as well as where they failed and why.
3 Developing a set of principles and a practical toolkit to improve our own ability to navigate change transitions by building a Change Mindset as we confront change and uncertainty as individuals, teams, or organizations.

In Chapter 1, I ask the question 'What is transitional change and why is it prone to failure?' The modern world offers us unprecedented choice, yet the more we have the less sure we become about defining what 'success' should be for us. Inevitably, this creates anxiety as we are faced with frequent and unavoidable transitions, which are moments when we must act despite great uncertainty. There is no easy formula to deal with this, but we can start by attempting to understand the paradoxes of change and the psychology behind our reactions to it.

Chapter 2 looks at our human experience of life as a metaphor for leading change. Research from human development, behavioural science and psychology all give us clues about how to prepare for and manage change in our personal and professional lives. Chapter 3 continues this theme by looking at the components of our life journey and how they form the basis for our change capabilities. Questions surrounding who we are, what we choose to do, how we give ourselves permission to act, and why we make the choices we do are universal and create a framework to develop a greater sense of agency and self-determination in the face of change. In Chapter 4 I start to build the Change Mindset framework in more detail, beginning with the core skills of courage and empathy. My interviews revealed that in moments of change it is courage that gives us the internal power to move forward. But we also need empathy to ensure we do so in ways that integrate the external context and the needs of others.

The proper mastery of these two skills is critical for a successful Change Mindset, but there are also traps and blind spots. These are the FAIL factors that we must learn to recognize and master: framing, asking, imitation and limitation. In Chapter 5, stories I heard from leaders who have been caught in these traps provide lessons learned about how to avoid repeating them ourselves, as teams, or across organizations.

Luckily, there are also helpful triggers that can boost our Change Mindset and our ability to navigate transitions. In Chapter 6 I explore these SPARK practices: spirit, partnership, alternatives, reason and knowledge, and look more closely at how to activate them.

Chapter 7 pulls together these concepts into a transitions masterclass where I present four powerful change archetypes: dreamers, drivers, shapers and sherpas. I believe that each one of us has a dominant change archetype that is linked to our life stage development and experience and whose natural power can greatly enhance our Change Mindset to navigate bigger and more complex change. Alongside the previous tools of courage, empathy, SPARK and FAIL, I show how these can help our 'change muscles' stay fit.

Of course, it is also important to actually put these tools into practice. So Chapter 8 offers a Change Mindset toolkit to improve decision making in uncertainty. Five simple but effective tools allow the reader to readily assess their current capabilities across a range of change factors. Assessments and worksheets provide space to analyse current change challenges and plan appropriate action. The tools can be used for individual assessment and reflection, as a coaching tool for groups, for teams to assess their collective change skills, or at an organizational level to foster innovation, agility or nudge culture towards greater adaptability.

These tools, instructions and templates are also available online for easy downloading and application in any individual, team or organizational context and include:

1 The change lifeline
2 The courage and empathy pyramid
3 The change readiness index
4 The archetype finder
5 The life stage ladder

And last but certainly not least, these new insights would not have been possible without the generosity of the leaders I interviewed for this book. I celebrate these 25 exceptional individuals in Chapter 9 with their top three lessons learned about change and one key piece of advice for others seeking to better navigate transitions and build their own Change Mindset.

In summary, we are all faced with crossroads in both life and business when we are forced to change something fundamental about ourselves. But often we find ourselves paralysed by lack of knowledge or insight. My hope is that this collection of stories, lessons learned, frameworks and tools will help the reader better succeed in their own key moments of change.

CHAPTER ONE

What is transitional change and why is it prone to failure?

Human nature makes the right behaviors really hard.
AMY EDMONDSON, HARVARD BUSINESS SCHOOL

This was the short answer provided by the Novartis Professor of Leadership and Management at Harvard University in response to the question posed by the title of this chapter. Transitional conditions trigger a series of unhelpful behaviours that make it surprisingly hard for us to react positively and rationally. But before examining why, let us first define transitional change.

What is transitional change?

Webster defines a transition as:

> The movement, passage, or change from one state or stage to another

In the context of leadership, I will define transitional change as:

> Any situation where we are forced to modify who we are and how we operate as the result of unavoidable, external and often unexpected events

Satya Nadella, CEO of Microsoft, identified such a threat when he joined the company, leading him to architect one of the best recognized transformations in modern corporate history as Amazon, Google and others began to erode Microsoft's dominant position. Faced with this undeniable need for change, Nadella galvanized his people to act together, transforming Microsoft from a traditional desktop software company (Windows) to a new cloud computing, services, gaming and innovation firm (Teams, Skype, LinkedIn and Azure).

Such transitional change situations have become more and more prevalent as we face growing complexity in our personal, professional and business lives. Emerging business models, global economic interdependence, unstable geopolitics, social movements such as Black Lives Matter and #MeToo, and accelerating megatrends such as climate change and sustainability all play a part. The global pandemic has put into sharp relief the fact that we control relatively little of our real external environment, and how we must constantly adapt to our increasingly complex and interdependent world.

This so-called VUCA world (Volatile, Uncertain, Complex, Ambiguous) is not new. Recognized as a model for the US Military to describe the so-called 'fog of war', it is the basis of a system that teaches soldiers specialized skills to become more agile and adaptable in extreme uncertainty and danger. VUCA has been the subject of management theories for decades but there is no doubt that the factors making up this acronym have all accelerated significantly in recent years.

What is new, therefore, is the expectation that all of us – not just elite soldiers – must now cope with living in a VUCA world as we manage the so-called 'new normal'. Today we are expected to manage complex technology from virtual meeting software to social media platforms, agile systems and AI-controlled processes. We are expected to remain online 24/7 to oversee work projects. We are increasingly monitored to ensure maximum productivity and efficiency in our work patterns (think Amazon warehouses), and software now even challenges our logic and corrects our decisions based on algorithms (think professional services firms). The average worker, often hired remotely, working from home and never having met their colleagues in person or having seen a real office, is expected to take decisions on their own, in remote situations, often with minimal training or supervision, and still be right. We are expected to navigate a much higher degree and complexity compared with our more 'linear' organizational life of a decade or two ago. This may not be the 'fog of war' but it is certainly becoming the 'fog of work'.

Thus, as we are faced with more frequent and complex transitions and change, we are forced to modify something fundamental about how we work, live, or interact with others. These transitions can of course be opportunities as well as threats. Indeed, the *Financial Times* reported in May 2021 an unexpected consequence of the Covid-19 pandemic that inspired the strongest start-up boom in Britain in a decade, with business incorporations up 22 per cent. The FT described our positive reactions to this transitional challenge: 'Some former employees have been forced to strike out on their own after losing their jobs, while others have reassessed their priorities during repeated lockdowns.'

Whether opportunities or threats, such transitions face us with uncertain choices that must be taken despite unknown consequences. The key difference between transitions and other 'change' is their imposed nature, which demands a conscious and deliberate reaction from us as individuals and as leaders.

Why is transitional change accelerating in today's world?

My colleagues at the futurist consultancy TomorrowToday Global have identified five major factors impacting our lives and our roles as leaders in today's world. The acronym TIDES covers technology, institutions, demographics, environment, and societal values (Codrington, 2010). Looking at these through our own lens of change and transitions, it is clear that each of these megatrends is contributing to the acceleration of transitional change.

Technology

Much has been written about the acceleration of technology. Today most of the world's seven billion people are actively using technology platforms every day in the form of Facebook, Amazon and Google in the West, and Alibaba, WeChat, and Weibo in the East. While these 'Super Apps' and platforms can greatly facilitate our lives, there is a well-documented dark side to them. The pressures from constantly being online and needing to respond to others is a known source of fatigue and burnout. The mental health issues associated with comparing oneself to a perceived peer group has been well documented in films such as *The Social Dilemma*. Platforms such as Instagram have come under scrutiny again and again for promoting unrealistic body images or lifestyles that tempt young people to fake or exaggerate their own reality. This backlash against Big Tech points to an increasing wariness from the public towards these organizations who know so much about our behavioral patterns and hold so much of our personal and financial data.

But there is more. The 2019 book *Invisible Women* by Caroline Criado Perez won the Financial Times and McKinsey Business Book of the Year Award for exposing data bias in artificial intelligence (AI). Even with the best design intentions, our algorithms can easily fall prey to the shadow of discrimination and skewed decisions (Criado Perez, 2019). Author Sherry Turkle of MIT has also flagged the dangers of digital algorithms, in her case as early as 1984 in *The Second Self* (Turkle, 1984). She has written more recently in *The Empathy Diaries* of the acceleration of this phenomenon as almost everybody on the planet now interacts with technology and feeds data into the matrix (Turkle, 2021). In another example, Sir Andrew Likierman shared with me how he has dedicated his post as the dean of the London Business School to investigating the role of human judgment in leadership. It is a brave attempt to tackle the thorny question of, as he says, 'what to do when you run out of data.' The *Harvard Business Review* has already published his work and this kind of analysis is going to prove ever more critical as we enter the more complex areas and moral dilemmas associated with Big Data, AI, and Quantum Computing.

On the positive side, technology has also greatly facilitated the international cooperation required to expedite the development mRNA and other viable vaccines against Covid-19. Hydrogen power, once an unattainable dream for clean energy, is now becoming a realistic potential alternative to fossil fuels for energy and mobility. And the reusable space rockets of Space-X have greatly reduced the cost and pollution associated with space travel and the deployment of further orbital and extra-terrestrial ventures. Governments are also leveraging technology more effectively today. Lord Parry Mitchell, the technology entrepreneur and member of the House of Lords, explained to me how he regularly advises the UK government on technology and digital issues. He has been instrumental in policies that have benefited education, data protection in the NHS and the national vote system, proving that Tech for Good in centralized government can be a powerful force for change.

The key point is that whether for good or evil, technology continues to accelerate and transitions abound in this area.

Institutions

The Covid-19 pandemic has made institutions the brunt of frequent criticism. When the WHO hesitated to declare the virus a pandemic and then failed to fully investigate the source of the infection with effective diplomacy, it lost much of its credibility. The EU has also come under attack from health professionals, the press and the public for a slow approach to its initial vaccine acquisition and deployment. In the financial realm, despite some headline grabbing fines by the EU, most governments have failed to effectively extract a fairer share of tax revenue from tech giants. Thus, the need for more effective management of transitions at the institutional level is clear. As Julian Birkinshaw of the London Business School has written in his book *Fast Forward*, institutions often find themselves playing catch up to business and society when it comes to transitions (Birkinshaw, 2017).

Demographics

Transitions and their challenges span all ages. The so-called 'millennials' have been much maligned for their 'snowflake' image of oversensitivity, lack of perspective and melting at the first sign of criticism or challenge. However, they will be the future global leaders running our businesses and governments, and will most likely bring a new and more sustainable mindset to the task. Despite being brushed off by the establishment, more and more aspiring young leaders are demanding improvements to inequality, injustice and accountability from the incumbent leaders.

At the other end of the spectrum, Lynda Gratton and Andrew Scott of London Business School talk about the second, third or even fourth career journeys we face in *The 100 Year Life*. Longer life expectancies and a trend towards continuing personal development for older professionals are creating a new cohort of potential teachers, mentors, innovators and entrepreneurs (Gratton and Scott, 2017).

Young and old will need to navigate multiple transitions as they move into these new roles and responsibilities.

Environment

The UN, the G-7 and successive COP conferences have struggled to create a coherent narrative or enforceable rules for carbon emissions, offsets, net zero and other environmental initiatives. The COP 26 in Glasgow failed to produce a credible transition plan from fossil fuel and barely managed to reinstate the previous 2015 Paris Agreement in a series of watered-down statements despite vocal protest by environmental groups.

But despite failures at COP26 and a lack of commitment from many of the largest companies and countries on sustainability initiatives, the environment remains firmly on the global political and commercial agendas. And some action is occurring. Activists like Greta Thunberg and movements like Extinction Rebellion regularly highlight the potential impact of climate change. Some recent ESG (environmental, social and governance) guidelines and activist investor pressures have accelerated the trend towards more responsible investing. Think tanks such as Moral Money created by Gillian Tett at the *Financial Times* are making inroads with strategies to support the UN's Sustainable Development Goals through smarter finance and fintech.

The challenge remains of course in the execution. Well-intentioned statements from COP26 or Mark Carney's GFANZ (Glasgow Financial Alliance for Net Zero) mostly lack action, or can fail to bear up under more detailed scrutiny. Companies remain driven by profits, consumers by cost, and the fragility of new attempts to balance these tensions are exemplified by cases such as UK fashion firm Boohoo, exposed for allegedly poor labour practices despite a positive ranking from MSCI, a leading ESG analytics firm. The key question for leaders and policy makers will be how to move from words to action in this difficult space of contradictions and necessary trade-offs. It is another arena of transitional change challenges.

Society

Nobody needs reminding of the recent shifts we have seen in societal values. Originating in the US, Black Lives Matter has become a global phenomenon and has led to some significant outcomes such as the conviction of police officers in the George Floyd case. But despite increasing justice in some sectors, other social inequalities persist. Many leaders I speak to feel unable to make a difference at the macro level, and simple micro solutions remain stubbornly out of reach. But the persistence of these issues again calls for a clear response from us as leaders of change.

... And black swans

'Events, dear boy, events' is how then UK Prime Minister Howard MacMillan explained to a journalist how the best-laid government plans can be derailed.

'Black swans', the extremely rare, unexpected events with severe consequences as popularized by Nassim Taleb in his book by the same name, are becoming more prevalent in our complex and interconnected world – the current crisis caused by the Covid-19 pandemic being the latest example (Taleb, 2007). Here again, more skilful change leadership will be needed.

What transitions do we face as leaders in a VUCA world?

So we see that the global context is forcing us to think differently about the choices we make. This disruption has made many of us question our values, our assumptions about life, and even our roles in society. In my research I encountered a host of such stories from leaders navigating change in one form or another.

Stories of personal transitions

- Changes in personal surroundings such as moving home, city or country
- Changing family arrangements such as home schooling or supporting elderly parents
- Forced job changes or loss of employment from the pandemic or economic downturn
- Significant personal changes such as divorce, illness, or bereavement.

Stories of professional transitions

- New work patterns such as WFH in the pandemic or hybrid arrangements
- Changes in work processes such as restructuring, automation or relocation
- Dealing with fundamental changes in business models due to technology and AI
- Onboarding and managing teams in new and hybrid ways.

Stories of leadership transitions

- Adapting to a new role or responsibilities in an organizational context
- Assuming leadership of new projects, structures or innovations such as Agile

- Managing external threats from: activist shareholders, competition, or supply chain disruption
- Failed entrepreneurial initiatives or product launches from unforeseen change.

All of these scenarios raise existential questions that bleed across all aspects of our personal and professional lives such as:

- How can I lead my teams and maintain engagement despite huge uncertainty?
- How can I make the right decisions on new projects or initiatives without complete data?
- How can I manage people in a WFH context that seems here to stay?
- What can I do to support bigger macro trends such as sustainability or equality?
- How do I ensure my own financial future and career development?

What leaders are telling me today is that they seem to know less and less despite expectations to know more and more about to these kinds of questions.

Our current education and organizational systems exacerbate the problem. Our professional roles value accomplishment with predictable outcomes and rarely tolerate experimentation or exploration, which of course entail more risk but are the cornerstones of navigating uncertainty. Our traditional reward systems often drive us to compete to win as individuals rather than collaborate to share broader collective results. And in an increasingly complex and uncertain world, especially in times of crisis, our natural survival instincts drive us to protect and guard our immediate perimeter, rather than explore new ideas and options that could help us evolve towards wider or more sustainable outcomes.

In the face of these externalities it is not surprising that we easily get blocked, opt for the easier choices, postpone decisions, shy away from new things, or actively resist and avoid change altogether.

I have witnessed this natural resistance and anxiety over many years of executive coaching and working with leaders. These significant change moments are risky and our ability to navigate transitions with clarity and confidence often remains out of reach for even the most 'competent' and otherwise successful leaders.

For further answers about how and why we react to change the way we do, I approached some leading thinkers on organizational behaviour: Amy Edmondson of Harvard Business School and Niro Sivanathan of London

Business School, who both study the psychology of change, uncertainty and its impact on decision-making.

What behavioural science can tell us about change and transitions

People don't resist change. What they resist is being changed. PETER SENGE

Interestingly, I found most conversations about transitions were more about failures than success. This made me wonder: 'Why do so many 'smart' people get stuck when faced with really important choices or significant new situations, and is there something we can do about it?'

Professors Edmondson and Sivanathan helped me understand more about how our brains react to external change and uncertainty, drawing on their expertise and some of the latest research in applied psychology and neuroscience.

First, they both concur that as humans we struggle in these situations. It seems the psychological cards are stacked against us when it comes to navigating change and uncertainty. Even as modern humans who, for the most part, live relatively unthreatened lives, we can still freeze when confronted with *perceived* danger from an unexpected change.

Professor Edmondson is the Novartis Professor of Leadership and Management at Harvard Business School, whose work investigates the role of psychology for leaders, teams and organizations when navigating change a VUCA world. We need look no further than the global pandemic for ample evidence that our increasingly interconnected world routinely triggers huge and unexpected change events. But as Professor Edmondson told me, 'We say we live in a VUCA world but we go about our lives as if it weren't.'

Professor Edmondson's short answer to the question of why these transitions are difficult was simple: 'Because human nature makes the right behaviours really hard.'

As we got into the topic, she explained that for all the adaptation skills and inventiveness we have as human beings, forced externalities that tip us into transitions still trigger our ancestral brain responses. As Professor Edmondson says, 'We prefer certainty. We also think we see reality as it is, whereas in fact we filter it through our own experience and therefore bias it, or at least colour the facts. And finally, we worry about status, saving face, and our reputation in the complex social ecosystem we live in, be it our professional identity or social position.'

Essentially, Professor Edmondson explained that 'imposed change and complexity generates a "threat response" as human beings', which happens in the amygdala part of the brain. Her research has proven that every adult experiences fear of criticism or rejection, and that we all remember moments when it may have happened. The resulting learned response is to avoid situations in which we are exposed, may look inferior, or potentially appear incompetent because we don't have the 'correct answers'. Essentially, when faced with change, we should acknowledge and accept that we will never have full certainty about our choices and the consequences of our actions. But this is a major challenge given our social conditioning.

Her advice to counter this 'amygdala hijack' is to develop more agile skills and mindsets. Externally, this means being more aware and in touch with our surroundings, and building greater 'fluency and agility'. Internally, she advises us to be more learning-oriented by asking questions, testing the waters, encouraging more thoughtful debate, and using 'smart experimentation', be it as a personal practice or in teams and organizations.

The shorthand for this is Professor Edmondson's concept of 'psychological safety'. It aims to create an environment that provides the important 'cover' we need in a group context to operate, especially in uncertainty and change. The term was coined in the 1960s from early research in organizational change by Schein and Bennis, who referred to the need to create psychological safety for individuals in order to feel secure and capable of change. Edmondson contributed to the field in 1999 by introducing the concept of team psychological safety, defined as 'a shared belief held by members of a group that the team is safe for interpersonal risk-taking', and demonstrating a clear link between team psychological safety and team performance (Edmondson, 1999). The importance of Edmondson's research was later highlighted by a study by Google in 2012, named Project Aristotle, that explored the most important drivers of high-performing teams in that organization. So-named from Aristotle's notion that 'the whole is greater than the sum of its parts', the study was an important step towards our understanding of the role psychological safety plays in high performing teams. The researchers found that *who* was on the team mattered less than *how* the team worked together. They identified five dynamics of effective teams, of which psychological safety was by far the most important. In fact, it even underpinned the other factors (dependability, structure and clarity, meaning, impact) (Rozovsky, 2015).

The project confirmed causation showing that higher-performing teams felt a greater sense of belonging through psychological safety than the other factors. The key features of this safety include a sense of group identity, shared goals, a culture of respectful challenge, and a belief that anyone in the group can speak up without rejection or fear of recrimination. Subsequently, psychological safety has become widely recognized as the most significant factor for the success of high performing teams.

In her 2019 book *The Fearless Organization* and elsewhere Professor Edmondson has written extensively about further useful tactics and practices that help groups establish greater psychological safety in a work or social context (Edmondson, 2019). We will later explore some of these but the key point is that we overwhelmingly react to forced change by resisting or retreating in some way. A conscious effort is therefore required for us to get out of our comfort zone and embrace change when it confronts us. This can manifest as accepting an unforeseen career challenge like Gillian Tett heading to Moscow without questioning the attendant risks or uncertainties. But for most of us, absent an unusual level of self-confidence, we face unfavourable odds when it comes to actively navigating such transitions.

Professor Niro Sivanathan of the London Business School offered me a different lens on this question, drawing from his expertise in behavioural psychology and heuristics. In particular, he studies how the mind operates around decision-making and where cognitive bias can impede our ability to make proper judgements, including in situations of transition and uncertainty.

The biases he researches are so-called 'systematic patterns of deviation from norms or rationality in judgment'. These occur when individuals create their own subjective reality that can then unwittingly dictate their behaviour. This sounds ominous but the good news about this apparent dysfunction is that it also helps us to quickly make useful connections between our previous experiences, thereby creating mental shortcuts to effectively navigate common life situations.

These cognitive shortcuts then become 'heuristics' and while they provide an excellent survival mechanism for shortcutting *known* situations,

Sivanathan provides a plethora of examples where they can also paralyse us in the face of *unknown* situations or forced change such as transitions.

His essential point is that people struggle with transitions because it creates internal conflict.

The trap we fall into is that we are not quick enough to adapt to new external shocks. Our behavioural 'toolkit', which is how we learn to deal with situations based on our past experience also makes up our core identity. As a result, if we need to 'drop our tools' in response to a new change, our identity also becomes challenged, creating even greater perceived risk. Yet while dropping tools seems fundamentally counterintuitive, it is what can save us in uncertainty. In the 1949 study by Organizational Theorist Karl Weick of fire fighters in Mann Gulch, Montana they metaphorically and literally did just that. Smokejumpers are the specially trained wildland firefighters who are dropped, often by helicopter, into live fire areas. They use various types of heavy equipment in their attempts to control the blaze, and core to their training is the principle to always keep their tools with them in order to have the best chance of survival in dangerous and fast changing conditions. Yet in this case one of their leaders advised them to drop their heavy fire fighting tools in order to move faster into a burned-out area that was believed to have a lesser chance of attracting the flames again. Some firefighters chose to keep their tools and disobey the new orders, but found their retreat slowed by their heavy tools. Most tragically perished when they were outrun by the fire in their attempts to escape. But the others who followed the new, counterintuitive, order managed to survive by moving faster. It was a risky choice but in the context of that extreme uncertainty it was correct one (Weick, 1996).

In the world of business and leadership, when faced with similar external threats or uncertainty, Professor Sivanathan told me we too require a different script and should 'drop our tools'. Unfortunately, in these situations, our instincts, our prior experiences and our ego all send us powerful signals to preserve the status quo, and we 'stick it out' using our previous behaviours hoping for a positive result. Justifying ourselves through our existing behaviours confirms our identity and this seems to be more important psychologically to us than the ability to switch tools or tactics. We shy away from potential failure in the form of ridicule or rejection, even though doing so may be the only way to generate the new solution we need, save our own lives.

Professor Sivanathan cites many other heuristics, or mental shortcuts, as common (yet unconscious) blockers to transitions. Among some of the most common are:

- *'Escalation of commitment'* that makes us continue investing in projects or ideas despite evidence of poor outcomes
- *'Availability heuristics'* that make us overweight more easily accessible information such as stories or images
- *'Affective forecasting'* that highlights our inability to forecast future emotions, thus impacting our judgments and decisions.

Professor Sivanathan uses these examples in his teaching and consistently proves to 'smart' executives across cultures and professions that they all suffer forms of 'change denial'. He likes to test his student's own biased 'norms' with simple questions such as their perceived proportion of Ivy League dropouts who become successful entrepreneurs (very few, it turns out, despite the stories of Steve Jobs, Elon Musk or Mark Zuckerberg), or estimating the distance covered by taking just 30 steps and doubling the distance each time (it turns out this takes us 26 times around the equator).

What is the risk of this change resistance for leaders?

Psychological safety, heuristics, and other biases are clearly risk factors for individuals experiencing personal transitions. But what about for leaders in organizations as they shape their teams, make investment decisions or evaluate risk? Are these professionals protected from these traps by their strategic plans, risk management tools and decision-making techniques?

According to Professors Edmondson and Sivanathan, it turns out that as leaders we face the same biases and blocks as in our personal capacity. Worse still, as leaders we often have even fewer coping mechanisms relative to the situations we face, and there are greater consequences of failure. Firstly, and obviously, leadership actions by their nature create broader impact because they involve decisions that affect others. The impact of failure is also more consequential given the resources and authority deployed by the leader. So it is ironic that many leaders lack the training or mechanisms to navigate effectively during complex change despite the higher stakes involved.

Not only do leaders often lack the attributes for transitional change but other factors also come into play, with significant consequences. Sometimes leaders end up being isolated from reality in the executive suite, which denies them crucial feedback and soundings from the front line that could help them lead change more effectively. In other cases, leadership roles come with a set of (often unrealistic) expectations to 'have the answers' because of seniority, experience, assumed knowledge and authority. But these attributes are often not present, and in any case are of limited use in truly transitional change. In the most extreme cases, I have seen leaders actively avoid feedback and ignore the facts out of fear of appearing incompetent and attempting to protect their position and egos. All of this, of course, becomes irrelevant in true transitions (unknown futures, uncertain outcomes).

Leadership expert Margaret Heffernan argues in a *Financial Times* article entitled 'Fear of losing a top spot at work will hinder you' that, 'Far from being spurred on to be more ambitious, top-flight executives often hunker down to protect their rank'. This is another version of not 'dropping tools' (Heffernan, 2017).

All this points to an even greater need for those in positions of leadership to gain better insight about navigating transitions and test out new 'tools'.

Professor Sivanathan likens this practice to flight simulator hours. He cites how we have been able to reduce pilot error in air accidents from 65 per cent to 30 per cent over time due primarily to more realistic flight simulators starting in the 1980s (Leher, 2011). This increased learning through experience helped defuse many of the heuristics pilots normally experience and allowed them to better tackle real unexpected flight situations. The movie *Sully* provides a vivid illustration of how each of the 20,000 hours of flight experience racked up by that pilot was a small metaphorical deposit in the bank against which a large future withdrawal could be made – in his case an emergency landing in the East River of New York. Professor Sivanathan argues, and I agree, that despite the value of the investment, few leaders so diligently practise uncertainty scenarios to build up their bank balances.

In conclusion, Professor Sivanathan points to the Covid-19 pandemic, where a confluence of biases has played a key role in our inability to adapt. All the signs were pointing to a major global threat, yet it took humans way longer than it rationally should have to react appropriately – whether it was closing wet markets in Wuhan in China, declaring the virus a pandemic at the WHO, acquiring adequate PPE supplies in the UK, or anticipating sufficient vaccine purchases by the EU.

Professors Edmondson and Sivanathan provide excellent insights into the subtle psychology of change and why discontinuities are hard for us as humans no matter our level of education, intelligence or experience.

Other writers and experts broadly reach the same conclusions on this topic. Margaret Heffernan also wrote in her bestseller *Wilful Blindness* how we tend to 'ignore the obvious at our peril' as leaders (Heffernan, 2011). Historian Niall Ferguson added a societal lens to the change problem in his book *Doom* where he explored the vulnerability of systems in how catastrophes unfold. He includes Covid-19 and flaws in our networked world as examples (Ferguson, 2021). Finally, a McKinsey report published in May 2021, a full 14 months after the beginning of the pandemic, found in a survey of 100 executives that 90 per cent envisioned a future of hybrid work. Yet two-thirds (68 per cent) still had no detailed plan for how to do it (De Smet et al, 2021).

Having looked at these organizational and systemic dynamics of change, we can see that the answers – or attempts at them – must start with us as individuals moving to action in the face of uncertainty. The question for us as change leaders is: How can we more deliberately overcome our natural aversion to change, and what lessons can we learn from people like Tad Beckwith, Charles Handy, or Gillian Tett, who instinctively step across this invisible line into new unknown territory, despite what we know from the experts?

Navigating transitions – light at the end of the tunnel

A successful transition will occur when we are able to move forward with a degree of clarity and confidence, even if we can't know the full outcomes of our actions in the face of significant change. Successful transitions involve building the mindset and attitude that move us from good intentions to effective action. It is the intentional development of this Change Mindset that creates a sense of self-determination and the ability to act more decisively in the face of uncertainty.

The subsequent chapters of this book are focused on building the Change Mindset which is that particular combination of attitude and aptitude that sets apart those who thrive in uncertainty, overcoming the anxiety associated with transitions and navigating uncertainty to reach successful outcomes.

Often this mindset revolves around finding something positive during otherwise paralyzing change. This notion was well captured by retired American teacher Kitty O'Meara (not to be confused with the homonymous 19th Century writer), who turned to writing during lockdown in an effort to curb her own anxiety amid uncertainty. Her resulting poem 'And The People Stayed Home' became widely shared on the internet, featured on Oprah Winfrey and praised by Deepak Chopra. When asked about her inspiration, O'Meara said: 'I saw the maps of the receding pollution over China and Europe and thought, with my love for the Earth, that was at least one good thing' (Nicolaou, 2020).

Like O'Meara, most of us will have asked ourselves a question at least once during our personal or professional lives along the lines of: How do I embrace this unexpected transition, and can I use the experience to learn something new? Yet we are trained from a young age to spot problems rather than grasp opportunities, to be right in the face of uncertainty, and to appear competent at all costs.

This paradox of ambition versus anxiety is a common leadership (and human) condition, especially in today's VUCA world.

Yet we must act. As Andrew Likierman adroitly reminded me: 'Transitions used to be voluntary acts of change. Today they are a necessary part of our existence.'

Summary of key points

In this chapter I have defined transitional change as 'any situation where we are forced to modify who we are and how we operate in the world as the result of unavoidable, external and often unexpected events'.

I showed why in our VUCA world we are faced more and more with these kinds of scenarios, and how the expectations on us to navigate them successfully as adults and as leaders have increased exponentially in a time of global turbulence.

We then heard from leading world experts in psychology and neuroscience about why as human beings we find such moments of change difficult. From biases to heuristics and our need for psychological safety, we are wired to seek stability and maintain predictability.

In the next chapter we will begin to make sense of this paradox by exploring life's natural stages of development, and what they can teach us about making change potentially less difficult by developing a Change Mindset.

CHAPTER TWO

Our shared human experience as a metaphor for leading change

In the last chapter we defined transitional change and showed why in our VUCA world we are faced increasingly with these kinds of scenarios, with rising expectations on us to navigate them successfully despite uncertainty. We heard from experts in psychology and neuroscience about why, as human beings, we find such moments of change difficult, often due to our learned preferences for stability. However, we also noted that many successful leaders do find ways to thrive in uncertainty despite this natural conditioning.

In this chapter I will examine some established psychological frameworks about life's natural development stages. We will see how we can learn from these as a metaphor for change leadership, and how they can also provide us with the tools to begin building a Change Mindset.

The road not taken

We know that, as humans, we all naturally transition through a series of life stages. These stages are made up of experiences that occur during a particular time frame and during which we form ideas, attitudes, and beliefs about ourselves and the world around us. We grow up in a particular environment and family milieu. Our schooling may then take us elsewhere, to colleges or universities in other cities. We then choose a career path or get our first job, often based on a combination of education, opportunity and luck. We build our professional experiences through a series of roles or projects, sometimes across different industries or locations. And along the way we make choices about our interests, hobbies, lifestyle and relationships. We pass through early childhood into adolescence, adulthood and then into maturity, navigating a series of personal and professional transitions that cause a mix of tension, uncertainty or excitement as we adjust and mature.

Thus, our life stages encompass experiences that can be physical (travel, work, meeting others), emotional (experiencing successes and failures), or psychological (key moments that form our attitudes, beliefs, likes and dislikes).

Metaphorical forks in the road will also punctuate these life stages. Here, we find ourselves suddenly facing a choice, perhaps to take on a new job, to move to another city or country, to associate with new people, buy a house, or start a family. At each of these forks we will face a known and a lesser-known 'path'. We may choose 'the road taken' – what our parents did, what our friends are doing, what seems popular, or we may opt for 'the road not taken' – travelling more widely, doing volunteer work, taking sabbaticals, making unexpected career changes.

Much has been written about the allure of the 'Road Not Taken', from the oft-quoted poem of the same name by American poet Robert Frost, to any number of books and articles about disruption and change. Popular literature and anecdotes from successful maverick leaders encourage us to explore more divergent options when faced with a crossroads in life or business. These reflect the call to action that is innate in our human drive to explore the unknown. But as we saw in Chapter 1 there is an equally powerful human instinct when faced with the unknown, to stay the course and keep a steady hand on the tiller. This reaction reflects our natural anxiety and hesitation in the face of change, and our aversion to uncertainty.

However, if transitions are the basis for personal growth and our ultimate fulfilment as human beings, what is the effect of the increasing uncertainty and crisis that is our common reality today? Crises force us to reassess our values and sometimes prompt us to reinvent ourselves entirely. But how does this current context affect our appetite for such reinvention, or taking the path less trodden? Does this help or hinder us as we try to build a Change Mindset?

Our choices in uncertainty will depend largely on how confident or adventurous we are feeling during our stage in life, whether we feel the need for a change, and how much we know about the perceived risks and rewards of each option available. We like to think we have control over our choices in these circumstances, but uncertainty often hijacks our ability to accept and manage these transitions.

Whatever choice we make, the essential experience from our life stages can be a natural training ground for navigating these transitions, and can teach us valuable lessons on how to face choice as leaders.

When I spoke to other leaders about their own experiences in these moments, I encountered examples of people firmly choosing the 'known' path when facing change, sometimes successfully, but often not. I also met people who had taken entirely unexpected paths, metaphorically choosing 'the road not taken' to explore unknown alternatives and possibilities when confronted with change. These more adventurous leaders also experienced successes and failures, but in the context of change and transitions, the bolder approach generally yielded more effective results. But the stories from both groups held valuable lessons about how to make better choices and increase our confidence in the face of the unknown.

One common reflection from these leaders was how many had looked back in moments of uncertainty to mine the personal lessons learned in their earlier years. Previous life stages had, in many cases, provided guidance. For example, reflecting on how they had developed their sense of self early on might remind them of their stance on some key issue that could now rein-force their choices. In other cases, choices made previously about their lives and careers, or how they dealt with unexpected setbacks, could steer them towards better alternatives now. In other words, the natural development stages of these leaders as human beings contained key insights about navigating change later as adults. This is more than simply reproducing what we have experienced before. Rather, it is the reflective and focused experience of rewinding the clock and paying close attention to some of those early shaping moments. Doing this can rekindle key lessons and boost our ability to be more courageous about change today. This in turn allows us to seek the road not taken more often and to greater effect. Satya Nadella is known for saying 'your life experience will teach you if you listen'. With this hypothesis in mind, let us briefly explore the psychology behind our human development stages and what it means for us as leaders of change today.

Life stages: our shared human experience

Psychology and anthropology offer us various frameworks to explain our human experience. Early social scientists such as Carl Jung explored human development through archetypes, the collective unconscious, and psychological type (the basis of many personality assessments still used today, such as the MBTI). The goal of our life experience for many of these early thinkers was what Jung termed 'individuation' – bringing together all our life experience into an integrated whole to achieve our aims not only as humans but as leaders in our chosen professions.

What are these development stages, and what can they tell us about leadership and change? First, let us define them. Jung was the first to categorize our life experience into broad psychological chapters (Jung, 1970).

Stage 1: Childhood

Up to age 15 or so we progressively distinguish ourselves from others and begin to shape our own identity. This stage is associated with mimicry as we imitate role models and others in order to fit in, be part of an identifiable group, and become validated. As adult leaders, we often retain an aspect of this desire which, as we will see later, can both help and hinder us in the context of change.

Stage 2: Early life

From 15–40 we gain independence and explore the world, becoming specialized in a particular domain. From a leadership perspective we build our career and reputation through work and also make important life choices to build social and professional networks. The lessons learned in this process can prepare us for some change but do not yet give us the insights or judgment to navigate bigger transitions and uncertainty.

Stage 3: Midlife

The decade from 40–50 is associated with our most significant achievements as we apply our practiced skills and expertise. Our ability to lead and drive change is enhanced, yet it can also be a time of important tensions. We are professionally established yet may begin to ask questions about 'what's next'. We feel competent and confident but realize we are aging and so become anxious about achieving our bigger dreams. Psychologically this is referred to as letting go of youth and confronting the concept of our 'shadow', the darker side we all have in our personalities and the blind spots we typically develop as the flip side of our expertise and accomplishments (Jung, 1969).

Stage 4: Maturity

After age 50 we often have the opportunity to more fully reconcile our life's experiences and develop a sense of purpose and fulfilment. By this stage we have experienced both successes and failures, and are often better able to manage the highs and lows of leadership and life. We can also make use of these experiences to lift others through mentoring and coaching. We become effective leaders of change with a longer term and more integrated perspective.

Most of us will recognize the arc of our own experience from these short descriptions. I believe each stage offers its own lessons to help lead change. But there are also blind spots and traps along the way, as academics and psychologists like Erik Erikson, Elliott Jaques, Daniel J. Levinson and William Bridges found. These experts extensively researched the risks and challenges associated with evolving across the life stages, including concepts such as 'inevitable changes' (Erikson, 1950), 'midlife crisis' (Jaques, 1965), and 'transitions' (Bridges, 1991). These frameworks and concepts remain widely applied today in the context of leadership and organizational change.

Thus psychology literature provides ample evidence that each life stage provides enabling factors in the context of change (I will call these benefits), as well disabling factors (I will call these blind spots).

What are these factors and how can we make use of them in the context of leading change?

Benefits and blind spots of the developmental stages

Stage 1: Childhood

CHARACTERISTICS

While we are not yet 'leaders' in our childhood, these early years form the basis of our later mindset and identity. We notice parents, teachers and other influential people around us and emulate their characteristics. In some cases, we may also deliberately choose to avoid these character traits, but generally our early role models and their attributes will re-emerge in our own behaviours later in life. These attributes can appear consciously and unconsciously as we channel them into our own behaviors as adults.

BENEFITS

This stage can serve us well as we learn from our early role models about values, behaviors and social skills. Such early lessons stay with us throughout life and act as a compass in times of change to help us navigate uncertainty. As we will see later, attributes like strong social skills, respect and curiosity learned early on can catapult our capacity to navigate change later in life.

BLIND SPOTS

The risk of early imitation is that we can also adopt the less helpful habits and attributes of our role models. We know that children imitate their parents and elders, so if that behaviour is negative, it can have a negative influence. Common examples include poor health habits, unjustified prejudices, excessive focus on materialism, or unrealistic expectations about achievement. Unless we are aware of these potentially unfavourable influences, we may perpetuate them later in life rather than establish our own sense of self. I have worked with many executives who continue to imitate the behaviors or expectations of their superiors (i.e. organizational 'parents') as they seek approval and validation, irrespective of the relevance or achievability of those demands. I also see the negative consequences of imitation in organizational cultures that disable challenge and block criticism of the status quo, forcing managers to toe the company line. Examples of this systemic corporate dysfunction are numerous across industries from energy to banking or the automotive sector where imitation and lack of challenge allowed a dominant leadership culture to cause financial and reputational damage because of an unhealthy parent-child management culture.

Stage 2: Early life

CHARACTERISTICS

Most young adults want to be seen as unique individuals, known for something distinctive. To achieve this, most of us will choose a particular direction for our education, develop related skills, and then find work or a vocation that uses our expertise to create the impact we seek. Through this process of testing ourselves and through trial and error, we discover what we are good at and apply these strengths in these chosen domain. We shape our identity, begin to express more of our own unique ideas, and find ways to apply our strengths in a more deliberate and useful way. We progressively become 'experts' in what we do, for example as lawyers, doctors, artisans, teachers, or as parents and leaders in our communities.

BENEFITS

Managed well, this life stage allows us to express ourselves as distinct human beings building on our early influences while becoming the professionals and leaders we want to be. We evolve in our work and life to approximate the ideal we have formed for ourselves. This desired state can be material, financial, social or even spiritual. Our drivers can be helping or supporting others through managing and coaching or we might be energized by a big idea (eg equality or justice) or furthering our professional expertise (eg science or law).

BLIND SPOTS

This stage can be valuable in many ways, but the risk of excessive differentiation is that we lose the ability to flex, listen and integrate the views of others. We may also fail to understand the wider context. Leaders who become the sole 'expert' in their domain or who focus on a deep but narrow skill can often become trapped in their own narrative. We saw this happening at a systemic level leading up to the 2007–2008 financial crisis which Gillian Tett describes in *The Silo Effect* (Tett, 2015). She examined how so-called experts failed to spot major systemic risks because they had become too specialized, despite having access to unlimited data and being hyper-connected by technology. But despite this deep specialization, the system was in fact unconsciously fragile, contributing to the 2007–2008 global financial crisis and its aftermath. I have also seen many leaders who become so 'expert' in their personal capacity that in addition to becoming blind to the bigger picture, they regress further by failing to seek feedback, ignoring data that doesn't fit their world view, and rejecting challenge. This is all to the obvious detriment of their effectiveness as change leaders, especially during major transitions.

Stage 3: Midlife

CHARACTERISTICS

This later stage can drive our greatest achievements in our personal and professional endeavors. It is the time when many of us choose to strike out on our own and build our own businesses or projects. It is also when we are likely to be called upon to support and guide others in their own development, including our children, families, friends and colleagues. We may also begin to evaluate our achievements more critically, perhaps questioning our past personal and professional choices. But the right attitude and mindset can keep us growing and contributing into our later careers.

BENEFITS

Confidence and experience are the main drivers of success at this stage. This is when we widen our networks and maximize the impact of our knowledge and expertise by sharing and learning from others across a wider sphere of influence. We typically move into more senior leadership roles, and as a result create greater impact as we build capabilities, businesses and teams. If we focus and make the right choices, our life experience and prior knowledge come together in a nexus of achievement in our chosen domain. Personally and professionally we now have the potential to make a real difference.

BLIND SPOTS

The risks of this midlife stage are clear. When we should be at the height of our power personally and professionally, this stage often provokes the opposite effect. Frustration, regret, uncertainty, doubt and even fear are common feelings at this delicate stage of adult development. We naturally begin to question our prior personal and professional choices, assessing our current achievements and attempting to see what's next for our future transitions. The threat response to change and uncertainty that we saw in Chapter 1 is liable to come into play in these moments, and a deliberate effort is required to counter them. Unless we can accept our failings and unrealized goals with equanimity, we risk feeling inadequate and underperforming. We need to give ourselves time and space to reflect on our life in a balanced and empathetic way. This can be difficult, especially for overachieving and successful adults who now find themselves a step behind their ambitions. Further risks occur if the natural desire to be recognized for our abilities and achievements becomes ego-driven rather than purpose-driven. We must be vigilant in maintaining a realistic yet empathic self-image, or we risk being overcome by our shadow.

Stage 4: Maturity

CHARACTERISTICS

For leaders who continue a deliberate journey of self-development, the process of individuation continues in later life as we build our presence in a wider social context and become the counsellors and mentors of others. There is great potential in the world for more such leaders in the future as the changing demographics discussed in Chapter 1 show. Increased life expectancy in many parts of the world will offer multiple career choices as described in *The 100-Year Life* by Lynda Gratton and Andrew Scott, also referred to in Chapter 1. They effectively challenge the traditional notion of a three-stage life of education, work and retirement (Gratton and Scott, 2016).

BENEFITS

There are many ways to accelerate our sense of fulfilment and individuation at this stage of life. Seasoned leaders often take on roles mentoring, teaching, or in public speaking. I see an increasing number of mature leaders, including women and minorities, now joining advisory boards or acting as non-executive directors for organizations seeking a greater balance of external views. The networks we naturally build over time can now be a source of consultation and ideas. Our extensive professional experience opens up new opportunities as others seek our expertise and insights. And we find ourselves with a credibility and gravitas that bring us naturally into situations of greater influence and impact. The additional time and resources we typically have available at this stage allow us to explore new work, perhaps completing further educational qualifications, participate in charities, or teach at a local college. Gratton and Scott offer tools and guidance about how these multiple new careers may play out, optimistically theorizing that they will be a great source of deeper purpose and meaning for those who actively prepare and those they lead through change.

BLIND SPOTS

Envisioning a multi-faceted post-retirement life will only be possible if we have the health and resources that allow it. Yet the courage, stamina and money that are prerequisites to maintain an active role into later life are by no means guaranteed. Some if these factors may be outside our control, such as health. Other constraints such as financial resources or family obligations can also restrict our options. So planning and focus are required to remain successful in our later life. And of course, in many parts of the world the social structures and freedom to act are simply not present today. Individuation assumes a free and enabling environment, but this is not yet a universal reality.

What life stages can teach us about navigating transitions

To understand how we can realize these benefits and avoid blind spots in transitions, it is important to revisit the psychology of life stages. What is key in life stage theory of human development is the emphasis on the potential for positive change at any stage. Neuroscientists have proven through MRI scanning of the brain and other research that adults can demonstrate neuroplasticity. Contrary to previous beliefs about personality being fixed and brain development becoming largely static after adolescence, we can in fact rewire ourselves to learn new patterns from lived experiences. These recent findings have been particularly useful in the context of therapy, rehabilitation, and adult learning. In the context of leadership development where the focus is to explore potential for continuous learning and fostering innovation or transformation, the consequences are worth considering.

The relevance of these frameworks for navigating transitions and building a Change Mindset is this: if, as individuals, we can be more self-aware about our life stages and then use the lessons they teach us, it gives us the freedom and the ability to control our reactions during change to make better decisions. This insight can help us at crucial moments when we face a fork in the road, and counter our natural aversion to uncertainty described in Chapter 1.

It became clear in my conversations with leaders about this question that strong parallels exist between what we learn from our natural life stages, and the skills and mindsets we need to successfully navigate the major changes we encounter in business. In other words, our natural human development can be a powerful metaphor for our development as leaders of change.

Life stage lessons in practice

So, what can be learned from these life stage experiences? What are the practical skills and actions to successfully navigate change throughout life, including the difficult period of midlife, so we can continue our path to individuation? One leader I spoke to epitomized for me the successful application of lessons learned from this notion of life stages.

Professor Sir Peng Tee Khaw provides an example of an individuated life with lessons learned at each key moment of his own life stages. He is a Consultant Ophthalmic Surgeon at Moorfields Eye Hospital in London, a world-renowned National Health Service (NHS) hospital. Together with the adjacent UCL Institute of Ophthalmology, Moorfields is the oldest and largest centre for ophthalmic care, teaching and research in Europe. Professor Khaw's activities extend well beyond the surgical care he provides for patients. He advises governments and is a world-renowned researcher in glaucoma focusing on surgical treatments that have had a profound worldwide impact on patient outcomes. In 2013 he was awarded a Knighthood for services to ophthalmology, and he and his team have been awarded over 20 national and international prizes for their research.

I first saw Professor Khaw in action at a charity fundraising event for a new paediatric eye centre at Moorfields Eye Hospital. The evening included dinner and a series of speeches, most of which had the usual PowerPoint slides and scripted comments. But when it came to Professor Khaw he projected one simple photograph and told us a story. The picture was of a young girl who was a patient at the hospital. He recounted how her condition had come about and the impact that her limited sight was having on her life and her schooling. He talked about the role that her family, who he knew well, played in supporting her. He explained how the new surgical techniques that were being developed at Moorfields had helped her maintain her sight for longer despite this incurable but treatable disease. The whole thing lasted less than five minutes but I am sure that most of the donations from that evening were triggered by his powerful and authentic presence to provoke change.

I decided to speak to Professor Khaw about how he learned such empathic communication and leadership skills, and his own journey of transitions within the context of his Asian upbringing to become a world-renowned clinician scientist.

As he described his life stage experiences, a strong pattern of curiosity and empathy emerged. He grew up in Malaysia in a traditional Chinese family culture after his grandparents had emigrated from China under difficult political and economic circumstances. This provided the first building block of his Change Mindset. As he describes it, 'Our early life defines and shapes us. In my culture your story begins with the people before you. That comes back to shape you as you make decisions in your life. And being aware of that is quite important for your future transitions and change experiences.'

But his family structure and Asian culture also created strong expectations early in life about focus, success and achievement. Professor Khaw had promised his lawyer father, who passed away in his early 50s, that he would pursue the same career. Yet as an adolescent his heart was not in law but instead he found himself strongly attracted to science and medicine. He told me about his hobby of assembling Airfix airplane models as a child and how it revealed his gift for seeing things spatially, fitting structures together and solving three-dimensional problems. While a career in medicine might be as respectable as one in law, there was clearly a tension between fulfilling the promise to his father and 'making his father proud', and pursuing what he was truly drawn to and evidently gifted for. As he says, 'You are very linked to your obligations in Eastern culture.'

These characteristics are still strong in the cultural and social fabric of his part of the world, emphasizing respect and humility before one's elders and being expected to follow their guidance and values closely. Self-determination and personal choice take on a different nuance than in the West, and can be restricted by these family and social conventions. But transitions and opportunities for change nonetheless remain an inevitable part of life, requiring an individual response by anyone experiencing them.

Faced with this dilemma at a pivotal moment at age 14, Professor Khaw found himself visiting an elderly Indian fortune teller after his father died. She was able to sense some of his inner turmoil and when examining his hands found some apparent mystical 'cross of healing', which she then insisted meant he must become a doctor and not a lawyer. He somewhat discounted the prescience of the fortune-teller, thinking his mother may have secretly briefed her or that he had let something slip in his conversation. But that moment helped him to 'polarize his thinking' as he described it, giving him the psychological nudge he needed to pursue his own inner path despite parental expectations.

Following that fateful palm-reading, Professor Khaw found in himself the self-determination to begin pursuing his true calling and re-orientated his studies towards medicine. He managed to gain the support and approval from his family despite his earlier promise to his father, drawing on other characteristics of his family: a sense of discipline, hard work, commitment to society, and humility in personal achievement. His mother in particular believed in doing things for the benefit of humankind, showing empathy and listening to others – in short 'doing good'. These sentiments acted as a catalyst and gave Professor Khaw the permission he needed to follow his calling into the field of medicine. Today, his work as a clinician scientist neatly marries his early attributes: curiosity about spatial structures, solving complex problems, and his desire to help others with commitment and compassion. We will come back later to the importance of this kind of psychological permission as a key skill in navigating transitions, and how paying attention to our environment and seeking external views can be a valuable trigger for action when navigating uncertainty.

Those early experiences and the psychological journey from childhood (stage 1) to early life (stage 2) clearly shaped Professor Khaw's future identity and career choices. He then consciously transitioned into his midlife (stage 3) by applying his expertise to achieve the outstanding successes he is known for in his chosen specialization. His later transition into maturity (stage 4) has achieved a high level of individuation that was reflected in his short speech at the fundraiser. These include a focus on the needs of others rather than himself; demonstrated expertise and credibility as a scientist; and the practice of empathy and humanity that are so important to influence and create impact on the 'bigger stage' of medical research, surgical innovation, and shaping global health policies.

I asked him about his advice for other leaders seeking to learn from their earlier life stage transitions. His response was, 'Find a strong motive, because this will drive you towards excellence'. He also suggests, 'Focus on the bigger game so you align your strongest true purpose in life with your actions.' Ultimately, he advises, 'Listening, being curious and finding out about other people. Be courageous and follow what your heart tells you so you align your strongest true purpose in life with your actions.'

I asked him what his next transition might be, his ultimate goal. His response? 'To influence the interactions that change people's lives for the better on this planet.'

I believe Professor Khaw's twin practices of passion for science and compassion for people (which he believes is key to modulate the darker sides of unrestrained passion that can lead to uncontrolled ambition, scientific fraud and disregard of people), are creating the conditions to accomplish this inspiring goal.

The role of synchronicity in transitions

You may think that synchronicity was first coined by the rock band The Police, but in fact it was Carl Jung who first published the concept in his 1952 paper 'Synchronicity — An Acausal Connecting Principle' (Jung, 1960). As a complement to his work on life stages, he defined synchronicity as circumstances and events throughout our lives that appear related yet lack a direct causal link. We experience these as important or meaningful coincidences that occur at unexpected moments. Because they are 'numinous', or psychologically and spiritually significant, these events often trigger some of our biggest transitions and moments of change, as unexpected events open new doors and create new opportunities that feel meaningful to us. In Chapter 1, Gillian Tett advised us to 'Give ourselves permission to roam and collide with the unexpected', which perfectly encapsulates this notion of synchronicity.

I believe synchronicity plays a key role as an *accelerator* to lessons learned during our life stages, but we need the right mindset and attitude to leverage these synchronous coincidences in our favour. With observation, openness and curiosity, we can realize the benefits of synchronicity by noticing and then taking deliberate action. When they are fruitful, moments of synchronicity seem to put us in the right place at the right time or help us find the courage to follow The Road Not Taken. Synchronicity is thus a strongly positive force that can move us towards individuation if we care to pay attention. Curiosity and trusting our intuition are two skills that can increase the frequency of these unaccountable events. But there are further practices that help us take full advantage of these opportunities, as I also discovered in speaking with Professor Khaw.

Synchronicity in practice

Professor Khaw told me a powerful story of synchronicity in his moment with the palm reader. But there are others. In particular, he shared a more recent instance from about ten years ago when he asked to meet a young gaming expert who had taught a computer to play and win video games. The idea of machine learning from repeated activity using huge data sets was a less publicized idea before the ubiquitous Artificial Intelligence (AI) stories that make regular headlines today. But Professor Khaw was curious about this idea and how ophthalmology might collaborate with this young mathematician. He was fascinated by his background story from chess prodigy through to games designer, PhD student and then entrepreneur, so he arranged a meeting with the young expert.

The collaboration was subsequently driven by an outstanding young trainee, clinician scientist ophthalmologist Pearse Keane at the NIHR Biomedical Research Centre. This work tapped the potential opportunities for the nascent concept of machine learning to be applied to the large data sets produced in the medical sphere, such as the high-resolution scans of the retina which contain huge amounts of multi-dimensional data. A well-documented collaboration followed that spearheaded research with the NHS to significantly accelerate diagnosis and treatment for ophthalmology and a range of other medical conditions. Medical databases remain controversial in an age of data protection and cybersecurity risk, but today the likelihood of further AI applications that will greatly benefit science and medicine are certain.

The young mathematician from Cambridge University and University College London was of course Demis Hassabis, the now famous AI researcher, neuroscientist, video game designer and entrepreneur who co-founded DeepMind. A child prodigy who became a chess master at age 13, he is a five times winner of the Pentamind Board Games championship and has been a UK Government AI Advisor since 2018. DeepMind was acquired by Google for $650m in 2014 and has since pioneered a succession of breakthrough scientific and technological innovations. These include AlphaGo, which replicates intuitive pattern recognition using neural networks. DeepMind has also been instrumental in fighting the Covid-19 pandemic through its research on virology and immunology. Its most recently developed predictive AI measures the folding nature of proteins with AlfaFold, including predicting protein structures on Covid-19 when no structures of similar proteins are available. This important work may lead to new therapeutic insights to this mutating virus, and Professor Khaw believes this work could be as momentous as the discovery of the DNA double helix by Crick and Watson in 1953, as it gives us the potential to predict the behaviors of some of the most essential building blocks of life.

Professor Khaw's instinctive curiosity and intuition that persuaded him to drive forward and facilitate this collaboration are examples of leveraging synchronicity – the ability to spot seemingly unrelated or spontaneous connections that can lead to wider and more significant outcomes.

Developing conscious skills to leverage synchronicity

A very different profile from Professor Khaw is educator and social entrepreneur Charlie Miller. In the realm of synchronicity he epitomizes for me the discipline of leveraging the unexpected. He is also an unparalleled storyteller who vividly brings to life the people and places he has experienced as an accidental entrepreneur throughout his career, and I immediately thought of him to explore this question further.

I first met Miller on a train journey to Paris in the 1980s. He was living in Vermont and importing baskets from Vietnam as part of an experiment to fund the building of schools and local communities there. His idea was several decades before the term 'social enterprise' became popularized by innovators such as Muhammad Yunus of Grameen Bank, who won the 2006 Nobel Peace Prize for promoting economic and social development in developing markets, and his related book *Banker to the Poor* (Yunus, 1999).

The day I met Miller he had recently returned from one of his visits to Vietnam and I had recently immigrated to live in America, moving there from Apartheid-era South Africa as a recent graduate. Both curious about people, travel and ideas, we found plenty to talk about as the forests of Flanders flashed by in a green blur through the second-class carriage window. As we parted at Gare du Nord he invited me to visit him in the clapboard-sided house he was renovating in Thetford, Vermont once we had both returned to the US. What he failed to mention was that it was truly being 'renovated', with, as yet, no plumbing, heating or installed windowpanes. He was living inside a plastic bubble in the living room while attempting various DIY projects, with only a small pot-bellied stove for heating and cooking. And when I finally got a chance to visit from New Jersey, where I had landed from South Africa, it was mid-February in New England.

Driving across the covered bridge that spanned a small stream below his house, I felt I was entering a scene from Henry David Thoreau's *Walden*. I turned up his steep driveway in the crunching snow, at the top of which

Miller greeted me with an axe in one hand and a steaming cup of coffee in the other. He had been splitting cords of wood around the side of the house and we spent our first weekend in Thetford stoking those logs into the pot-bellied stove as snow flurries occasionally blew in through the empty window frames.

The point about synchronicity is that Miller's US upbringing gave no hint that fortuitous events would play a major role in his later projects. He has an English Literature degree from Dartmouth College in New Hampshire, but it was a series of synchronous events that led him over his long career to be an English teacher in the US, then Greece, followed by Japan and finally Hawaii, where he taught at Punahou, which counts Barack Obama as one of its more recognizable alumni.

As we continued our wide-ranging conversations over the following years, I discovered how Miller's entrepreneurial and social initiatives were often the result of his ability to recognize and leverage synchronicity. I would often visit in the autumn when the cold air would sting your nostrils and the sharp light would play across the red and yellow shades of the New England foliage. We would rise early, make coffee in a battered Molino Italian coffee machine, pack the car with an array of arts and crafts collected on his travels around the world, and head to local county fairs under the sharp blue autumn sky. We would set up a stall with Peruvian hats, Vietnamese baskets, Mexican ponchos and Asian wind chimes. Neighbouring vendors would offer locally grown vegetables, old tractor parts, and garden furniture. I don't recall how much he sold of anything and the whole affair seemed an excuse to enjoy conversations with visitors. We spent many weekends this way talking and sipping hot coffee poured from a rusty army flask, amid the scattered bales of hay and oversized pumpkins. It was during these road trips along the back roads of Vermont in Miller's 1951 Rocket 88 Oldsmobile that I gradually unpicked the synchronicity of his life.

It had starting with being hired 'accidentally' three times in a row in his 20s and 30s. His initial foray into higher education after high school had Miller applying to Dartmouth at the behest of his railway industrialist father who considered that to be a 'proper' path in the family tradition. Despite not being 'Ivy League material' he nonetheless managed to graduate, as he says, 'Last in my class'.

His next accidental career move occcurred when he was inadvertently hired at Harvard University. While awaiting a friend at George Washington Hall and wearing jeans and a T-shirt, he happened to be sitting in an area where some interviews were taking place. A certain Mr. Foley walked past and said 'You're next' and proceeded to usher him into an interview room. After 30 minutes of rather general conversation Miller was asked if he wanted a job. He was not employed at the time so said 'OK'. Foley then said, 'Good. Doing what?' and Miller ventured 'Admissions?' having noticed such a sign on a nearby door. It was a brief experience once he realized the job was 'Not me' but the story again shows how keeping an open mind and saying 'yes' (rather than 'no' as most of us do when put in front of something unexpected) can trigger synchronicity and unexpected opportunities, like working at Harvard despite having no relevant qualifications. Without knowing it, those two experiences gave Miller a valuable network that would later open doors for funding his charitable endeavours.

The third accidental job occurred during an application to teach at Phillips Academy, one of the premier schools in New England. This time he did in fact want the post, but as the panel began to question him about the intricacies of *Finnegan's Wake* by James Joyce, Miller floundered and eventually said, 'Don't hire me, I'm not a PhD'. But the panel did anyway, recognizing from his humility and some stories about traveling the world that he would be good with children. His natural empathy counted more for the school than his academic credentials. The role brought out his natural talent as an educator which became quickly evident, triggering further assignments in Japan, Greece, and Hawaii from where he travelled extensively around Asia. These postings brought him into contact with cultures and people where education infrastructure was sorely lacking, triggering the idea for his NGO and educational projects.

Thus, his entrée into social enterprise through education was also due to synchronicity. It started while he was teaching in Japan, one day getting lost in Tokyo. He happened on the Vietnam Embassy where he went in to ask for directions. In talking with the woman at the front desk she offered him a visa, which he decided to use during an upcoming school break. Arriving in Hanoi, he found himself to be one of the first Americans in Vietnam in 15 years since the war. As he journeyed around, he again made unexpected contacts, this time in a local village that was producing lacquered baskets, which gave him the idea to try and sell them overseas and use the money to refurbish the school, which was in poor repair, and also help build the local village economy. In hindsight he realized that, as one of the first exporters in Vietnam when few foreigners could enter the country, he could have built a large, profitable business. But his goal was for educational impact, so he stuck to those baskets, selling them back at those weekend county fairs in Vermont where I first admired them.

Miller had discovered his natural strengths in a roundabout way as he passed through his life stages, but they had emerged as curiosity, empathy, storytelling and working exceptionally well with children. We will see later how curiosity and empathy in particular are key attributes for building a Change Mindset. But applying those attributes consistently in his midlife stage enabled Miller to act in moments of synchronicity, creating social enterprise projects in Vietnam, Honduras and Haiti despite having no 'core' skills for such businesses. Another key attribute that I have seen in Miller's projects is humility. Like Professor Khaw, he puts his ego aside and puts others first – the villagers and the students – which seems to make further 'luck' come his way.

Today, the small basket weaving business he invested in during that chance trip to Vietnam is a successful international manufacturing and design company. Miller himself has now also formalized his social enterprise efforts into a structure by creating The Children's Initiative. He has received several awards for transforming communities and student's lives through his founding of schools in Vietnam and Haiti and an orphanage in Ethiopia. I visited his latest project, a long-term rural development project in Honduras, in early 2020 to take photographs to support his fundraising efforts. Back in the US he sits on several non-profit boards and works with young people at risk in his local community in Portland, Maine.

When I asked Miller about lessons learned about synchronicity he told me, 'I wanted the experience rather than the outcome. These moments also show up something that people see in you but that you don't recognize in yourself.' As for advice on finding moments of synchronicity to build change skills: 'These moments of transition for me, are not about doing something else but becoming someone else. When you are naked and exposed in uncertainty you discover who you really are. And in these moments, with the right mindset, it is possible to fully be yourself – you don't have to wear the uniform.'

A final moment of synchronicity occurred on the way back from one of our county fair weekends, before I moved to Europe after a decade in America. Randomly opening the glove compartment of Miller's Oldsmobile I found a small plastic bag of white powder and made a joke about his new drug habit. He burst out laughing. It turned out to be a handful of ashes that Miller had stolen from his best friend's funeral, with the intention of giving him a 'proper burial' in a place he knew his friend loved, rather than the cemetery plot chosen by the family. He had absentmindedly thrown the bag there on the way back from the funeral and had been searching for it for years. His best friend had in fact been accompanying him around the back roads of New England for all that time and I can't help believing that had been a better resting place for him than being scattered to the four winds across the Green Mountains of Vermont.

Summary of key points

In this chapter, I have explored how psychological life stages can be a metaphor for leading change. Progressing through these life stages creates tension but can also be resolved through reflection around our lessons learned in the process. Benefits and blind spots can occur during these stages too, particularly in midlife when our willingness to flex our behaviour and embrace change sometimes dwindles.

We also explored the role of synchronicity when moments of coincidence and connection can create wider opportunities to leverage changes we face.

One key message about life stages is to remember that they do not replace or override one another. Rather, they transcend and build on each other. What this means is that we retain certain aspects of what we have learned and experienced before; for example, behaviours like imitating or differentiating. At the same time, as we mature these earlier drives become less significant and we develop new skills. These give us more options for leading change, for example through activating our ambitions or more integrative thinking.

The leaders I interviewed about their own transitions had all learned important lessons from their own life stages, helping them navigate change as they developed their leadership skills.

In the next chapter I will build on the life stages framework to translate them into more specific leadership skills and practices that can further build our Change Mindset.

CHAPTER THREE

Person, passion, permission, purpose: The four tenets of powerful change leadership

I hope for nothing
I fear nothing
I am free NIKOS KAZANTZAKIS

There is a windy hilltop that I visited in Heraklion on the island of Crete some years ago. The Martinengo Bastion commands the highest point of the city's old Venetian defensive fortifications and offers panoramic views across the mountains and the sea of Crete. But it was not the views that my wife, who has Greek origins, and I were after that day. Rather, it was a simple grave made of a few rough granite blocks and a modest wooden cross that sits on a small clearing overlooking the Aegean sea from the windy heights of the ramparts. Chiselled into the rough marble headstone is the inscription above. Nikos Kazantzakis, the giant of Greek literature whose works include *Zorba the Greek* (1946) and *The Last Temptation of Christ* (1955) was a controversial author during his lifetime. The Greek Orthodox Church threatened Kazantzakis with excommunication, which explains the location of his final resting place: he was denied burial in a cemetery. His epitaph is based on the philosophical ideals of the ancient Cynics, who rejected the conventional human desires of wealth, power and fame in favour of simplicity and a deep connection to nature.

Kazantzakis' protagonist in the story of *Zorba*, played memorably by Anthony Quinn, brings this epitaph vividly to life as he navigates the numerous setbacks and opportunities peppered throughout the story of travel, adventure and change. It captures the essence of a life that many of us might also aspire to – throwing caution to the wind and following one's instincts regardless of the consequences. In a way, it is the Mediterranean version of Frost's more stoic New England parable *The Road Not Taken,* and Kazantzakis extends us the same invitation in *Zorba*. The unforgettable image of Quinn dancing penniless on the beach in the final scene captures the essence of the Change Mindset in confronting transitions and leading change. He is a whole person, passionate and courageous about his undertakings. He has given himself permission to embark upon a series of risky but inspiring big ideas. He shows clear purpose in pursuing these dreams and he is fearless in the face of uncertainty, all the while living life to the fullest. In my conversations with leaders on the topic of navigating transitions, similar attributes were apparent, albeit it in a generally more modern setting: a clear purpose, a sense of freedom to act, courage in the face of adversity, deliberate use of one's natural gifts, and choosing to pursue something they truly believe in. Many of the leaders I interviewed for this book were like modern-day Zorbas.

But the other protagonist in the film, the narrator, is a young Greek intellectual who also teaches us lessons about dealing with change and transitions. He struggles with his 'internal no' and a lack of courage, hesitating and projecting worst case scenarios onto Zorba's big ideas. The sad reality is that the narrator represents many of us when it comes to our life choices and our reactions to change. When presented with more risky or inspiring options, our 'internal no' acts as a brake to realizing our true potential or embracing change in a more deliberate and courageous way. We select what seem to be the more 'acceptable' options in life, and choose what are deemed 'proper' professions in work. In the world of business, many executives I work with, though essentially capable in their roles, also become dominated by worry, introspection and inaction when faced with uncertainty. Often this is because they have been conditioned by their bosses and shareholders to make safe choices, always taking the more reasonable, studied, and planned approach. It is also a hold-over from our imitation life stage discussed in the last chapter.

But Zorba encourages us to think differently, saying in the book: 'A person needs a little madness, or else they never dare cut the rope and become free,' (Kazantzakis, 1952).

So as aspiring change leaders, how can we inject a little more 'madness' into our own lives to lead through the inevitable changes and transitions we face in today's VUCA world?

Translating life stages into change levers for action

In Chapters 1 and 2 we explored why our natural survival instincts put us at odds with change. We saw how, in our personal lives, we struggle to take actions that could enhance our outcomes when we face uncertainty. In our roles as leaders and professionals too we often fail to take clear action and find the right strategies when faced with change. We dither, defer, hesitate, delegate and often end up avoiding action altogether. We want to stay safe and preserve our status, so we create a façade of confidence to disguise our lack of answers or ideas. Even if we want to take on the change, ideas and solutions often elude us despite our best efforts.

Yet there are some who thrive in these moments of uncertainty. We saw how Professor Peng Khaw, social entrepreneur Charlie Miller, journalist Gillian Tett and author Charles Handy had learned to observe, adapt and act in moments of change and uncertainty.

But for most of us, such uncertainty can be daunting and goes to the core of who we are. Indeed, key moments of change and transition will often provoke fundamental questions about our life, work, values, purpose and our most important choices. Daniel Goleman, who popularized the concept of emotional intelligence in the 1990s after it was originally coined by psychologist Michael Beldoch in the 1960s, captured this sentiment in a post for the global talent consultancy Korn Ferry in the early days of the pandemic, writing: 'Millions of people have hit an existential crisis. The pandemic, coupled with racial tension, political upheaval, and a growing awareness of climate change, has brought us face to face with our own mortality. Why do I do what I do? Does my workplace value me? Do I value my own work? These questions are more and more common' (Goleman, 2021).

The leaders I spoke to for this book were unanimous about the need to be making bolder and more deliberate choices in the face of these existential questions. We saw in the last chapter how life stage theory can teach us helpful skills and practices to build a Change Mindset when we face moments of uncertainty. We identified attributes including curiosity, openness, observation, listening, courage and controlling one's ego. These are some of the ways we can be more 'present' to our surroundings to better navigate change. We also explored the role of synchronicity as a phenomenon that helps us grasp unexpected opportunities more deliberately at any life stage.

Yet the challenge remains that transitions and change are everywhere, and as the leaders we are the ones expected to provide solutions, even though there is no toolkit to reliably show us the way.

Perhaps we need to 'cut the rope', as Zorba suggests, but 'a little madness' alone will not solve complex problems. And recklessness is never a recommended leadership practice either.

Yet I have met many leaders who do share the sense of freedom that Kazantzakis invites us into. You may think these people are born with natural courage and self-determination, but I believe anyone can navigate change successfully with greater agency and purpose if they develop the right mindset and self-awareness.

To explore this further in the context of leadership, we can draw again on the foundational psychology from the last chapter to build a behavioral framework for change. I have reinterpreted this early work as a journey through life involving the following sequence of transitions:

- *Imitation* – the process of remembering our early role models and identifying the values and standards we saw in them, choosing these to guide us through adult life as change leaders
- *Differentiation* – the deliberate discovery of our natural strengths and attributes, and using these more purposefully to form our leadership identity and potential as change agents
- *Activation* – the process of building our confidence so we use our strengths more deliberately in moments of change to create opportunities, make lateral connections and bring ourselves closer to realizing our deeper professional ambitions
- *Integration* – the work of bringing together all of our professional and life experiences in a way that maximizes our impact during transitions, finding a shared context and a clear purpose both for ourselves as leaders and for those we lead.

We can illustrate this journey in four life quadrants as follows.

FIGURE 3.1 The journey to individuation

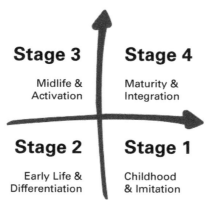

In testing this model through conversations with leaders and exploring their own choices in moments of change, four key leadership questions emerged for each life stage, from imitation to differentiation, activation, and integration:

- When a significant change requires us to evolve past *imitation* to define ourselves and our identity, the transitional leadership question is: Who am I?
- When a significant change requires us to achieve greater *differentiation* by discovering our unique strengths, the transitional leadership question is: What are my gifts?
- When a significant change requires deliberate *activation* of our strengths to navigate uncertainty, the transitional leadership question is: How do I realize my potential?
- When a significant change requires *integration* of our experiences into a clear sense of purpose, the transitional leadership question is: Why have I chosen this path?

Using this new vocabulary gets us closer to the answer of *how* we can practically overcome our aversion to change and begin to explore what we instinctively know about change to increase our confidence to act. This helps us align our choices with our values, mine the lessons learned from previous transitional experiences, and apply these to the change at hand. In this context, our framework for building a Change Mindset now becomes:

FIGURE 3.2 Developing a Change Mindset

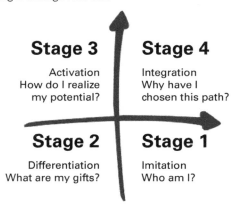

This revised framework now provides us with a more tangible set of questions to activate ourselves and build a Change Mindset when faced with change.

I believe that many of our change challenges and transitional dilemmas can be solved with this more deliberate approach to exploring the *who, what, how* and *why* questions. They are not existential traps, but powerful triggers in the context of change that can move us forward.

This mining of life stages links our current change challenges to our previous experiences, and is the key building block of an effective Change Mindset. It is cumulative experiences of change that builds our coping skills, and the essential questions of *who, what, how* and *why* can provide us with a roadmap for further insights and action at these moments. The process helps us navigate transitional changes because only we know who we are, what we want, and why. This in turn gives us the focus and rationale to act with purpose. It also creates belief. As Charlie Miller put it, in these moments 'We are not doing something else, but becoming someone else'.

When I spoke to Gillian Tett about her new book *Anthro-Vision*, (Tett, 2021), she shared an analogous insight: 'The 20th century was all about tunnel vision and silos. The 21st century I think is all about lateral vision.' Making connections and links across our life experiences helps to thrive in a more transitional world. It can also open doors for us to move more courageously onto 'the bigger stage' as Charles Handy described in Chapter 1.

The four tenets of powerful change leadership: Person, passion, permission, purpose

'The unexamined life is not worth living'

These were allegedly Socrates' words at his trial for impiety when faced with exile or death in 399 BC (Fowler, 1966). Choosing death before honour to uphold his own purpose and values in life was a courageous choice for the great philosopher. But his belief in the pursuit of wisdom through questioning and logical argument represents the essence of the Change Mindset that we are exploring in this book: questioning the status quo, taking bold action in the face of uncertainty, and staying open to new thinking even when our instincts pull us back to safety. As I read Socrates, he too made it a lifelong quest to explore *who, what, how* and *why*.

In today's context of leadership and change, I reframe these questions as four P's (person, passion, permission and purpose) to generate fresh insights about navigating transitions in a more 'examined' way.

Our Change Mindset framework now becomes the source of our power to tackle uncertainty as 'whole' leaders.

FIGURE 3.3   The Change Mindset in action

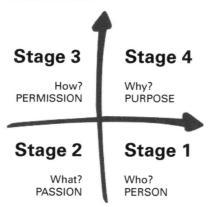

As we face change and transition situations, the four P's can now trigger action, as follows:

- *Person:* Who am I being in this change situation? Do I have my own voice or am I imitating something or someone else? How can I bring myself more fully into this situation?

- *Passion:* What knowledge, skills and unique attributes can I apply to this question? What am I particularly good at that can help me gain new insight?
- *Permission:* How can I create the conditions for deliberate action in response to this change? Am I feeling confident about my plan and my choices? If not, what is missing and what can I do to give myself more certainty to move ahead?
- *Purpose:* Why have I chosen this path for my personal and professional journey? How does this align with my underlying values and purpose? And how do I use this knowledge to inform my choices in response to change?

The concept of synchronicity acts a layer over all these questions as we seek to unlock further possibilities during change by leveraging unexpected moments of connection.

The interaction of these factors as we build our Change Mindset can be visualized in the following table.

TABLE 3.1 Linking life stages to the Change Mindset

LIFE STAGE QUADRANT	PRIME MOTIVATING BEHAVIORS	PERSONAL DEVELOPMENT FOCUS	LEADERSHIP QUESTIONS TO NAVIGATE CHANGE
1 - Early Life & Identity	Imitation	Person	Who am I?
2 - Early Career	Differentiation	Passion	What are my gifts?
3 - Midlife	Activation	Permission	How do I realize my potential?
4 - Late Career & Maturity	Integration	Purpose	Why have I chosen this path, do my actions align with my values?

We can also plot this as a chronological journey of learning about change as we experience life as follows:

FIGURE 3.4 Leading change over time

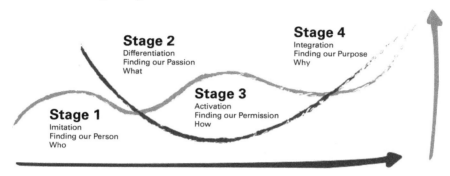

However we choose to use these different elements to navigate change, the key is to stay aware of our lived experience and learn from it as we journey through life. If we focus on our power to act in the face of uncertainty, we can unlock action by asking ourselves the right questions when we are unsure of how to proceed.

But what that does this framework look like in practice, and what can we learn from other leaders who have built their Change Mindset by mastering these skills? Let us take each factor – *who, what, how and why* – and illustrate them through stories.

Person: Who am I?

The question: At what stage do we transition from imitating others to defining a personal identity that can answer the question: 'Who am I'?

Lord Parry Mitchell is a member of the British House of Lords and shared a vivid story of the moment he was able to answer this question. The House of Lords is the independent second chamber of the UK Parliament, tasked with shaping national laws and challenging the work of government across a range of policy areas. As the Upper House of the UK Parliament, which itself dates back to 1295 AD, it is one of the oldest institutions for debate and decision making on legislative matters across the UK and, indeed, the world. In addition to this role, Lord Mitchell advises public and private bodies on future digital strategies for the UK. He also counsels entrepreneurs on digital strategies and dedicates time to supporting young leaders in their own technology startups. His background as a technology entrepreneur gives him a unique perspective on digital business models, big data strategies and data privacy.

How did he arrive here and how did he identify his 'person'?

Lord Mitchell grew up in North West London. His family had emigrated to the UK in the late 1890s and his father was a furrier who had a chequered career as a businessman. As a child, he found himself with few role models and chose to be a rebel at school, as he himself describes in his recent auto-biography *Some Fall by the Way*. The title alludes to the fateful comment made by the school headmaster to his mother suggesting that Mitchell was on track to fail most of his exams, which in fact he went on to do, failing six out of seven of his O-levels.

Aged 16 and suddenly needing a job, he applied as a salesman for the US home appliance company Hoover. On his first day at work found himself looking down what seemed to be an interminable row of semi-detached brick houses on a wet street in Wood Green. His job was to knock on every one of those doors and show his samples as he tried to fulfil his quota. At this very distinct fork in the road, he was suddenly able to very clearly answer the question 'Who Am I?' It was clearly not being a Hoover sales-man and he quickly understood that if he wanted to achieve anything significant, he would essentially have to transform who he was. He decided then and there he wanted to be an entirely different person – successful, wealthy and, in his words, 'To become Prime Minister'.

As a result of that moment Lord Mitchell decided to go back to evening school where he attained his A-levels and then a Bachelor of Economics degree with honours. He went on to successfully earn an MBA at Columbia University Graduate School of Business in the US, arriving in America with just $500 in his pocket and his admission form. On his return to the UK he worked his way into a role at IBM as a systems engineer and then hit his stride as a business leader. Lord Mitchell further shaped his identity as a serial entrepreneur by creating a series of ventures in the then nascent tech-nology sector of mainframe computer leasing.

Lord Mitchell subsequently transitioned into a series of roles leading to public service, spurred on by his childhood goal to 'become Prime Minister' and a drive to pursue politics. Through business and personal connections, he was able to become a founding member of the UK Social Democrat Party in the early 1980s, and although ultimately unsuccessful as a party, this new identity opened further doors. He was ennobled in 2000, rose to Shadow Business Minister and Chair of Labour Digital in 2013, sat on the Joint Select Committee on National Security from 2014, and became Enterprise Advisor to the government thereafter. Today Lord Mitchell is a major influencer of public policy and has further extended his work into the realm of educational charities, such as the Coexistence Trust which he founded to bring together Jewish and Muslim students to jointly explore common ground.

I asked Lord Mitchell about his lessons learned in answering the fundamental question of 'Who am I?', and what advice he had for others in this context.

His first piece of advice for others was, 'Be a contender – you have to work hard to create your own story.' Like Marlon Brando in *On the Waterfront*, he wanted to be something other than the surroundings he came from. Even though becoming Prime Minister was a step too far, the clear image he set himself served as a compass to make the courageous choices he needed over the following five decades as he reinvented his career in a clear example of consciously progressing beyond imitation. He also believes in 'Setting big goals and telling everyone about them, because that will commit you to deliver.' This self-determination reminded me of Charles Handy who also publicly declared himself, in his case as a 'social philosopher' because no label existed to describe the profession he had chosen. In striving to achieve his 'person', Lord Mitchell also believes, like Churchill, 'You must never, never, never give up.' He did inevitably hit bumps on *The Road not Taken* from his North London upbringing, but he has reframed these as part of the journey, telling me that his past failures were, 'A series of stepping stones on the way to success.'

But his most insightful comment on the question of 'Who am I?' was this: 'There is a different *you* in there if you look for it.'

In other words, we don't need to be defined by our family, our environment, education or background. It seems that in answering the 'Who?', personal reinvention is always possible, and at any age.

Passion: What are my gifts?

The question: At what stage do we discover our strengths, find a passion that differentiates us and answer the question 'what are my gifts?'

Martin Gayford epitomizes someone who has found his unique gifts and built a successful career around that passion.

Gayford is a prolific and acclaimed author and commentator, known for his major biographies and memoirs of artists such as Michelangelo, John Constable and Lucian Freud. He is also a long-term friend of David Hockney, with a recent book collaboration following the artist's move to Normandy in 2019 (which subsequently forced him to work in isolation due to the pandemic). *Spring Cannot be Cancelled* is an exuberant celebration of positivity in response to a year living under repeated lockdowns, disruption and fear, and the existential questions this raised for many of us (Gayford, 2021).

Gayford spoke to me from his home in Cambridge, about how he found his passion for art and writing, and what lessons he learned in the process.

Navigating change throughout life has also been a constant theme for him. Originally studying philosophy at Cambridge, he lost enthusiasm when he realized the limits of a practical career in that discipline. After some existential soul-searching he switched to history of art, which he felt was more aligned with his natural interests, learning an early lesson in the process: 'Find what you are shaped to do and have the courage to walk away from what doesn't fit.'

While seeking more ways to apply his newly discovered interest in art, he landed a role in journalism. Over a chance lunch with an arts editor one day he was asked, 'Is there anything else you would like to write about?' to which he responded, 'How about art?' This short exchange led to a long train journey from London to Liverpool and an extremely short deadline to submit a review for a Sickert exhibition. His passion for the topic and his excitement about this new opportunity helped him deliver a successful article on time, which led to further assignments outside his regular beat. Eventually he found himself spending more time writing about art than in the role he had been hired for.

Describing his journey into realizing his passion further, Gayford also described the role of courage when faced with the unknown, saying, 'Taking on a challenge requires nerve, and you won't move forward without it.' He likens this to 'stepping through the mirror as Alice did in *Through the Looking Glass*.' But the risk of such unknowns is worth the reward, he says, because in the process 'if you find something you love, you will do it every day'.

Other lessons learned include the need for unbounded curiosity and a drive to constantly be learning more about one's chosen area. As an example, he told me of a moment over tea with the painter Lucian Freud when the conversation turned to what it was like to be 'under the artist's gaze'. Gayford said, 'I'd like to try this experience,' and offered his services as a sitter. Seven months and 100 hours later, the portrait *Man with a Blue Scarf* was completed. 'It brought me one step closer to the actual creation of art,' says Gayford, and his book of the same title (Gayford, 2011) brilliantly captured the wide-ranging conversations over those 100 hours as Freud shared insights into portraiture and discussed artists such as Michelangelo, Vermeer, Titian, Goya, van Gogh, Mondrian, and Francis Bacon. Gayford's developing curiosity led to a further evolution in his work after *Blue Scarf*, to explore the three-dimensional world of sculpture and leading to a new collaboration with British Sculptor Anthony Gormley and the book *Shaping the World* (Gormley and Gayford, 2020).

Gayford provides an excellent example of someone finding a passion and acting deliberately through life to apply it in their work. Speaking to him about his many collaborations with Hockney, I also got the sense they are kindred spirits in their pursuit of a passion. Hockney's infectious enthusiasm about painting has grown over his 50-year career as he moved from the UK to America and now France, reinventing himself by working in oils, acrylic, digital art on iPads, and even stained-glass with the recent *The Queen's Window* in Westminster Abbey. Now into digital animation, these most recent transitions as an artist have occurred in his 80's, and he shows no signs of losing his enthusiasm for change.

For both Hockney and Gayford, discovering their passion has become a compass for navigating their personal and professional decisions in moments of change as they evolved in their respective careers.

Permission: How do I realize my potential?

The question: At what stage do we find the confidence to activate our strengths, giving ourselves permission to follow our deeper ambitions and answer the question 'how do I realize my potential'?

In 2015 I signed up for an organization development (OD) programme in Oxford and spent the next 14 months learning the essentials of applied behavioural science under the tutelage of the Dean, Dr. Mee-Yan Cheung Judge. She is the best example I have come across of creating permission to lead change.

Dr. Cheung Judge is a recognized expert in OD, having written and taught extensively on the subject as 'scholar-educator-practitioner'. Born in Singapore and now based in Oxford, she advises organizations and institutions on 'Balancing organizational effectiveness and organizational health'. When we first met, she was working on a client engagement to transform the capacity for creativity and innovation in the state of Singapore. In a country with a rote educational system and where hierarchy and obedience define 'good citizenship', the assignment seemed like a huge challenge when she told me about it. But Dr Cheung Judge had given herself permission to embark on this large-scale attempt to transform the culture of an entire government, recognizing that in order to compete with neighbours like China and South Korea, the nation state had to become less risk averse and bolder in its innovations.

At the conclusion of the NTL programme I invited Dr Cheung Judge for a coffee to ask her how I might now best apply the important concepts we had explored together. I expected a list of clever techniques for my next consulting engagement but instead she said simply, 'Andy, start with your gifts.' What she meant of course was: find what you are really good at, and give yourself full permission to use that to make the difference in your work. So it wasn't about tools but rather about talent and deploying more of who we fundamentally are by using our intuition. She calls this 'using the self as instrument'. As we build greater confidence about ourselves as leaders, this is where the power to create change lies. This may sound easy but of course it is a lot harder than applying a toolkit or checklist. Throwing away what we know to explore new territory without the manual, or 'dropping our tools' as we saw with the Mann Gulch firefighters in Chapter 1, can be liberating and rewarding. But it also requires losing our ego and giving ourselves full permission to trust our instincts, take risks and be willing to expose ourselves as leaders.

Someone else who has mastered permission is Martin Lutyens. Lutyens and I were colleagues at Watson Wyatt when I was working in the International Practice out of Paris and San Francisco, and knowing his track record for creating permission I decided to reconnect with him to explore his insights. Lutyens spent most of his career as one of the most senior advisory partners at the consulting firm Watson Wyatt (now Willis Towers Watson) where he advised boards on sensitive and high visibility matters of executive remuneration and corporate governance.

He told me how in that environment you are paid to have your own voice, putting forward your arguments with conviction and clarity in matters that are often financially and reputationally sensitive.

One of his lessons learned was to entirely trust his instincts in moments of uncertainty, in order to access intuition and judgement. To illustrate this he shared a story about rehearsing for a major presentation at a conference in Los Angeles where a professional coach had been brought in. At that time, Lutyens would always speak from a small pack of index cards with bullet points as cues. 'I had been talking for about eight minutes and the coach said, 'Stop. Can I have your cards?' He tore them up and put them in the bin, saying, 'Right, you can carry on now.' Lutyens decided to try the experiment and to his surprise, he told me, 'It actually worked.'

Lutyens may not have had much choice about permission to change given his cards were shredded, but nonetheless the metaphor to 'throw away the cue cards' stuck and served him well as he further built his expertise advising his most senior clients. With this principle he habitually pushed the envelope, giving himself and his team leeway to innovate with new services and try out different approaches to meet client needs as the world of corporate governance evolved and grew more complex. Permission played a key role in his ability to navigate change and adapt.

Lutyens is also the great nephew of the celebrated British architect, Sir Edwin Lutyens. In another display of permission (and in the spirit of *The 100 Year Life*) he decided to accept an invitation to become a trustee of the Lutyens Trust, the charity dedicated to the study and preservation of Sir Edwin's works. Successfully marrying his business career with his interest in the arts, he is now Chairman of the Lutyens Trusts in both the UK and US, steering their educational, conservation and fundraising activities – and mostly without cue cards.

Permission clearly runs in the Lutyens family, and Lutyens also shared with me how Sir Edwin gave himself permission as a young man to take up architecture, despite very limited formal education or training. He did complete two years' study at the South Kensington School of Art and nine months apprenticeship in the office of a then fashionable architect but remained largely self taught. With this limited toolkit, Sir Edwin went on to become the most sought-after British architect of his day and create some of the world's most iconic buildings, among them the Viceroy's House (now Rashtrapati Bhavan) in Delhi and the Cenotaph in London. Both required the ability to seek out and execute these nationally important commissions and neither would exist without him having trusted his incredible instinct for proportion and perspective, which was a vital ingredient of his work. Quoting a comment by one of Sir Edwin's colleagues, Lutyens told me 'He seemed to know by intuition some great truths about our art' and added, 'He had some lucky breaks but seems to have learned to just trust his instincts. I believe if you can do that, you'll do fine.'

These stories provide lessons about how to give ourselves permission to act in moments of change, regardless of how challenging or risky the situation may appear. Metaphorically throwing away our cue cards and trusting our instincts to try something new are the keys to creating the right conditions to succeed. Without this permission to step outside what we know, our value as change agents will remain hidden under a shroud of conformity.

Purpose: Why have I chosen this path?

The question: At what stage do we transition from activation to integration, bringing together our life's experience into a clear sense of purpose? And how might we share this with others to help them navigate change – as individuals, teams or organizations?

The ultimate ability to lead change is to do so with purpose and at scale, engaging groups, organizations or even society in some form of transformation. Such a clear sense of purpose was abundantly clear to me during my conversation with Annmarie Lewis, OBE and Founder of UK-based and award-winning social enterprise Rainmakers Worldwide. The social enterprise offers women and young people from challenging and diverse backgrounds – including those affected by prison, the care system and homelessness – access to work and business opportunities to become entrepreneurs.

How did she come to formulate these transformational ideas, and what allowed her to realize them with such notable success?

At age three, Lewis was already forging her own purposeful path. She alarmed her nursery school teachers by 'staring at school books all day' until her parents were called in. They realized after having her recite a few lines that she was actually reading rather than staring at those books. This thirst for knowledge and her quick mind continued to serve her well, and she told me how her purpose was in fact 'revealed' to her early in life as a mission to 'Elevate people through the principles of justice'. This ideal manifested itself before she was 10 when, aged 6, she brought home a few of her classmates from a peripatetic Travelling family who were being bullied due to their appearance. She insisted to her mother they be given access to wash facilities and be fed and clothed again before going back to their community site.

Later, after being a standout student in her adolescent years, she quickly found her niche as a social entrepreneur as she searched for a vehicle to actualize her purpose and improve justice for young adults from marginalized backgrounds. Her clarity of purpose also enabled her to become the first black woman to join the UK prison service as an officer in a young offender's institution and then later create Rainmakers.

I first met Lewis when she brought a group of former youth offenders to meet a team of asset managers in London as part of a strategic offsite. Her presence was designed to be a provocation for the investment experts to think more broadly about their possible future clients and where future investable wealth might be generated. The exercise was not as far-fetched as it sounded. Many Rainmakers 'graduates' have gone on to launch successful entrepreneurial ventures in fashion, music, business and technology.

Lewis told me about how this happens.

> Many prison leavers, especially the youth, are actually the smartest kids and most entrepreneurial in their peer groups. But they lack opportunities to express this and are often bored in their underserved environments, with complex needs unmet. Because of the multiple flaws and failures in the system, crime and associated affiliations often create the most interesting and realistic outlets for them, despite being obviously wrong. But if you can point that energy and intelligence to something more creative and structured, these kids can become amazing business leaders.

During that strategy offsite we also talked about the amount of global wealth waiting to be passed down to next generation, $15 trillion according to one estimate (Reyburn, 2019). A significant proportion of this will be in the hands of this new generation which demonstrates a far greater appetite for impact investing, alternative asset classes and philanthropy than today's asset management client base. This future wealth will also be generated by the young entrepreneurs like those from Rainmakers, whose diversity of view, experience and backgrounds will also come with non-traditional values and expectations about managing money and what do with it. The impact of these new trends on the banking and investment industry is already being felt through structures such as ESG funds, crypto and NFT assets, and impact investment vehicles.

So how did Lewis find such a clear calling to improve justice and then create the opportunities to make it happen, successfully navigating a series of transitions to build her impact? During a conversation at her home in London, we explored this question together.

First, she talked about how her Jamaican father and her mother, who also has Scottish heritage, gave her early insight into the value of diversity, creating a potpourri of cultural experiences from family gatherings to mealtime recipes that reflected their Anglo-Caribbean roots. Next, witnessing the non-traditional roles taken on by her extended and multi-cultural immigrant family showed Lewis clearly at an early age that anything is possible in how we choose to live our lives or create impact with others. Finally, her courageous choices to work with under-represented, underserved communities and those affected by homelessness brought her face to face with poverty, violence and crime. This revealed to her the pressing need for greater equality and access to opportunities in society.

These powerful influences, coupled with end-to-end justice experience spanning 25 years, combined into her clear purpose: to trigger a societal shift in justice, for which Rainmakers Worldwide has been a key foundation step. This instinct for justice has guided all her key decisions later in life.

I asked her what advice she had for others seeking to uncover their own purpose and create a bigger narrative to underpin their lives and drive change. 'To create a purpose,' she told me, 'find a calling and then focus relentlessly on it.' Finding our calling is not an easy task but if we take Lewis' example it starts with reflecting on our childhood influences and the moments that formed our worldview, including what is important to us and what change we therefore believe we can make in the world.

She also believes that having a purpose 'creates your own unique opportunities and shapes your destiny' as our interests and energies naturally place us in the right place at the right time. She illustrated this principle in a story about unexpectedly finding herself in front of a group of PWC executives to pitch an idea for her social enterprise. She was in a PWC location that day by chance, and happened to share her idea about Rainmakers during an informal conversation. The person she was speaking to was aware of a senior partner meeting happening that day which was looking at new investment opportunities, and so spontaneously invited her to share her vision with them.

Her natural energy and the words she found to describe her vision unlocked the opportunity and she was granted the funding she needed.

Lewis is also a strong believer in the power of observation and the importance of paying close attention to what is happening around us as we shape our values and purpose, saying, 'You have to recognize the pivotal markers in your life so you can learn from them.' In her case this included learning early on about the value of multiculturalism, reflecting on the role of different values and attitudes, and seeking experiences of diversity through volunteer work in her local community. These deliberate observations and experiences helped her form a view about the growing injustice in society, and from there it became a question of using the power of language and acting on her conviction to be a change advocate, as she did at PWC.

But alongside her drive and energy, I also see a remarkable humility in Lewis. She takes nothing for granted and always stays open to feedback, which as we will see later are trademarks of a strong Change Mindset. To keep one's ego in check, she says, 'Stay close to those trusted people who remind you who you are and tell you the truth, both the good and the bad.'

Today, Lewis is a valued and experienced consultant in the fields of entrepreneurship, criminal justice and diversity and inclusion for young people. She underpins her purpose with rigid qualifications, holding degrees in criminal justice, youth community work, applied anthropology and leadership. She frequently speaks about her work at the London and Warwick business schools and works at a range of universities, including the Oxford and Cambridge summer schools. In her current role as Head of Culture and Strategic Leadership in the Youth Custody Service, she is working to transform the culture in the UK justice system.

At the end of our interview I asked her what her ultimate personal goal is. Without hesitation she replied, 'I want to die empty. I want to deposit everything within me that was meant for this world'. Her ultimate aspiration, she told me, is 'To create a learning institution that is specific to systems and culture change in society.'

Here is someone so committed to her purpose that she wants to use the entirety of her skills, energy and time to fulfil that calling. I have no doubt that her focus and commitment will achieve the impact she has envisioned.

The shadow side of who, what, how and why

We are probably among the first generations in the developed world with the freedom to actually determine our life choices. It can seem almost indulgent to explore the questions of *who, what, how* and *why* as we contemplate a change of career, a move to another country, starting a new businesses or embarking on a portfolio lifestyle. Many people around the world do not yet enjoy this degree of freedom or self-determination in their local contexts, though I believe that as globalization and freedom of information continues to connect us, these choices will become tangible for an increasing number of people. The internet has vastly increased access to information and education, and technology now allows us to start a business from our laptops or even smartphones. With barriers to choice about or lives and work steadily diminishing, unprecedented new opportunities are inviting us to become more self-determined, purposeful and able to trigger transitions – even in underprivileged societies such as we saw with the Grameen Bank project in Chapter 2.

Yet, ironically, too much choice can also lead to no choice. As I spoke to leaders for this book, I discovered that despite greater opportunities, many fail to trigger their own transitions. Given the chance to quit our job and start a business, or embark on volunteer work, or try out teaching, many of us still fail to test these new – and perhaps more satisfying – avenues. Ironically, when we embark on a new transition, exploring *who, what, how* and *why* can even backfire. What are these conditions that disable our Change Mindset, and how do they cause us to derail?

Person: The shadow side

As leaders, if we fail to develop a clear self-image and identity in response to the question 'Who am I?' we are likely to remain in a cycle of imitation, emulating or even pretending to be people we are not. And although imitation is a childhood association, in these circumstances it can persist well into adulthood and often unconsciously undermine our confidence and effectiveness. I have coached many executives who are still emulating earlier but now irrelevant role models. They might twist themselves into conformity to be accepted in a dominant organizational culture, sometimes even in the C-suite. They may unconsciously continue to 'please' a parental figure, now transposed psychologically onto a boss or key customer.

The converse is also true. Leaders who formulate too strong a definition of 'Who am I?' are equally likely to become trapped when it comes to navigating transitions.

In addition to misguided imitation, some leaders compound the problem by remaining locked in their adolescent behaviours and personas of 'maverick', 'disruptor' or 'class clown', which masks their true identity and limits their potential as adults. Lord Mitchell may well have 'fallen by the way' in this fashion had he not decided to take charge and reinvent his identity more firmly when he was 16.

Lord Mitchell in his early years neglected his studies and chose a role as the 'disruptor', which nearly stalled him until he decided who he really wanted to be. But he also confided to me that later in life his vaulting ambitions also came at a cost. His absolute clarity about 'who' in the form of 'becoming rich and being Prime Minister' began to affect his family and his personal relationships. The adrenaline and power he experienced constructing increasingly important business deals began to dominate his life. His relentless drive contributed to a series of personal and professional setbacks including divorce, falling out with colleagues, and precipitating several business failures. Eventually his entrepreneurial zeal brought him close to burnout. As he told me with total honesty, 'I forgot the role of happiness'.

But on his 45th birthday Lord Mitchell declared that it was, 'The first day of the second half of my life'. He had learned lessons. He remarried and pledged to himself never to repeat the happiness-eroding decisions of his previous life. He set up another business which was also in computer leasing but was much less demanding of his time. And of course he re-emerged into politics by way of the House of Lords. It was a conscious decision to de-stress and enjoy family life. Now approaching 80, he is the happiest he has ever been. His family bring him great joy, and being a member of the best club in London is also 'none too shabby'.

Yet for many leaders, finding such deliberate balance remains out of reach. The two opposing extremes of poor self-determination at one end of the spectrum or over-reaching ambition at the other, will either limit our ability to develop our own voice or make us so over-confident that we become prone to misjudgement and mistakes. Finding the right balance between living one's true and real identity, 'Who am I', while releasing our earlier perceived role models and their associated expectations, is something that many leaders struggle with, often well into middle age.

Passion: The shadow side

Costas Markides is Professor of Strategic Leadership at London Business School. He also teaches executives about the role of passion as an accelerator of performance (Markides, 2021). Yet in his lectures, which I have sometimes helped to facilitate, he wisely cautions us to be realistic about this lofty sounding goal. Most of us, he says, will not discover our deepest passion in a sudden and convenient flash of insight. The exhortation from leaders and authors to be 'passionate' in our personal and working lives as a panacea to our various problems and insecurities has become an overused cliché, and rarely works if forced. Professor Markides sensibly advises us to develop our interests *over time*, using trial and error around things we are naturally attracted to, and experimenting widely before eventually honing in on what we really care about. Sometimes, we may eventually find a passion in our work, but often we don't, and we should never fake it. In other cases our emotional energies may be drawn to community work, coaching a sports team, teaching, or pursuing an important hobby – all of which are valid sources of 'passion'. Some people will find their ultimate fulfilment as parents or members of their extended families, which are natural sources of happiness. But the point from Professor Markides' teaching is that any of these energizing sources are valid for our eventual fulfilment. The key is that passion should never be mandated, seen as an end in itself, or appear inauthentic.

While such inauthenticity is a trap, the full expression of our passions – while fully authentic – also comes with the requirement for great courage and determination to fulfil it, as well as the risk of disappointment if we fail. For those of us who do manage to craft a career and a life around what we love, like Martin Gayford or Annmarie Lewis, passion can come at a price. Gayford himself cautions, 'You have to sacrifice something in order to make things happen,' and 'often you have to carry on despite tremendous discouragement from your immediate surroundings'. He persisted through a period of submitting applications to magazines and newspapers which routinely came back with rejection slips, before being accepted on his first attempt by the Courtauld Institute of Art in London to study history of art where he could finally apply his passion for the subject. Lord Mitchell persisted through his night school sessions to achieve his A-levels, which eventually helped realize his passion for achievement as he went on to attend Columbia and then become a successful entrepreneur.

Permission: The shadow side

While not giving ourselves permission to embark on transitions can be a serious brake to our progress, the opposite is also true. Giving ourselves too much permission can result in maverick behaviours, narcissism, alienating others and taking on unnecessary risk.

In Chapter 1, Professor Edmondson of Harvard shared the practices of establishing psychological safety. These include positive framing, constructive challenge, and asking good questions. One of her colleagues, Chris Argyris, renowned for his research about organizational structures, has studied the risks of the opposite condition: being too sure of one's convictions, especially in situations of uncertainty. In his book *On Organizational Learning* (Argyris, 1999), he labelled the terms 'advocacy' and 'inquiry', believing, rightly, that curiosity, openness and good questions (inquiry) are the most effective in creating dialogue and options during uncertainty. Conversely, excessive confidence, strong opinions and pushing for action (advocacy) quickly shuts down debate, limits choices, increases the likelihood of errors, tunnel vision, and bias in our decisions.

But unfortunately, as Professor Edmondson reminded me, 'Research shows that inquiry is a rare beast'. By this she means that while permission is key to triggering action and decision-making in situations of significant change, if we don't moderate our own advocacy with openness, questions and debate, we will miss the exploration and weighing of options that are so crucial to good judgment.

Purpose: The shadow side

Purpose has become a popular notion in leadership circles, but it too has a dark side when overly relied on. Peter Docter is the Chief Creative Officer of Pixar Animation. In an interview on NPR about Disney's film *Soul* he refers to the difference between passion and purpose (Doctor, 2021). The former can be translated as 'What do I love?' whereas the latter is the far more powerful 'What was I born to do?' The shadow side of purpose is the simple fact that most of us know what we love, but far fewer will find a clear and authentic purpose in our working or personal lives. In fact, finding purpose is a broad and existential question that many of us might never succeed in answering clearly. Yet today the management gurus and strategy consultants tell us with confidence that purpose is a pre-requisite for any kind of effective leadership, and especially leadership during change. But as Professor Markides reminds us, these bigger questions about ourselves and our reason for being are a life's work. They cannot be achieved through a training course or a single coaching session. Nor can they be mandated by an overly zealous CEO or a management consultant's report.

In the worst cases, executives may be under such pressure to have purpose that they contrive one in order to appear inspirational and 'on script'. Yet a business or personal purpose, if we do find one, must be clear, authentic and deeply felt. Commitment and discipline to seek what is important to us is the key to formulating and living a real sense of purpose. This is hard work and can require many years of reflection. It also requires consistency and commitment over time. Many leaders simply find this too hard to sustain, but as Annmarie Lewis has found out on several occasions, straying too far from our purpose sets us back fast. In her words, 'When you surrender to your calling, the doors fly open. As soon as you put yourself first, they will slam shut again.' So purpose is a privilege as well as a responsibility.

I advise leaders at all levels to exercise patience with this important question, and not to feel obliged to attach themselves prematurely to a purpose (or someone else's) for the sake of appearances. Such a false identity cannot be sustained and will ultimately fail.

Finally, not every role in life and business requires significant purpose, and not every leader has the makeup to be evangelical or iconic in their expression of it. Good management and proper execution skills may be entirely sufficient to do our jobs in most cases. It may be sufficient in our current state to 'be our job description' until we can find a higher order journey.

Summary of key points

In the last chapter I explored the life stages theory of Carl Jung and others to extract parallels and lessons for navigating change today. In the transitions between these life stages we naturally learn lessons as we move from imitation to differentiation and then to activation and integration on our journey to individuation.

In this chapter I augmented these principles to create a more specific framework to build a Change Mindset for transitions in the context of Leadership. The *who, what, how* and *why* of our life stages translate into the leadership questions of *person, passion, permission and purpose,* guiding us as we tackle important moments of transitional change in our personal and professional lives.

Activating these key elements can increase our chances of success when outcomes are unknown yet decisive action is required. But there is also a shadow side to these factors that we must remain aware of as we consider our choices.

In Chapter 4, I will look more specifically at two attributes that can further build our Change Mindset: courage and empathy. We will see how the deliberate practice of these additional skills can create a powerful personal change compass to navigate change.

CHAPTER FOUR

Building a Change Mindset through courage and empathy

We are not what we know but what we are willing to learn.
MARY CATHERINE BATESON

Bateson passed away in January 2021 having spent much of her lifetime documenting observations about human development. Her invitation to adopt a learning stance throughout our own lives reflects one of the key attributes that I found among successful change leaders.

Bateson's focus on a learning stance was no doubt influenced by her mother Margaret Mead, also a cultural anthropologist who, like Carl Jung, spent her life exploring how human beings and societies function during periods of disruption and transition. Mead developed a deep conviction about our innate ability to succeed with change at any stage in life. The quote often attributed to her in this context is: 'Never doubt that a small group of thought-ful, committed citizens can change the world. Indeed, it's the only thing that ever has' (Mead, 1982).

Inquisitive to the end, Bateson and Mead both believed that an essential willingness to learn is the most reliable predictor of our ability to navigate transitions successfully. Many leaders I spoke to for this book confirmed this principle about adopting a learning mindset. But mindsets are intangible and nebulous things. Yet they are key to shaping the right behaviours in uncertainty, as Professor Aneeta Rattan of London Business School says in her work on leadership. 'It's imperative that organisations understand their peoples' mindsets because our ability to do our work and to do it well is shaped by the mindsets we hold. Under conditions of stress and challenge and difficulty, it is mindsets that differentiate peoples' responses.' (Rattan, 2021)

Unfortunately, most of us lack the curiosity and conviction of Mead and Bateson to practice and maintain such a learning mindset. Our daily preoccupations and stresses tilt us towards procrastination and avoidance rather than action and inquiry when we bump up against new challenges. This is a dangerous stance which, at the collective level, quickly translates into organizational conflict and inaction. We can see this almost daily as we read about political horse-trading, protectionism, trade wars, blaming migrants for economic failures, and other defensive or self-justifying behaviours among leaders across business and politics.

Yet the key to navigating transitions well so that we can achieve positive outcomes lies in our mindset. We need to adopt a more open and curious attitude towards the outer world, while maintaining realistic self-awareness of our inner beliefs, attitudes and potential biases. Thus, navigating external transitions requires us first to provoke an internal change in ourselves. It is our ability to hold an honest internal dialogue with ourselves that will determine whether we can or cannot develop an effective Change Mindset.

Unlocking our Change Mindset

We are what we repeatedly do. Excellence, therefore, is not an act, but a habit. WILL DURANT

Here the American writer and philosopher Durant is paraphrasing from Aristotle's *Nichomachean Ethics* and capturing the essence of what I will examine in this chapter – how to build a Change Mindset through greater self-awareness and deliberate practice. In the last chapter we explored the lessons we can learn as we transition through our life stages, and how we can use those as a basis for navigating future changes. We looked at the questions of *who, what, how* and *why* and the leadership questions they infer:

- *Who* am I being in this change situation?
- *What* unique knowledge, skills and attributes can I apply?

- *How* can I create the right conditions for action?
- *Why* have I chosen this path and do my actions align with my values?

These questions gave us an augmented framework for decision-making during change linked to the questions of *person, passion, permission* and *purpose*, using self-inquiry for better outcomes. In my conversations with leaders about what specific skills they used to take action in uncertainty, two additional attributes emerged as a consistent theme: *courage* and *empathy*.

Why courage and empathy?

Why were these two attributes so particularly important in managing transitions?

For leaders such as Martin Gayford, Lord Mitchell and Annmarie Lewis, courage was the common denominator that helped them define themselves with clarity in their chosen fields (art historian, politician, social entrepreneur). It generated the power to move forward during uncertainty, helping them stay the course in moments of doubt by saying 'yes' to what felt right. It also allowed them walk away from what was 'not them' as Gayford put it.

As an illustration of making these more powerful choices, Gayford shared with me some of his conversations with British Sculptor Antony Gormley who, as a young man was variously an archaeology graduate, a hippy backpacker, and a Buddhist monk before turning to art and sculpture. By casting around for an identity yet being courageous enough to walk away from what was 'not him', Gormley was able to define himself through trial and error, eventually becoming the globally recognized sculptor we know today. In similar fashion, Annmarie Lewis found the courage to launch Rainmakers despite limited social enterprise experience, but based on a deep conviction that there was significant untapped potential in the world of young offenders. As for Lord Mitchell, he found the courage to walk away from that rainy street as a Hoover salesman and recommit to his studies, becoming a successful entrepreneur as a result. Professor Khaw found the resolve to radically alter his own life path and transition into medicine at an early age after encountering his Indian fortune-teller.

Thus, it was courage that made these leaders ready to confront difficult and unfamiliar circumstances, cutting through fear and paralysis. Courage provides us with the power to act with purpose and strength in important moments of transition.

As for empathy, it was what helped these leaders act in a way that engages with the world around them, providing wider perspective and incorporating the views of others. By asking questions, understanding the needs of others and challenging our own assumptions – which are often biased or flawed – empathy gives us a reality check to test and re-evaluate our own choices during transitions.

Used together, these two attributes sharpen our 'true north' to make better decisions in moments of change. Once we place them in our change toolkit we can begin to deliberately practice courage and empathy to better evaluate options, make decisions, and trigger action.

With this new insight, we can now layer courage and empathy into the Change Mindset model that links to our life stages of imitation, differentiation, activation and integration. Courage and empathy now make us ask some harder questions about our choices and their potential consequences, and layering these attributes into our decision-making can increase our chances of success while reducing the risks of failure.

We can illustrate these new elements in the Change Mindset model as follows:

FIGURE 4.1 Courage and empathy

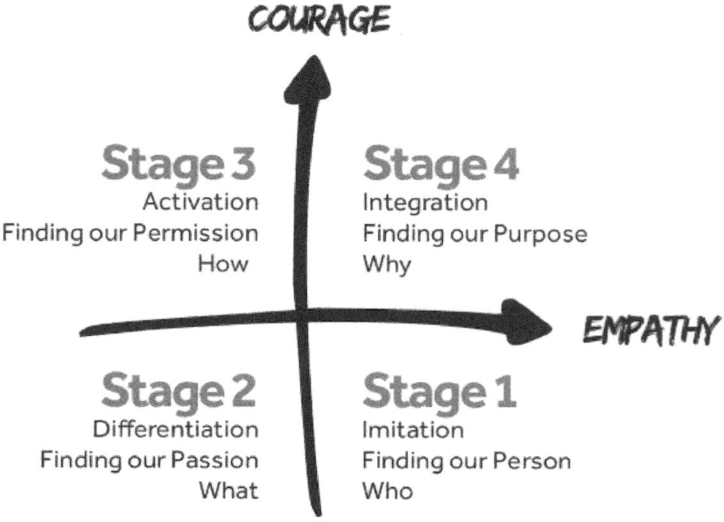

COURAGE

Stage 3
Activation
Finding our Permission
How

Stage 4
Integration
Finding our Purpose
Why

EMPATHY

Stage 2
Differentiation
Finding our Passion
What

Stage 1
Imitation
Finding our Person
Who

But what do courage and empathy look like in practice, and how can we develop them more deliberately to access their power? Let us look at each in turn.

What is courageous leadership?

Winston Churchill provides us a helpful starting point here, saying, 'Courage is rightly esteemed the first of human qualities, because it is the quality which guarantees all others' (Churchill, 1931). In the context of leadership, courage is thus the first and most critical determinant of whether we are able move from good intentions to effective action during moments of change and transition.

Yet courage is often in short supply in today's world. Many of us feel disempowered by seemingly constant unexpected shocks, be it climate events, political upheaval, social polarization or the Covid-19 pandemic. We feel increasingly isolated in our virtual and hybrid work routines, lacking the human contact that fosters peer reviews, debate and support for new ideas and actions. Business and political leaders also seem unsure how to adapt their policies and strategies to more rapidly changing global conditions. And for everyone it feels much easier to point fingers at a perceived enemy or wait to be rescued by some benevolent power than to take action ourselves.

But the courageous leaders I spoke to had found ways to become the architects of their environment rather than victims of it. They had built their courage through a strong sense of self and clear values. They worked hard to control self-limiting beliefs. Some found courage early, like Professor Peng Khaw reorienting his studies as a young student, while others took many years and almost 'fell by the way' before developing theirs, like Lord Mitchell. But over time they all found a way to deliberately build courage as a response to challenges, risks and opportunities.

This deployment of courage to tackle uncertainty may seem obvious. Few would argue that courage is not an important leadership attribute and that having more of it will make us better change agents. But most of us find it difficult to be courageous all the time, and especially under stress and uncertainty. So how can we build our own courage more deliberately as part of our Change Mindset?

Taking heart

The poet David Whyte teaches executives about courage in a rather unique way. He discovered the power of words early in life, influenced by the changing landscapes of his native Yorkshire and the Anglo-Irish ancestry of his parents. His boyhood imagination was fired to explore story, legends and mythology, inspired in part by the mysteries of *Calypso*, the ship skippered by pioneer marine biologist Jacques Cousteau in the 1970s that featured in a weekly television series of the time. These aquatic adventures prompted Whyte to study Marine Zoology, stationing himself in the Galapagos Islands in his early 20s, the first in a series of courageous personal transitions. After several more career experiments he decided to explore the universe of the human mind rather than the world of undersea creatures, and found in poetry the power of words as a means to explore and explain the challenges of change and transformation. Today, Whyte is a professional poet recognized for his powerful insights into life and its myriad challenges. Sought out as a business consultant, he also brings these insights to life in organizations, teaching executives about change, courage and transitions. His global consultancy, Many Rivers, guides large corporations such as Boeing in their use of language as a way to explore the future of their industries and the role of leaders as they navigate disruption.

I spoke to Whyte in Oxford during one of his lecture tours on Courageous Conversations, where he reminded me that 'courage' comes from the French *'coeur'* – heart – ultimately deriving from the Latin 'cor', which was thought to be the 'seat of all emotions'. Courage for him is therefore not a matter of heroism or storming the ramparts but a more deeply seated, reflective and personal discipline. It guides us in being more true to ourselves and acting according to our deeper values and convictions. According to Whyte, courage is an attribute of spirit, where we look into the 'heart' of ourselves to define what is most important. Courage helps us define how we will tackle unforeseen challenges with clearer thought and bolder actions. Defining courage and courageous acts also requires the right framing. How we talk about our courage during change will define how we act. As Whyte reminded me, 'We cannot enter the world for which we do not have the language.' Or, quoting Wittgenstein, 'The limits of my language mean the limits of my world' (Wittgenstein, 1922). We must therefore define courage for ourselves in ways that have specific meaning, building our capability to push the boundaries of our own identity and what we believe is possible for ourselves.

Whyte likens this capability to 'captaincy', which he defines as 'the place where the ship meets the water'. His metaphorical ship is of course our life and the water is the fluid external world we must navigate as it passes around us and forces us to change and adapt. A courageous hand on the tiller of our own lives and an understanding of these external 'currents' is therefore how we can more effectively navigate change, interacting with the world a more connected and deliberate way.

What courage will mean for us and how it manifests in our own personal actions will be specific to each of us. For some like Lord Mitchell, it will be the courage to launch new business ventures and to fearlessly fight for his beliefs to influence government policy. For others such as Annmarie Lewis, it will be the courage to build social enterprises that lift up others. And for yet others like Tad Beckwith, it was the personal courage to cycle single-handedly across the remotest parts of Asia to forge relationships between young people across cultures and borders.

Courageous coaching

Yet to effectively build our own courage is not an easy task. I asked Peter Hogarth, founder of The Change Partnership and an executive coach to many global CEOs, about this question. I have known Hogarth since I set up my own business 15 years ago and he has been a stalwart and generous mentor as I gradually built my own practice. Over the past 25 years Hogarth has helped many executives, more seasoned than me, build their leadership capacities, including the key skill of courage, which he defines neatly as 'pushing the boundaries of where you can be taken seriously'.

Yet when asked how many of his clients had been successful in becoming truly courageous leaders, he was more sanguine. 'The most consistent, and depressing, trait I find among senior leaders is the phenomenon of self-limiting beliefs. These are entirely self-generated notions that, when challenged, are almost always invalid. Yet they remain blind spots for many even in the C-suite.' I asked Hogarth what advice he has for leaders caught in this trap, and he was equally clear on the remedy: 'Ask yourself what you would do if you had absolutely no fear, and then use that picture to craft a different story for yourself.' This kind of powerful question is the essence of Hogarth's executive coaching work. It is about asking ourselves what might be possible, forcing a deeper interrogation of ourselves, and then taking deliberate steps towards that new horizon. This links back to giving ourselves permission to activate our strengths to drive change, rather than waiting to be rescued by a job transfer, a promotion, or the advice of a management consultant. In David Whyte's collection of poems *Pilgrim,* he describes this courage to act as 'Giving your fullest attention to the step you are taking right now.' (Whyte, 2012).

So, this is the first element of a successful Change Mindset: the brave choice to challenge our own self-limiting beliefs and to move a step further towards our potential through courage.

But what does courageous leadership look like in practice?

Courageous leadership in practice

If you want to know the reason you can't get something done, just look in the mirror. TIM COOK

Tim Cook, CEO of the world's most valuable company at the time, Apple, made this statement while being interviewed by David Rubinstein, the billionaire businessman, philanthropist and co-founder of private equity firm Carlyle Group on his Bloomberg streaming show *How to Lead.* In it Rubinstein explores questions of leadership with C-level executives and he was asking Cook about building on the legacy of his late boss, Steve Jobs.

Cook's response is a good example of courageous leadership in practice. He placed the responsibility for setting Apple's strategy and delivering results squarely at his own door. He spoke of how leaders must set direction, show conviction and continually take courageous actions to drive performance, always leading by example. He also said we must be accountable for our decisions and choices, and when things go wrong, as they inevitably will, the first place they must look is 'in the mirror' – meaning at ourselves. This is sound advice, and I see too many leaders sidestepping this responsibility, pointing the finger at others, or blaming 'externalities' such as the Covid-19 pandemic or Brexit when things go wrong. Cook essentially measures himself against his own yardstick of performance. In turn, he is setting the bar for Apple's other 147,000 employees. There is no room for self-limiting beliefs at this level, and Cook's leadership style requires deep courage.

Where else can we look for demonstrations of courageous leadership during change? I witnessed a more personal example of it working with Laura McKeaveney at the global pharmaceutical company Novartis. There, she formerly held positions as Global Head of Patient Engagement and Global Head of Human Resources for Novartis Pharmaceuticals. We got to know each other during a series of leadership initiatives at the company, and I got back in touch to ask her more about how she developed and deployed courage as a leader of transformation during her time there.

She started with her own story of growing up in Northern Ireland in the 1970s and 80s during the so-called Troubles. Life was modest, and McKeaveney's father was a Baker in Belfast, starting work at 4a.m. to support a family of five children. However, a number of setbacks affected the family, including her father's health, leading to some financial difficulties which resulted in McKeaveney taking on night work after school to help out. As the eldest in the family she took this in her stride thanks to the role modelling of her mother, who valued education and her faith above all else. 'For a young girl in this environment,' she would say, 'only education will get you out of here'. Following her mother's sound advice, McKeaveney completed her school studies, in a school uniform having had its hem dropped several times to save money. During this time she worked part time to help support the family financially, and yet went on to become the first in her extended family to earn a university degree. Ironically, even with these newly minted qualifications she was forced to take a receptionist role as her first job, because it paid more than other professional positions. But it meant that she could carry on supporting her family.

These early transitions built a natural courage and resilience in how she saw the world, which was further shaped by her daily experiences in Belfast where danger was never far away. Which side of the street she chose on the way home from school could mean the difference between being caught in gunfire or arriving safely in time for tea: 'You took a risk every day, whether it was a bomb or a bullet,' she told me. Once, on her cross-border commute, a group of paramilitaries in balaclavas stopped her on a back road. Their subsequent search of her car might have been a death sentence had they found the rosary she kept in her glove compartment, but after some questioning, they let her go. Some time later, while on business in Hong Kong, she received a phone call informing her that her house had been burned down. The police had no explanation other than that her daily commute across the border to work for an American company 'may have raised suspicions'.

After these powerful experiences, McKeaveney might easily have let self-limiting beliefs begin to dent her confidence and restrict her choices. She could have blamed her environment, the conflict, her family's circumstances, or being a woman in the 1970's. Instead, she courageously continued her education with a second degree and an MBA, and went to work despite the dangers of border crossings. She lived with open eyes, realizing that 'In order to live my life I might need to lose my life, but I took the risk.' Contemplating the remains of her incinerated home, she told me, 'I realized I had two choices, decide that I was a victim, or decide that this was an amazing opportunity to start again. And very shortly afterwards, I went to England.' Her mantra became, 'I've got one shot at this, let's go for it' and over the following decades she continued to deploy courage and self-determination when faced with transitions, which culminated in her holding the most senior HR role in Novartis Pharmaceuticals, a $50bn plus business unit in the Novartis group with over 100,000 employees.

More recently, McKeaveney has again transitioned to a new path, moving away from profit driven organizations and into volunteerism, health initiatives in Africa, and women's education. In Northern Ireland, as chair of the charity Tinylife, she leads the board in support of the CEO whose team deliver services to parents caring for premature babies across Northern Ireland. These more recent transitions, she says, are her way to use her experience and insight to 'pay it forward'. 'Though the odds were stacked against me earlier in my experience, I had a wonderful life and career. Now, I feel a need to pause and reflect about how to fall forward into a new chapter and start giving back.'

McKeaveney's courage to seek these new horizons reminded me of a passage from *Walden* by Henry David Thoreau, who too advocates exploring beyond our immediate surroundings:

> Men come tamely home at night from only the next field or street, where their life pines because it breathes its own breath over again. Their shadows morning and evening reach farther than their daily steps. We should come home from far, from adventures, and perils, and discoveries every day (Thoreau, 1854).

McKeaveney never hesitated to embrace 'adventures, perils, and discoveries every day' from her early days in Belfast, and there is growing evidence in the modern literature too that courage is becoming a more critical leadership skill in times of uncertainty and change. In *Grit* Angela Duckworth explores the value of 'grit' over talent, using examples from sports and business to highlight the role of resilience and perseverance in successful change (Duckworth, 2017). In *Daring Greatly* Brené Brown reminds us that when faced with transitions we also face vulnerability. But she challenges us to reframe this as a strength that can bring more purpose and meaning to our lives. Hers is essentially an invitation to become more courageous during change (Brown, 2012). Jeff Crowther, the Lonely Planet travel writer and author of the original 1960's hippy trail writings, was known for courageously exploring the world at a time before Google Maps and AirBnB. His passion for writing and adventure led to him to author the *Lonely Planet Africa Guide*, featuring his iconic hand-drawn maps and crowdsourced tips for cheap hostels spanning the continent. His courageous spirit and thirst for new experiences was captured in a recent *Financial Times* obituary following his death in 2021: 'The hardest part is making the decision to go in the first place. The rest is easy, and will turn into one of the best buzzes you've ever experienced' (Jenkins, 2021).

Courage therefore is one consistent building block I see in leaders who navigate complex change successfully. They develop it by looking in the mirror as business executives, by taming their self-limiting beliefs, and by taking action despite the odds. And they always persist, knowing the benefits of their efforts will be great. In the words of another great travel writer:

Courage is grace under pressure. ERNEST HEMINGWAY

What is empathic leadership?

Courage is inarguably a prerequisite leadership skill during change and there are numerous examples of leaders who display great courage in the face of change and adversity, for example CEOs Jeff Bezos at Amazon and Elon Musk at Tesla. But relying on courage as the sole method for tackling change and transitions has its limitations. At best, courage can power action and overcome barriers. But at worst, the collateral damage it can cause includes alienating employees, angering investors, creating excessive risk or even destroying businesses and reputations. Change efforts driven solely by courage, and that hinge on purely tangible metrics such as financial results or business growth, may fail in the wider context due to a lack of the second key attribute of empathy.

As an example, Uber's focus on profit and its protracted battle over drivers' rights and gig working contributed to the demise of founding CEO

Travis Kalanick. At Amazon, a well-documented culture of low empathy has repeatedly triggered bad press and employee protests over rigid and demanding working conditions, along with attempts to unionize that have been repeatedly blocked by company lawyers. Such leaders may be very successful when measured by certain metrics: profitability, growth or shareholder returns. But they are less admirable when measured against a broader set of metrics, especially in light of the growing trend towards multi-stakeholder governance and the need for greater workforce engagement. Leaders ignore this reality at their peril. CEOs who make courageous business decisions without empathy may alienate their more savvy investors, fail to forge key new partnerships, and be unable to attract the best talent and tap into the discretionary effort that is so crucial for innovation and performance.

We know that organizations are made up of people who need to feel achievement, purpose and belonging to do their best work. Feeling part of a greater whole requires more than just acting together, and the leader's role today is increasingly to consider the needs of others on whom we rely to achieve results. Leaders who show empathy alongside courage understand the key interrelationships across groups and the role this plays in improved performance.

In 1624 the English poet John Donne wrote in *Meditation 17* that 'No man is an island'. In the essay he reflects on our human need for interdependence: 'any man's death diminishes me, because I am involved in mankind, and therefore never send to know for whom the bell tolls; it tolls for thee' (Donne, 1624).

This reminder of our lifetime reliance on others to achieve our goals goes to the heart of why empathy is key to effective group dynamics. We are all 'involved in mankind' and empathy can act as a multiplier of courage in our quest to navigate transitions. As leaders empathy helps us see the more subtle, ambiguous and complex nuances that play out during change. And it allows to respond to these with greater intelligence and relevance in our decision making.

In the past, lack of empathy in business was easy to ignore, but social media and an increasing desire by Millennials for more meaning and authenticity at work has highlighted its increasing importance. A new Global Empathy Index, which defines empathy as 'understanding the emotional impact a company has on its staff and customers' was published in the

Harvard Business Review in 2016. The index is based on an analysis of internal culture, CEO performance, ethics and social media presence across 170 companies on major financial indexes. The results indicate that companies with empathic cultures retain the best people, create environments where diverse teams thrive and, as a result, achieve greater financial returns. It is not surprising, therefore, that top ranked employers are often also the top financial performers.

I firmly believe in empathy as a source of competitive advantage – something leaders have underrated and must begin to better acknowledge. Empathy is our ability to understand other people's emotions, predicaments and challenges by putting ourselves in their shoes and taking an active interest in their concerns. Researchers are increasingly publishing about the positive role of empathy in leadership effectiveness, showing that these skills allow them to better understand the perspectives, opinions and concerns of not only their employees but also stakeholders and customers. Furthermore, empathic leaders have the advantage in changing environments, as they are more willing to observe, adapt and do things differently. This adaptability is particularly advantageous in cross-cultural situations and can reduce the risk of misunderstandings, mistakes or offending others during business interactions. Empathy, therefore, can be taught and then actively developed by any leader.

But what does empathic leadership look like in practice? Let us examine some historical and modern examples.

Empathic leadership in practice

Que Sais-je?   MICHEL DE MONTAIGNE

We can trace the role of empathy as indispensable for human change as far back as 1580, when Michel de Montaigne published *Essais*. These were a series of reflections on politics, economics and the changing nature of human society in his time. He used empathy as a cornerstone for his philosophical and political writings, distilling this into his famously humble question, '*Que Sais-je?*' or, 'What do I know?' Montaigne's *Essais* provoked changes in his lifetime as nobles and traders considered his insights about business, politics, governance and power. His writing went on to influence leaders and academics who still use his insights to shape their views on government, law and society. Simply starting with such a question as we embark on any change journey will help lay the ground for a more successful outcome, because through empathy we are more likely to consider the views of others, remain open to new information, and avoid the biases and assumptions that otherwise block our path.

Four centuries after Montaigne, Dr. Anthony Fauci also used empathy to navigate change as the Chief Medical Advisor to the White House during the Covid-19 pandemic. Previously at odds over which policies would effectively combat the crisis, the current US Administration began to take Fauci's advice more seriously. But tensions remain as he navigated between the conflicting views of special interest groups, Big Pharma, antivaxxers and the World Health Organization. Today, Fauci must still work hard to balance the multiple and competing demands of these stakeholders to continue navigating the uncharted waters of the global pandemic.

How has he done it? There is a back story to Fauci's success in navigating transitions. Empathy has been a hallmark of his leadership style since he began as head of the National Institute of Allergy and Infectious Diseases in the U.S. in 1984. He has been an advisor to every US president since Reagan and in a recent interview on National Public Radio he shared how empathy has helped him succeed over those years (Fauci, 2021). In a striking parallel to today, he cites another moment when there was little understanding about a novel virus outbreak, yet tremendous global concern about its deadliness. It was the AIDS pandemic of the 1980s and Fauci wanted to get a better sense for what was causing this new disease at a time when discussing sexually transmitted diseases was both taboo and feared. He used his empathy as a weapon, becoming the only leading health figure to visit the Castro District of San Francisco and Greenwich Village in New York, talking to the affected groups about their fears and concerns and gaining valuable insights in the process. His empathy and desire for understanding allowed him to sidestep biases and begin to formulate new and more effective strategies. Fauci's subsequent research uncovered how HIV progresses to AIDS through the destruction of the body's defence systems. Alongside other important outcomes, his work led to the creation of the President's Emergency Plan for AIDS Relief, an initiative that addressed the epidemic globally and ultimately helped save the lives of many living with HIV.

In the same interview, Fauci spoke of another confrontation, this time during a protest by activists on gay rights, and again he used empathy. Rather than calling in the police to disperse the crowd, he went outside and asked the group to select a few leaders, inviting them into his office to discuss their issues and concerns. Today, Fauci is deploying his empathic leadership style to seek more diverse views and widen collaboration between stakeholders as he tackles the ongoing uncertainty about the current pandemic.

The role of self-empathy

There is one further important aspect to the power of empathy as a change enabler: empathy towards oneself. During our interview, Laura McKeaveney described her own practice of self-empathy, telling me how at moments of important transition she will reflect on her achievements and lessons learned, including views from others in the form of old 360-degree feedback reports. Why is this important to her?

> What lies ahead of me is probably the most important part of my career, so I often ask myself, 'What have I learned and how have I grown?' But this isn't always easy. There was a certain expectation in the early days of my career to 'do things a certain way', or 'be a certain type of leader'. When your sense of self hasn't matured, you often compromise in order to be successful. But it's never too late to learn and grow, and it is often those painful cringeworthy reflections that lead you to choices that allow you to be your best self.

This has led her to important insights about knowing oneself and embracing change. 'Your best teachers are often your subordinates,' she told me as one example, 'the courageous ones who have found their sense of self.' Or, 'It can be very satisfying to be right. But it can be more satisfying to be kind.' Looking backwards to look forwards in this way is a well-known leadership tool. But it applies equally well to our own personal journeys through change, as we cast an empathic eye over our past in order to better prepare for the future.

The New Zealand-born screenwriter and director, Jane Campion, has also spoken about self-empathy – in her case as a tool to spur creativity as a writer. She is best known for the success of her 1993 film *The Piano* which was nominated for eight Academy Awards, won three, and made her the first female director to win the Palme d'Or at Cannes. Creative professionals like

Campion often require safety and encouragement to tackle uncertainty and generate their best ideas. Speaking to the *Guardian* about her most recent film *The Power of the Dog* she said, 'If you are too anxious or panicky about things, that's the real stopper for the creative flow. In my experience, you've got to trust processes you don't even understand, in creativity and in life, because the brain is always a few steps behind the instinct.' (O'Hagan, 2021).

Such anxiety is even more acute for leaders in times of significant change and uncertainty. Yet if we can trust our instinct and the process in these moments, while practicing self-empathy like Campion, our best ideas will still emerge. The film's 12 Academy Award nominations and Campion's statuette for Best Director must partly be due to her effective deployment of empathy as a leader.

Combining courage and empathy to build a powerful Change Mindset

Some of us are naturally courageous and build empathy over time. Others may be naturally empathic, building courage as they experience life. In rare cases, leaders will naturally develop both attributes in tandem. But for most of us, we must work hard to learn these skills and then apply them consistently in moments of change. I spoke to two change leaders who had developed both these attributes, but in a different order. Here is how they did it.

Building empathy from courage

For Peter Hogarth, founder of the executive coaching firm The Change Partnership, courage came early during his time at a British military school that instilled in him discipline and self-reliance. It was during that time that he also discovered his natural gifts for mathematics and a penchant for solving complex problems. With these attributes and a newly minted degree in hand, he joined a Big Four accounting firm and after a series of quick promotions was made partner at the early age of 31. It was largely his courage for volunteering to take on the most challenging and complex projects that enabled this rapid trajectory. He shared several examples with me during our interview about how he did this. One breakthrough assignment he took on was working with the British government in the pharmaceutical sector to create new accounting concepts that aligned global drug sales with return on capital. The engagement involved challenging the status quo of a very powerful industry with a vocal lobby. His proposals, viewed as contro-versial at the time, would create a global industry standard that is still in place today. Without courage the changes would most likely not have happened despite their intellectual merit. At another point Hogarth found himself appointed by the CEO of Société Générale to set up their UK Investment Bank, again requiring courageous conversations across the Channel with multiple high-level stakeholders to overcome obstacles. Yet another story involved him joining the London Stock Exchange and creat-ing innovations such as the order driven system for share trading that revolutionized trading in the UK and helped cement its position as a global financial centre. The courage developed in Hogarth's early years enabled these subsequent professional achievements in complex situations where the stakes were high and the various key stakeholders were not always aligned.

But it was Hogarth's later transitions that developed his empathy, widen-ing his impact as a leader of change into new areas. Over a business lunch with the owners of an executive outplacement firm, the topic of executive coaching emerged. At the time the profession, at least in the UK, was in its infancy. The opportunity to grow and professionalize something new appealed to Hogarth's problem-solving skills, but coaching executives was unfamiliar territory. However, it proved to be a revelation. 'I just loved it,' he told me. 'Within three months I was completely hooked. Why? I'm very interested in people, very interested in problem solving, and fascinated by business so it was a natural transition at that time in my life.' This experi-ment led to the creation of The Change Partnership in the mid 90s, which was soon advising over half of the UK FTSE 100 companies, creating a new benchmark for executive coaching in the City of London.

For Hogarth, empathy now became the core of his work as he dedicated himself to supporting executives through their own changes and transitions. I asked him how he built this new skill in his mid-career. 'First of all, it was playing to some very deep-seated things that I believe in: Always do your best. Embrace problem solving. Choose good people. Second, I was working with some really different people than myself and learning and feeding off them. So there was novelty. But most important, I discovered that commit-ment, empathy and positive regard are the keys to great coaching, so I decided to always approach people with that in mind.'

In the 1950s the American psychologist Carl Rogers expanded on earlier work by Stanley Standal and popularized the term 'unconditional positive regard' (Rogers, 1951). His theory advocates unconditional support towards others in the context of client-centred therapy as a method to accelerate healing. In the context of executive coaching, unconditional positive regard becomes a key lever to accelerate personal and professional development. The belief that every person has the potential to improve their leadership skills, and that the solutions for doing so lie mostly within themselves, is the basis of the most effective coaching. For Hogarth, his own empathy and positive regard for others allowed him to quickly get to the essence of any executive's development needs. 'Empathy gets me to the nub of a problem very quickly' he told me. 'Clients say, "You come in here without the faintest idea how to deal with the issue, I talk for 20 minutes, you don't say a word, and then you hit the nail on the head!"' How does Hogarth achieve this? 'Deep listening and empathy are the lynchpins of my relationship with clients, right the way through.'

I asked Hogarth his advice for others who may have relied on courage and drive to succeed in their careers, and who now want to develop greater empathy to expand their change skills. 'There's lots of advice I could give, but I tell you what is really important,' he told me, 'and that is to follow your soul.' Hogarth spoke of the countless executives he has coached who simply felt stuck in their careers, despite high intelligence and excellent qualifications. Many had done the same job for years despite feeling unsatisfied or unrecognized for their contributions. Others had a dream to change to something more meaningful, yet lacked the conviction to do so. Hogarth believes we must all be more willing to can practise self empathy so we change direction and walk away from safe and unchallenging situations like yet another promotion that further embeds our current ways of working, or an annual bonus that acts as a pair of golden handcuffs to our inner potential. What advice does he share with such leaders? 'You have to seriously take stock: ask yourself, "Am I really enjoying this? Am I developing and improving my skills? Am I being a better person as a result of it?" Carl Rogers called this 'congruence' - attempting to align our outward presentation with our inner felt-sense'. Equally important for Hogarth is allowing ourselves and others to make mistakes as we experiment with change. This is something executives typically shy away from, but, as he reminded me, 'Mistakes are where you improve. In America, where I've done a lot of coaching, nobody cares if you lose or fail. It's seen as a rite of passage, and they just say: 'What did you learn?' So you've got to be brave. You've got to follow your conviction. And don't worry if it goes wrong because something inevitably will and you will learn something important in the process.'

This is very sound advice that I have been lucky enough to benefit from over the years as Hogarth has also nudged me through my own transitions from the corporate world towards starting my own business, joining the London Business School, and now writing on leadership and change. A few strong challenges from him have helped me over the biggest hurdles, but it has been his consistent empathy that allowed me to sustain belief in my endeavours.

I asked Hogarth, now a very youthful and energetic 70-year-old, what was next for him. 'There are other things in me yet,' he told me, 'but I haven't quite worked out what they are.' To me this is a sure sign that his courage and empathy remain undiminished, and that he will deploy them both to great effect in whatever he chooses to create next.

Building courage from empathy

Some leaders, like Peter Hogarth, possess natural courage that propels them through their early achievements before developing their complement of empathy to navigate change later in life. But the opposite pattern often occurs too.

Arthur Bastings is CEO and founder of Arthur Bastings Collective, a Singapore and Palo Alto based collective that combines private equity and venture capital structures to build businesses, focusing on young founders and early-stage ventures, particularly in the creative sector. A veteran media and entertainment executive, he has held senior leadership roles at MTV, Viacom, and Discovery Networks during their international growth phases. I came to know Bastings as we worked together to build his leadership teams in some of these international ventures.

In contrast to Peter Hogarth, Bastings' journey began with a natural core of empathy. He told me the story of his early life growing up in a small, rather conservative Dutch town, and how as a teenager his self-awareness and sense of empathy began to shape him. 'I think we all come into life pure and relatively unformed, but in my teens I already had a strong sense of who I was and realized this rural Catholic environment was not me. I was also gay and it became quite clear that at some point I had to move on to live my own life and be true to myself.' This need to express himself more authentically – an early experience in self-empathy – led him to the US where he completed his studies at Johns Hopkins University. Shortly thereafter he joined a fledgling music channel called MTV, becoming head of International Strategy in his early 20s and then pioneering the channel's expansion outside the US in subsequent years.

Bastings found himself increasingly using his natural empathy as the core of his leadership style in a succession of roles in those creative environments. He learned the importance of listening, dialogue and feedback to get the best out of his creative and commercial teams. And he used his own empathy and cultural sensitivity to work effectively across global boundaries to attract and motivate talent across multiple business lines. What were some of the empathetic tools he deployed at this point in his career? 'Feedback is key,' he told me. 'Accepting feedback is something a lot of people don't know how to do. Either they're not comfortable with it, or at worst they openly reject it. Most of us require quite heavy "friction" before changing our behaviour. And feedback is the most empathetic way to do it.'

When most of his peers were competing within a narrow range of technical skills, Bastings' openness to change and experimentation with new behaviours helped him craft a more engaging and authentic leadership style, which helped him move into MD and then CEO roles managing multiple divisions and diverse global teams. He pins this success on his deliberate deployment of empathy, his humility and always being open to advice from others. 'One thing I've learned is that with empathy we can learn from anybody, even our mediocre bosses. What is that person doing? What impact are they having on the organization? Is that what I want? What could I do differently? Our teachers can also be many things: a relationship, a colleague, a friend, a book you read. But it's always about being open.'

Bastings' deployment of empathy in environments like MTV and Discovery was the key to engaging teams during those early growth stages, where rapid change and uncertainty pervades the workplace. His self-empathy also helped him learn about self-care and the importance of mental wellbeing, for himself and for others. He understood early how mental health affects organizational performance, well before our recent awakening to this topic. He advises leaders to avoid the 'sprint' leadership style too common today that races to achieve goals and drive change in times of crisis, inevitably to the detriment of people and the business. 'With more of a marathon mentality you learn to trust your instincts, trust the journey and trust the outcomes, even when you're not sure about your choices. It is a better long term business strategy but it also requires a lot more patience and empathy.' These behaviours are not easy when the spotlight is on us as leaders to act fast and aggressively, particularly in times of rapid change when the pressure to perform increases even further, as in today's VUCA environment.

Over the years, Bastings' empathy also drew him into the realm of spirituality, which led him to his current view that life and business are both a balancing act. 'Life is like a chair with four legs: intellect, emotion, spirit and body. Most people have an unevenness in these four dimensions, but all four legs need to be developed to be successful. The same is true for organizations.' An early adopter of meditation and mindfulness, Bastings used these principles in business as a way to help him integrate teams, explore shared values and define a greater purpose for himself and the people in the organizations he led. 'That's been a decade's work but it's transformed how I show up as a leader. It's made me reflect more deeply on why I'm here and how I can make the most of things for others. We're all ultimately here for the same thing, which is personal growth and to help each other.'

You may wonder how meditation is relevant to driving large scale business transformation, as Bastings has done. Most leaders find this kind of subject matter too uncomfortable and intangible. We want to grab our tools, analyse the options and move to action rather than trying deeper reflection and questioning ourselves before acting. Like Hogarth and Handy, Bastings likens this to staying 'close to one's soul' in the pursuit of change. Bastings' belief, after years of reflecting on the question, is that our success as change leaders emanates from a wider set of conditions as we become more connected with our surroundings, in tune with those around us, and open to being challenged about our beliefs. 'The question is: Can you see the universe around you and how it is unfolding? Can you be in greater flow with that universe in order to make good things happen?'

Whether we choose to embrace this level of thinking in our own leadership practices the key point is that the power of empathic leadership inhabits the same territory as what Bastings describes. It requires lowering our ego, accepting external views, and trusting a larger set of conditions that lie outside our control for change to happen successfully.

Having succeeded in leadership primarily through empathy, Bastings has further transitioned to be become an entrepreneur in his own right, deploying courage as the new tool in his leadership arsenal. I asked him how he had discovered and deployed this new skill.

I've been blessed with wonderful teachers who helped me deepen my consciousness. Organizations too are like people, they have a journey, whether they're conscious of it or not. I resolved to take this approach for my new venture. It's about purpose, it's about people, and it's about cultural values. Legacy organizations find it very hard to switch gears, but to stay relevant we must ask ourselves, 'What kind of organization do we want to be? What does this mean for us as a management team, for us as a group, and for each person?' This requires both empathy and courage.

There is now a hard edge to his vision for the Collective that requires courage and conviction, especially in the current global business context.

What will drive success in business is entrepreneurs, their vision, their ambition, and how I can help them grow as leaders. I want the Collective to be a successful private equity structure with a mentoring space. I'm interested in pursuing this ecosystem of entrepreneurs as an organizational principle. If we can help entrepreneurs pursue their journey without being acquired and subsumed by the likes of Disney or Discovery, we can preserve their agility and creativity. I love the idea of deploying capital, but with a strong focus on entrepreneurship and social impact.

Setting up this kind of entrepreneurial structure, finding backers, securing funding and locking in partners requires courage beyond what Bastings started with in the Dutch village of his childhood. But like Tim Cook at Apple, another openly gay and visibly successful leader, Bastings is frequently looking in the mirror to test his own leadership courage as he explores this new territory.

Towards the end of our interview, I asked Bastings what advice he has for other leaders seeking to build courage on top of empathy to drive change and transformation. 'Step into this area with genuine curiosity. Big transitions are more about your legacy than immediate return on capital. Also be part of a community and contribute to the broader picture. We're all part of society whose health ultimately can't be delegated to governments or institutions. We all have to participate, so you will need to step up and do your part.'

I see Bastings as well ahead of the curve when it comes to these emerging business practices and the future of work. With the advent of the Covid-19 pandemic, collectives and ecosystems like his will likely become the norm as we aggregate talent from around the world into diverse teams who collaborate in hybrid and asynchronous work spaces to create the next waves of innovation. And empathic leadership – focusing on people, purpose and planet – will remain the key to attracting and engaging this new pool of talent. And for anyone in doubt about these shifts and new ways of working, figures from consultants MBO Partners show that between 2019 and 2020 the number of Americans saying they 'plan on becoming digital nomads over the next two to three years' increased by almost a fifth. A further 49% increase occurred during the Covid-19 pandemic itself, with over 10 million people in the US alone (Brown, 2021).

Thus, the journey from empathy to courage is as valid as from that from courage to empathy. The essential lesson in building a successful Change Mindset is to recognize the importance of both these levers to accelerate our transitions. For Hogarth and Bastings, the need for deliberately empathic and courageous leadership in today's organizations is clear. As Bastings concluded in our interview, 'Younger generations, the Millennials and Gen Z, is where the future of business lies. And this talent is looking for careers and deployment of skills in settings that are more balanced – emotionally, spiritually and commercially. That must come from the top. If I'm at the head of an organization, I am at the apex of the energy pyramid. That is a responsibility as well as a blessing. So if you're not modelling authenticity and a growth journey yourself, you can't ask others to. This is why I take my own development so seriously. You can't delegate that.'

Courage and empathy as the new drivers of business change

When I spoke to leaders about courage and empathy they clearly rose to the surface as two key attributes in leading successful change. Yet those I interviewed were also rather exceptional people, so you may wonder if these skills, especially the more 'soft' notion of empathy, are as applicable to the general leader, or indeed the general reader? The answer is that we have increasing evidence that these skills are becoming recognized as essential to lead change across the wider world of business.

In one example, Chief Innovation Officer of Société Générale, Claire Calmejane, was quoted in 2020 saying, 'The skill of the future is empathy' (Cundy, 2021). More recently, Google chief innovation evangelist Frederik Pferdt cited empathy as 'a major skill needed in growing an innovation mindset, and helping business leaders come up with better solutions' (Balinbin, 2021). British journalist and author David Goodhart in his 2020 book *Head, Hand, Heart* divides human aptitudes into head (cognitive), hand (physical) and heart (emotional), also arguing that these have become badly out of balance with too much power associated with logic and not enough for essential human needs such as empathy (Goodhart, 2020).

Gillian Tett of the FT has also frequently examined the role of empathy in business, notably in her book *The Silo Effect* and more recently in *Anthro-Vision* where she explores evidence of empathy as a key capability for business leaders. She describes one experiment at Google that blends anthropology, psychology and data science in an attempt to better 'inoculate' Internet users against misinformation by understanding the unintended consequences of data-heavy search processes that often create inherent biases. Inserting people with qualitative skills into such traditionally quantitative research has 'made Google techies understand what they don't understand with their data tools.' Tett's conclusion? 'We need more empathy for strangers to survive and thrive' (Tett, 2021).

The MIT Psychologist, Sherrie Turkle, also reinforces these conclusions in her book *The Empathy Diaries,* reminding us that the 'engineering mindset' is too linear and 'we need empathy to augment the algorithms'. Her original insights about the dangers of the digital world go way back to 1984 in her earlier book *The Second Self.* In a recent interview with the *Financial Times* she explained: 'The empathic position is not, "I know how you feel," but rather, "I don't know how you feel,"' (Foroohar, 2021).

Even the legal and technical worlds of corporate governance have embraced more empathy. The recent move away from shareholder primacy as espoused by economist Milton Friedman in 1962 with his book *Capitalism and Freedom* and towards multi-stakeholder governance reflects a shift towards more empathic business strategies. Indeed, the International Business Council lobbied in 2018 for a shift towards multiple stakeholder strategies and has since nudged businesses into thinking more purposefully about the role of their organizations in society. Their *Compact for Responsive and Responsible Leadership* has now been signed by more than 140 CEOs and incorporates factors such as long-term value and sustainability using the UN Sustainable Development Goals (SDGs) as a roadmap (Mathuros, 2017).

It seems that in the 'new normal' business is increasingly becoming a bellwether for the well-being of society, rather than simply a profit machine for its owners. In one example, BlackRock CEO Larry Fink, in his recent annual letter to CEOs, labelled ESG a 'fundamental reshaping of finance' for 'accountable and transparent capitalism' (Fink, 2021). In fact, the 'S' in ESG infers empathy as we aim for improved social practices in business. ESG itself could eventually represent a new kind of 'empathy for the planet' as we develop more purposeful, aligned and sustainable business practices globally.

And as we begin to embrace more empathic organizations, results are beginning to show. Recent McKinsey research examining the most effective leadership behaviours during the pandemic revealed the priority for CEOs 'being' rather than 'doing' in how they interact with their executive teams and boards. This is new and somewhat existential territory for business executives, but 'how leaders are showing up' at this moment of global uncertainty seems to be having as much impact on employee engagement and performance as anything in the strategic plan. And leaders seem to be getting the message: further research indicates that CEOs are now spending a significant portion of their time on the 'softer' areas such as purpose and engagement to sustain performance (Dewar et al, 2020). In a final example, during a December 2020 webinar on *The Future of Business*, former McKinsey global partner Kevin Sneader even used the 'L' word, referring to 'Love' as a new skill for CEOs (Sneader, 2020). Employees led by such CEOs were apparently four times more engaged. But there is clearly more work to be done: less than 50% of the same respondents felt their wider organizations were exhibiting these traits.

Perhaps the best advice for CEO's attempting to build these new empathic organizations can be found in the well-known saying attributed to author and activist Maya Angelou: 'People will forget what you said. People will forget what you did. But people will never forget how you made them feel' (Gallo, 2014).

Summary of key points

It was clear from my research on leading change and transitions that cultivating both *courageous* and *empathic* leadership are key to leading change effectively in today's VUCA world.

Learning and deploying these practices can augment the change lessons we have already learned from our earlier life stage transitions as described in Chapter 3 (*who, what, how* and *why*).

This process of looking forwards, as well as backwards to lead change, now shows that:

- Hindsight provides us with lessons about change from the experience of our life stages

- Foresight occurs as we apply courage and empathy to consider future actions
- Insight comes from combining these factors to make better choices in our present change challenges

The most successful leaders I spoke to had learned to blend these key attributes in an agile and dynamic way to unlock the ideas and options required when faced with significant change and transformation challenges.

In the following chapter we will look at what gets in the way of using these skills as change levers, and then in Chapter 6 how we can overcome those blocks to build a more robust and reliable Change Mindset for the future.

CHAPTER FIVE

The FAIL behaviors: Transition traps and how to recognize them

Only those who dare to fail greatly can ever achieve greatly. ROBERT F. KENNEDY

In the last chapter we explored stories from leaders who had built a Change Mindset by deliberately developing courage and empathy in moments of transition and change. They used these attributes in their personal lives as they faced career choices or life stage changes, and in their professional roles leading others when confronted with business challenges or opportunities. When we paired courage and empathy with the previous life stage change model, we created a holistic map for change. This involves first asking ourselves the questions of who, what, how and why in a given change situation. We then apply the filters of courage and empathy to evaluate our options and actions with greater focus and insight. This approach helps us tackle what I have called transitional change – situations that are outside our control yet demand a clear response from us as leaders.

The key skill in this process is balancing the sometimes-opposing forces of courage and empathy in these circumstances. We need the courage to act with clarity in times of change. And we need empathy to lead others with care and collaboration in these moments. This interaction can be represented chronologically in the Change Mindset model as follows.

FIGURE 5.1 Building courage and empathy over time

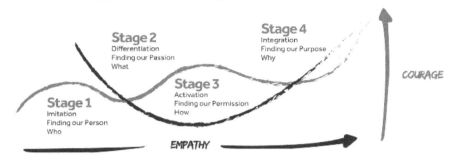

For most leaders, courage tends to build throughout our lives and careers. Despite the odd setback, we generally gain confidence with experience as we shape ourselves through imitation (who), differentiation (what), activation (how) and integration (why). Hence the fluctuating but overall rising trajectory with time showing courage as a skill which increases across our life stages. Empathy, on the other hand, is something that appears to start high, dips, and then increases again. We experience strong empathy early in life during imitation (who) in family relationships and as we explore our identity (what). Empathy appears to surge again in later life with integration (why) as we seek meaning and purpose through wider connections, 'paying it forward' and harmonizing with our surroundings. However, empathy can often dip in our early to mid-career stages as we focus on building our expertise, reputation, and impact (how). Hence the bowl-shaped timeline.

We will examine the evolution and interaction of these two factors again in Chapter 7 as we explore how to further strengthen our Change Mindset. But for now, I will focus on how we can develop our courage and empathy during change, looking first at traps that can slow us down, and then in Chapter 6, the triggers that can mitigate these to increase our impact.

Transition traps: What gets in the way?

Once we know that courage and empathy are required for transitional change, applying them may sound simple and logical enough. But putting them into practice consistently and with skill requires both focus and determination.

Almost every leader I spoke to shared their stories of failures and frustrations while attempting to manage change. This is because truly transitional moments demand that we take risks, move into unknown territory and change ourselves in some significant way. We will often be forced to question our own judgement, our previous experience, or to give up something we feel is important to us like status, power or control. Sometimes these moments make us re-evaluate our entire professional careers as we suddenly realize we may not have been true to ourselves, and that our previous choices have been driven by imitation, inertia or even fear. But these are also powerful moments when we can reflect, learn and ask ourselves the harder questions about what we really want our lives to look like, whether personal or professional.

We have seen many instances during the global Covid-19 pandemic of how unexpected external shocks have forced people to question themselves and their priorities. This relates to the existential crisis highlighted by Goleman in Chapter 3. Some have found that their work no longer fulfils them or that they are in the wrong profession. It has been well documented during the pandemic that unprecedented numbers of professionals have quit their jobs, changed occupation, or moved cities in response to such realizations, so much so that it has been termed the Great Resignation (Homegardner, 2021). And it is not just adults and corporate executives experiencing this, who generally have the means to change tack, start new ventures or relocate. Many new graduates and Millennials are launching micro-businesses or collaborating in new sectors such as home delivery, health, fashion, fitness or 'upcycling'. In just one example, Silverstone-based Lunaz in the UK re-engineers and electrifies classic cars, modernizing Rolls-Royces, Bentleys and Jaguars for a more sustainable future. Founded in 2019, it has grown significantly thanks to investments from the high-profile Reuben and Barclay families, as well as David Beckham, himself a serial entrepreneur (MIPTV, 2021).

But making such wholesale changes in our lives and taking these kinds of business risks does not come easily. The personal mindset needed to act in these key moments of change takes courage, effort, and clarity. Instead, as we saw in Chapter 1, change triggers our survival instincts and makes us shy away from action as we become defensive, doubt our choices and avoid making decisions. Indeed, if courage and empathy were easily acquired and applied, dealing with these unexpected twists and turns in life would be simple. The reality is that our instinctive aversion to change and the threat response it triggers remain our dominant default when faced with the unexpected.

How can we become more aware of these blocks and what might we do to overcome them?

Beyond the threat response to change we read about in Chapter 1, I wanted to explore whether there were other triggers that block us during change, and how as leaders we might mitigate against them. In speaking with executives about their 'failed' moments of change, I found four common behavioural errors that seemed to occur repeatedly when navigating transitions.

If we can become more aware of these, and be more vigilant about how and when they occur, we can choose to react with alternative behaviours and strengthen our Change Mindset in the process.

The four most common transition traps, which give us the acronym FAIL, are:

- Framing: failure to dream big enough
- Asking: failure to explore all of our options
- Imitation: the danger of mimicry and pleasing others
- Limitation: imposter syndrome, the inner critic and the fallacy of not good enough.

I will examine each of these in turn and then in the next chapter explore the alternative behaviours that can help counter these blind spots.

Transition trap 1: Framing the future

In 1926 T.E Lawrence wrote in *The Seven Pillars of Wisdom*:

> Those who dream by night in the dusty recesses of their minds wake up to find it was all vanity, but the dreamers of the day are dangerous men, for they act their dreams with open eyes and make them possible.

The essential question about how big we are willing to dream forms the basis of our power to change, and determines our subsequent actions. Yet when I questioned leaders I have coached or consulted with about their own dreams and personal ambitions, they often have difficulty engaging fully with the question. We know about our natural aversion to risk from Professors Edmondson and Sivanathan in Chapter 1, and how our default psychology makes us shy away from committing to anything significant that has big unknown outcomes. But it can also hinder us when we are trying to imagine possible futures for ourselves such as a big career change or an innovative new business idea like Arthur Bastings launching the Arthur Bastings Collective or Tad Beckwith cycling across the Tibetan plateau. Daring to think big and declaring our hand raises the possibility that we may be wrong and will fail. Often the self-limiting doubts related to our self-esteem impede our imagination. As a result, we mostly stand by and admire the 'dreamers of the day'.

Most leaders I spoke with about this trap had experienced it at some point in their lives. Those who had consciously transitioned from imitation (who) to differentiation (what) had more clarity and confidence in defining and acting on possible alternative futures for themselves. But at times even they found themselves struggling. They suddenly had to become beginners again as they learned a new skill or took on a new role. They had to be vulnerable as they learned about a new sector, built new relationships, or searched for the resources that would bring their ideas to life. The possibility of rejection and failure was a clear and present danger at every stage of their new projects, and forward movement required tenacity and perseverance. This was true for Gillian Tett and Martin Gayford as they found themselves rejected during repeated work or academic applications. It was true for Annmarie Lewis and Arthur Bastings as they reworked their business plans multiple times before launching their new ventures. And for Anthony Gormley and Lucian Freud, it required testing and re-testing their personal identities.

Understandably, most 'successful' people would want to avoid the loss of power, status or reputation that these challenges entail. Over time, our identity as adults becomes intertwined with our job title, our status, our wealth and our past successes. We therefore reject the possibility of losing these, even if there is a potentially bigger game to win. The risk of failure can become an impossible psychological outcome to accept, and we default back to our current circumstances. I have coached many executives whose power, ego and narcissism has progressively gotten the better of them in this way, often without them realizing it, leading to paralysis in their mid-careers about 'what's next'.

So the first and biggest transition trap is 'framing', where we limit our imagination and fail to dream big enough for ourselves. What does this look like in practice?

In my own case, I was also a victim of this transition trap. Despite having wide experience across several business sectors working with recognized companies and having lived and worked in several countries, when it came to reinventing myself it took several attempts. My background should have made the idea of transitions quite accessible. But it was not until my 40s that I was able to envisage an alternative future for myself as an independent consultant, let alone act on it. Even then, the actual shift was partly by design, but mostly by default as I found myself in the middle of a company reorganization with the arrival of a new management team that spelled imminent change for most of the incumbents. So even though I had been dreaming about something like this for about a decade, what made me finally jump from the day job into running my own business was a confluence of events, and I can only take partial credit for instigating that transition. I see this inadequate framing behaviour as an all-too frequent trap for many other mid-career professionals.

I wanted to explore more about this trap and so turned to a former colleague who I had also approached for advice when I was considering starting my own business. We had worked together in the early 2000s at the early Fintech start-up Egg Plc, which was owned by the UK's Prudential insurance company. As the Chief Financial Officer, Stacey Cartwright had successfully overseen its IPO following a successful career moving up the ranks as a business executive at PwC and Granada Media. When I shared my consulting business idea with her she had moved to a subsequent role as CFO at Burberry, the UK luxury fashion retailer. Over a glass of champagne, which happens to be her favourite beverage, I quizzed her about whether she thought I had any chance of succeeding with my own company one day. To my great surprise her response was affirmative, but more surprisingly she expressed her admiration at my courage, suggesting that she could not contemplate such a bold move from Burberry. I laughed, thinking she was simply exhibiting British humility. Yet her response was interesting and so I asked her to elaborate, 'I am sitting here with effectively a pair of golden handcuffs in my current role. Burberry is a top luxury brand. I travel the world doing investor roadshows. I attend events and meet famous people. The risk of trying something different on my own compared to the track I'm on at the moment just seems crazy and I could never do it.'

I am sure Cartwright could have transitioned easily into her own venture after Egg or from Burberry, but the psychology of this conversation intrigued me. While entirely confident in her own abilities and with no lack of imagination, the corporate conditions she was working under were effectively creating a transition trap even for someone with such exceptional capabilities and track record.

The trap didn't last long however, and Cartwright subsequently moved on to be CEO at Harvey Nichols, successfully transforming another luxury retail organization into a modern, digitally-enabled and highly profitable B2C business. When I interviewed her for this book about her subsequent experience of transitions, it was from Dubai where she was in the process of setting up her own consultancy as a non-executive director for a variety of global organizations. I asked her how she had unlocked those golden handcuffs.

The light bulb in the last year or so has been: why do I need to be in London? The old days as a non-exec meant having a calendar which basically said, 'I need to be in London because I'm attending the board meetings and audit committees for Savills. Then I need to go to Dublin to see my Irish board.' And then New York to see my New York board. It's just snowballed this year and now I've got a couple of Middle East companies to complete my portfolio and I realized it really is 'work from anywhere'. In the process you can also be very focused on what's important to you.

Clearly, she has now jettisoned the golden handcuffs ten years after our conversation about my tentative consulting business launch. But it took her a decade and some deep reflection plus a pandemic to envision that she could fully reimagine her career and lifestyle with the right framing.

Fortunately, these kinds of reframing are becoming increasingly feasible for more people and Cartwright is by no means alone in saying, 'All of a sudden people are craving different things in their life. You reach milestones in your life where you think, "I've been working so hard, it's round the clock, and it's relentless. And although I love it, I want a bit more balance." It's about getting really clear on what's important to you.' She also had the insight to move onto new things at the right moment. 'You've done all the restructuring and the re-engineering and the innovative thinking. And it becomes harder and harder to reinvent yourself. So to avoid becoming stale I said to Angela (Ahrendts, then Burberry CEO who went on to be SVP Retail at Apple), "I want to go before I reach my sell-by date."' I asked Cartwright what gave her the conviction to take this step after so many years as a successful corporate executive. 'When you get excited about the end prize that you're looking to achieve, the excitement carries you through.'

This is what I mean by 'future framing'. It is thinking big and out of the box and working towards an 'end prize', something we too often fail to do adequately for ourselves.

Her advice for other mid- or late-career executives seeking to reframe this bigger stage for themselves and open up their imagination was this:

Ask yourself: what do you really want? What do you want your life to look like? Then you can work backwards if you have defined what you want to be doing in five years' time. Use a milestone in life such as a birthday to say, 'When

I turn 50, or 60, I'd like to be in this position – what do I need to do now?' The excitement of the eye on the prize then gives you the energy and the courage and wherewithal to get there. And if you've done that a few times in your life, the next one is less daunting. It becomes a virtuous cycle. Take that risk and even if it's a disaster, the lessons learned are invaluable. And that gets you to the next thing.

Cartwright makes the crucial point that the requisite conviction and clarity doesn't manifest in an instant. She and others I spoke to had fostered the ability for future framing over time, and despite not always getting it right, always worked hard to bring their ideas to life in moments of change. Nor had they done this in a vacuum. Many reminded me about the importance of external feedback and advice to gain the right perspectives when planning a big change. 'You need to open up to others, be able to listen and put yourself into neutral so you can hear really good advice. And then don't be afraid to move from safety to risk – often this is when we learn the most.' Such moments of pause or doubt can make us feel vulnerable at the time, but they are prerequisites to moving forward successfully.

Today Cartwright is a sought-after NED working for a range of organizations who recognize her extensive experience and expertise. But even for somebody with such solid credentials, there are moments in their careers where a transition trap can still impede or limit their potential. In my case it took a solid push out of a corporate role and some very good advice from a few trusted colleagues like Cartwright to trigger the leap into a more risky venture. At other companies where I have worked, such as Disney, Sony and Saatchi & Saatchi, I came across many intelligent and qualified executives whose careers were also clearly becoming stale, yet who were unable to find the wherewithal to widen their horizons to imagine a better future for themselves.

Failure to frame the future ambitiously enough is a powerful transition trap to be avoided. The key lesson is to guard against our natural tendency for inadequate future framing, and to keep our eyes above the horizon to be on the lookout and aspire to bigger ideas and possibilities for ourselves, especially in times of transition.

Transition trap 2: Asking for options

The second transition trap I encountered in my conversations was the failure to consider and embrace sufficient alternatives. This is a crucial Change Mindset skill to cultivate and uncover less conventional solutions when faced with complex change. The creative world of performance art and music is the best place I have found to illustrate this phenomenon, starting with the American choreographer Twyla Tharp.

Tharp started dancing in the 1960s in outdoor spaces because she and her young ensemble found it hard to get hired to perform at established indoor venues. A pioneer in both modern dance and ballet, Tharp has enjoyed a long and influential career including collaborations with Film Director Miloš Forman (*Hair, Amadeus, Ragtime*) and musicians Billy Joel, Frank Sinatra and David Byrne.

In the recent PBS American Masters documentary, *Twyla Moves,* examples abound of where she found herself caught out by a lack of alternatives and options when faced with change (Cantor, 2021). She speaks about how she had to overcome the challenges of being a young and unknown dancer, without the options available to more established artists. She talks about how she had to create alternatives for herself and her troupe through their style and technique in order to break through. She also reminisces about creating her first unpaid and spontaneous performances in outdoor spaces, on rooftops and even in subway stations to gain initial visibility as an artist. Always asking about what other options might be available, she was ready to perform on any surface and to any audience to gain experience, learning adaptability in the process. 'Uneven territory was our proving ground,' she says in a vivid metaphor for the importance of adapting to different terrain as leaders of change.

Tharp also says of her early experiences, 'You can learn from anything', referring to how she explored further alternatives by creating a unique 'relaxed' choreography style that had never been seen before. Because she lacked the typical physique or abilities for pure ballet, she chose to differentiate herself by calling on her own unique gifts and attributes – flexibility, athleticism, and creativity. Rather than trying to imitate other top dancers, she reinvented dance in a way that played to her strengths. 'It's not a question of new steps and styles but of expanding our ordinary movement.' Her speed and creativity led to techniques, which she then adapted to different scenarios to form her unique style. In a vivid example of exploring options, she took on the challenge of writing a choreography piece for Russian dancer Mikhail Baryshnikov in the 1970s. While the public expected a show of classical technique, Tharp chose to completely re-educate him in her new modern style. The reception was outstanding, but her alternative approach took great creativity and courage.

Tharp is also known for other innovations, including forming one of the first all-female ensembles. It was a way to bring the unique strength of each dancer to the fore in a shared group performance. Avoiding traditional male leads in this way allowed Tharp to explore what each female dancer could bring to the stage, and to then create new and alternative moves and narratives to suit them.

Moving from dance to music, a further example of challenging existing standards and seeking options to successfully change comes from Jazz legend Miles Davis. He shares some of his stories in another art documentary, *The Birth of the Cool* (Nelson, 2019). Davis is known for constantly reinventing his music and in doing so remaining at the forefront of jazz stylistic developments. From the cool jazz movement of the 1950s he moved on to the more hard driven, rock styles of the 1960s, and even into hip-hop and pop in 1970-80s to which critics were not always receptive. For him, the most important attribute for good jazz improvisation is the search for alternatives, using trial and error and experimentation. The courageous step here is to let go of entirely of what has made us successful so far. As he says in the film, 'Even what you love needs to change.'

Dance and music are of course easy places to draw on examples of creativity and reinvention. But these lessons in adaptability clearly extend into the realm of business and leadership, where generating alternatives is often key to survival during change. I saw this in the story of Fred Prysquel., who may not be a household name for some, but is the French designer behind Vilebrequin Fashion, the iconic swimwear company which will be forever associated with the carefree optimism of the South of France in the 1960s. After founding the label, Prysquel.'s designs quickly became the *de riguer* luxury men's beachwear brand for the following decades, and have been sported by celebrities and royalty from Jack Nicholson to Leonardo DiCaprio and Prince William. The brand has more recently extended the range to women's and children's designs as well as sportswear and accessories as it continues to reinvent itself.

I interviewed Prysquel. at his home in St. Tropez where he created his brand 50 years ago. It was the 50th anniversary of the brand and limited editions of swimwear were being showcased in all the local boutiques, including custom men's beach shorts for over 4,000 Euros. Like Tharp and Davis, his story is one of constantly seeking alternatives in the face of changing conditions. Starting with his Jewish family's multiple relocations across Europe to escape German occupation in the Second World War, he experienced uncertainty and the need to adapt quickly early in life. He safely saw out the end of the war but emerged with no clear plan for what to do next.

Yet he was blessed with a creative spirit, and meeting some people involved in the early days of motor racing piqued his interest in the sport. His gifts for relationships and writing came together and he became a journalist and photographer in the early days of Formula 1 in 1962. Halfway through our interview he disappeared inside the house and emerged back onto the terrace clutching a well-worn leather diary. As he turned the pages, I saw it was filled with autographs and hand-written entries, mostly words of thanks from the many racing legends he had known and photographed. Those inscriptions and the black and white photographs tucked in between the pages re-awakened a sense of the excitement, speed, and danger from those earliest beginnings of motor racing.

But Prysquel.'s true calling, which was to become a globally recognized fashion designer, also emerged serendipitously during his military service as a young recruit stationed in Senegal. Coming from a family in the textile business, Prysquel. couldn't help noticing the bright patterned fabrics worn by men on the beaches of Dakar. He asked an African friend to fashion him a pair of beach shorts from local material, partly inspired by the board shorts he had seen in early American surf movies, with a looser cut and a drawstring. The resulting look using those bold African colours was in stark contrast to the short, monochrome and figure-hugging swimwear worn in Europe at the time. His new swimwear design was about to disrupt the entire Riviera beach scene back home.

Sporting his new creations in St. Tropez on his return to France in the early 1970s, they sparked immediate interest at the local beach clubs and he knew he was onto something. That iconic town became his base and together with his young wife he built the fashion brand around the new idea of colourful and 'free' beachwear. He adopted the name and logo *Vilebrequin*, meaning crankshaft in French in a homage to his time as a Formula 1 journalist, and over the following two decades his instincts to always seek alternatives remained the key to his survival in the competitive and fickle world of fashion. New market entrants, American competitors, changing tastes in fashion and changing business economics all forced Prysquel. to constantly reinvent his business model. He changed fabrics, colours, designs, suppliers, manufacturing bases, distribution partners, and financiers frequently to stay ahead of the game. His persistence and focus paid off, and he eventually sold the brand to an international fashion group after a long and successful run. The company has since moved further into new designs and social initiatives, partnering with the RED branding that supports AIDS, and with the Polynesian charity *Te Mana O Te Moana* that works to protect global marine life.

It was Prysquel.'s willingness to let go of his former identities and move in sync with unexpected opportunities that were the keys to his success. Without these abilities he would have been victim to the second transition trap of failing to explore sufficient options during change. I asked him what advice he has for other leaders facing transitions in their own businesses and feeling a lack of alternatives. 'When faced with uncertainty or dead ends, we must not dig our heels in. This is about paradoxical planning. We must balance passion with pragmatism,' he told me. He summed up this paradox with characteristic French flair, *'Il faut toujours avoir un plan, mais sans avoir un plan.'* In other words, have a plan but always keep your options open.

The key to avoid the second transition trap of is therefore to constantly explore our options, including seeking new and unconventional avenues, when faced with challenges in times of change. This may sound obvious, but it involves a difficult skill: maintaining forward momentum and actively evaluating choices under uncertain, unpredictable and risky conditions. Doing so means being ready to fail until you succeed again with a new approach, like Miles Davis. It also means reinventing your business model and your personal brand when faced with disruption, like Fred Prysquel. And it means creating new tools and techniques that play to our strengths when our other skills fall short, like Twyla Tharp.

The importance of this 'optionality' has also begun to appear in the management literature. One recent example is the work of Adam Grant, the Wharton School University of Pennsylvania Author and Organizational Psychologist. In *Think Again: The Power of Knowing What You Don't Know* he writes how in a turbulent world, success depends not just on cognitive horsepower but also cognitive flexibility and the ability to question our convictions. His essential message is that we must seek alternatives in the face of blocks and setbacks, yet retain the flexibility to change our minds when things don't work out as expected. (Grant, 2021)

Transition trap 3: Imitation and the danger of mimicry

I wish I'd had the courage to live a life true to myself, not the life others expected of me. BRONNIE WARE

Ware is an Australian author and motivational speaker who wrote *The Top Five Regrets of the Dying* after working as a nurse in palliative care for terminally ill patients. The top regret that she documented among her patients, shown above, reflects the risks of the third transition trap: imitation. The failure to become the person we want to be, because we feel the need to mimic some external, imposed standard, is a common trap for many leaders. In the context of navigating change, imitation can also be a debilitating trap if we are unable to trust our own judgment and follow our instincts because we are too influenced or constrained by the views or expectations of others.

As we saw in Chapter 2, the first life transition we experience is from imitation to differentiation. The psychological theory is clear that our early influences shape our behaviours and attitudes through early role models such as parents, teachers and figures of influence who create the templates that shape our world. Then, as we mature, we gain in psychological maturity and begin to discover our own personality and preferences, allowing us to move away from these early influences.

However, many leaders I have worked with still find themselves unconsciously mimicking the behaviour of others in order to be validated, to fit in, or to please their bosses, clients, teams or friends.

Such imitation comes in many guises. Sometimes we will be tempted to imitate leadership behaviors we see around us because they seem 'right' or 'better' than our own. We find ourselves aping those we read about in the management literature or see on TED talks. Along with the black turtlenecks, these people always seem to have the more powerful arguments and confident body language. We can also find ourselves being swayed by a forceful leadership personality or a dominant company culture that expects assimilation to be seen as 'playing on the same team'. The trap of course is that our innate human need for acceptance and belonging pushes us to mimic such behaviour. In the worse cases, I have seen entire organizations coerced into dysfunctional patterns that are promoted by the behaviour of just a few leaders at the top. The negative consequences of such collective imitation can be significant. Well-documented examples include companies that condone unconventional leadership behaviours such as at Wells Fargo where client acquisition numbers were fabricated, incited by overly aggressive sales targets set at the top. Other examples include toxic, hubristic or sexist cultures shaped by leaders at companies such as WeWork, Uber or Facebook, many later exposed by brave (mostly female) employees who chose to speak out. Julie Lythcott Haims, in her book *Your Turn* argues that avoiding the urge to please others, which often entails imitating them, is key to our sense of worth (Lythcott-Haims, 2021). One way to check our propensity to imitate, she advises, is to 'Sit with yourself for a quiet moment and ask, "What would I do if no one were judging me?"'

The transition trap of imitation, in whatever guise it appears, will smother our own personalities and limit our power to change or adapt on our own terms. Finding our inner voice and having the courage to honour it is not easy when we are increasingly bombarded by corporate 'values', what is deemed 'politically correct', or social media images of other people's apparently perfect lifestyles (see Facebook) or grandiose achievements (see LinkedIn). Accounts of yet another Silicon Valley unicorn launched by a 20-year-old is enough to depress anyone over 30. But despite these unhelpful pressures to achieve, we must struggle with uncertainty to find our own voice through trial and error and over time.

An example of how to avoid mimicry and stay true to oneself was brought to life for me by another former colleague. Before we worked together at Saatchi & Saatchi, Siobhan Stanley had trained from age 10 at The Royal Ballet School in London, later gaining a place in the Royal Ballet, Sadler's Wells as a soloist and performing there for an impressive 15-year span. She later transitioned to more contemporary dance performance with the prestigious Rambert Dance Company, before turning her creative talents to acting in theatre, film and television. When Stanley and I worked together in advertising she was honing her skills as an executive coach, which she then expanded into a standalone business, helping executives increase their personal presence and impact using performance techniques for clients like Google and the BBC, where we also collaborated.

When I interviewed Stanley for this book, she had yet again reinvented herself as a professional painter, creating hyper-realistic oil canvases of Renaissance scenes. But she adds a twist, inserting real contemporary portraits of multicultural sitters that imbue each work with a striking juxtaposition between classic and modern.

I asked Stanley how she had been able to reinvent herself in so many courageous ways, avoiding the trap of imitation in ballet, modern dance and acting. Such hyper-competitive professions are known for the pressure they place on performers to imitate or emulate the top 'stars'. This can also be a very seductive place, endowing its professionals with a cachet and mystique that is hard to surrender. Yet Stanley left those worlds to move into the more risky and potentially less glamorous arenas of business, then professional development, and now art.

She described this as an act of 'skin shedding' and an antidote to the pressure to emulate others or trying to be someone you are not. 'There are always moments in life where you feel a change coming. They are not always obvious but the key is to hear them and then listen to them. You know they are going to be disruptive but often they end up being delicious accidents that open doors to really finding out who you are and allowing you to then become that person.' I asked her how to know we are making the right choices in these moments of change. 'It's also a question of being very clear about what to say yes to and what to say no to. There is no answer given to you so you have to trust your instinct. It's about really tuning into what is important for you. Can you get your internal radio back onto the strongest signal of who you are? You're searching mindfully and carefully for exactly the right wavelength, a bit like sharpening the focus on a camera lens.'

This is a key life skill, as these moments of potential independence can occur at any stage in life. Witness Stanley's coaching career that started after two decades of dance and performance. Or her painting career that started well into her 50s. As she reflects on her previous incarnations, she told me what was driving her now was the question: 'What will impact the big picture?' That question is leading to her next incarnation which is to study to become a Justice of the Peace in the UK. This is another example of someone 'paying it forward' as she becomes an integrated and powerful change agent in her later life. 'In some ways, it feels like a full circle,' she told me, 'Because the theatre of the court will not be dissimilar to the stage of a dance or movie performance. It will again be about preparation, practice, and performing at your best for an important audience.'

I am confident that Stanley will dance her way successfully around the important legal matters she will be addressing, while letting her paintings continue to express her creative core. Despite having been in some of the most ego-challenging professions, in no way has this person let imitation or mimicry limit her power to change.

For me, the key insight from Stanley was this: any leader who is ambitious, gifted and wants to reach the peak of their abilities will inevitably compare themselves to others. But equally inevitable is the likelihood that someone else will always be one step ahead, better, faster and more recognized. This can sometimes have a positive effect by inspiring us to improve ourselves, but more often such comparisons and the resulting anxiety they create disables our ambitions and paralyses our actions.

I see this often in highly skilled and competitive professions such as banking, professional services, and of course sales. However, copying others' behaviours (or business models) in an attempt to succeed is a fallacy. We will rarely outperform others simply by replicating their methods. And we will never reap the benefits of our own (most likely valid) judgments if we follow the crowd. Twyla Tharp would never have been a successful dancer had she tried to perfect conventional ballet moves. Miles Davis would not have remained relevant when the popularity of jazz seemed to wane in the 1980s if he hadn't recruited younger and more electric-oriented guitar players. And Stanley herself may not have pursued coaching, painting or justice had she succumbed to the transition trap of imitation.

So, while it is natural to be influenced by others, it is equally important to inhabit our own persona as adults. In the context of change, it is even more critical to behave according to our own values and standards and not those of others. This is the only way we can 'show up' as authentic and believable in times of change, not by trying to copy the best student in the class.

As writer Samuel Johnson warned as far back as the 18th Century: 'Almost every man wastes part of his life attempting to display qualities which he does not possess' (Johnson, 1752).

Transition trap 4: Limitation and the imposter syndrome

The often-cited condition of imposter syndrome was originally coined by Pauline Clance and Suzanne Imes in a 1978 article *The Impostor Phenomenon in High Achieving Women*. It has been a cornerstone of professional development and leadership coaching ever since and captures the essence of the fourth transition trap: the doubt we often harbor about our own abilities (Clance and Imes, 1978).

Even the most successful leaders I have worked with have at times experienced some level of self-doubt. Some question their 'right' to occupy a certain role or position. The worry of not being 'good enough' will recall painful memories for anyone who has failed a school exam or a job interview. And even the most experienced leaders will know these moments. I have already noted bumps in the road experienced by Gillian Tett and Martin Gayford. In their case perseverance won out, but the journey was not easy. According to Tett, 'You need to be very good at projecting yourself and being confident and grabbing center stage. And you need to know a lot of people. In my case I didn't, but I just had this absolute tenacity and inner obsession and drive about exploring the world. I had absolutely no expectations whatsoever about what I could or could not do. But in retrospect, this was incredibly liberating.'

Tett clearly never fell victim to the fourth transition trap of self-limitation, thanks to her counterbalancing perseverance. But for many leaders, repeated rejection, failures, or criticism will accumulate into doubts about their core abilities, eventually causing fear and paralysis in the face of challenge or change.

This trap is of course rooted in a lack of self-belief which can have many sources. The surprising fact is that many otherwise competent professionals can easily develop a sense of insecurity about their abilities over time. Peer pressure, competitiveness, unrealistic targets, a demanding boss, or inflexible company cultures can all play a part. It gets worse too, when leaders progress within organizations. This often occurs as they rise to more influential positions, gain access to greater resources, and thereby enhance their power and influence. Yet it is often such people, for example top partners at global Big Four firms, who tell me they feel like 'insecure overachievers' or fret about their 'personal brand'. I also see successful lawyers, doctors and bankers lament their perceived underachievements, blaming 'the system' without realizing that they in fact make up 'the system' and have full power to challenge and potentially change it. Several very qualified CEOs have even admitted to me they 'don't deserve the role'. But in most cases, a deeper conversation will reveal that the facts rarely justify these fears. Nonetheless, this common trap occurs often for many leaders, and especially in times of change, uncertainty or disruption.

As I mentioned before, one of the questions Peter Hogarth asks his CEOs is 'What would you do if you had no fear?' This is a revealing coaching question that gets to the core of limitation and the imposter syndrome. When asked casually, most of us can easily articulate ideas or dreams we have about our future, our business, or our personal interests. But when challenged on why we haven't acted on these visions, we bring out a long list of reasons why it 'wouldn't work'. We cite our own lack of knowledge, resources, skills or contacts to make the change. We say, 'the time isn't right', or 'I'll do it next year', or 'as soon as I've saved this amount of money'. Powerful coaching techniques like those deployed by Hogarth can usually pinpoint why such blocks occur, what gets in the way of action, and how we can begin to formulate coping strategies.

Small, achievable steps can then move us towards what may at first appear to be an unattainable dream.

Most often, what is at play is a fundamental limitation we imagine. But in a given change scenario, if we really push ourselves to evaluate the likelihood of our imagined worst-case outcomes (I'll be destitute, I'll lose my house, my reputation will vanish) we realize they are in fact very unlikely to materialize. More often, the consequences of 'failure' are likely to be a bruised ego or a hiccup in our otherwise successful life or professional trajectory. Discovering a big idea or being inspired by some fresh ambition is a tremendous gift. So, limiting ourselves by not taking bold permission to act is a wasted opportunity and an all-too-common derailer caused by this transition trap.

Actress Helena Bonham Carter offers us a lesson on silencing the inner critic as she navigates the tricky transitions in and out of character roles for her work: 'To know a character, I focus on objectives rather than adjectives', she says. This is wise advice that goes well beyond the world of acting. Don't try to be someone else but focus rather on what you are trying to achieve and how it fits 'the story'. She admits however, that it is not an easy task. The imposter syndrome is never far away: 'I do my homework to attempt to silence my very loud inner critic, the Party Pooper' (Bonham Carter, 2020).

Recent research suggests useful new insights on this topic. Neuroscience is building on the psychological safety research that Professor Edmondson shared with us in Chapter 1, offering further tools that help us feel safe to experiment and embark on change. The psychologist and CEO of the NeuroLeadership Institute, David Rock, has explored additional factors that either exacerbate or mitigate our self-limiting triggers. His paper 'SCARF: a brain-based model for collaborating with and influencing others' from 2008, posits five factors that neurologically shut down our ability to react in the face of change (Rock, 2008). The essential idea behind each letter of his acronym is as follows.

- Status: our relative perceived importance compared to others
- Certainty: our ability to know and predict future events
- Autonomy: our sense of control over such events
- Relatedness: how safe we feel in the presence of others as we experience change
- Fairness: how fair we perceive the exchanges between people to be in these circumstances.

'SCARF' is one of several emerging models that use this new neuroscience to help us understand what triggers psychological self-limitation and how we might quieten our inner critic. One key insight is that psychological 'pain' activates the same threat response area in our brain as physical pain. Both conditions trigger our survival instincts so, in other words, a perceived challenge to our status, rank, power, or a lack of certainty caused by change is interpreted neurologically the same as a physical threat or event. It is no wonder then, that our inner critic, which routinely presents us with vivid images of our unrealistic, worst-case imagined scenarios, wants to effectively shut us down in the face of change.

Self-limiting beliefs and imposter syndrome in fact played a large part in Charlie Miller's journey to becoming an accidental entrepreneur. He was honest enough to admit that his rejections of various promotions offered at the most prestigious schools like Phillips Andover and Harvard were more the result of self-doubt than any arrogance or eccentricity.

> At the most prestigious secondary school in America they pleaded with me to stay,' he told me, 'offering me Deanships and plum positions. I was convinced they had no idea who they were dealing with – an imposter. On reflection they probably knew exactly who they were getting, but at the time I couldn't see it. An early transition was perhaps missed. But I'm not sure it was. In two years I was teaching in Japan, while starting up my import business from Vietnam.

There is also a curious flipside to the limitation trap. Martin Gayford pointed this out to me, calling it 'misconstruing our abilities.' Overcoming our imposter syndrome is key to avoiding paralysis in moments of change, but Gayford also believes there is a risk of being overly bullish about our abilities to move mountains. 'Once a certain level of success is achieved, it is easy to believe that something is good just because it's by you. But it's no use being bold if you have nothing new to offer. You need to produce something that people want.' Indeed, Lucian Freud once told him, 'The amount of time devoted to something is in fact irrelevant. The only thing that counts is whether it's any good.' Gayford calls this paradoxical state 'escaping our own virtuosity.' It is the honest and self-aware state in which we manage to sidestep the transition trap of limitation through courage, yet remain clear-eyed about our actual abilities.

Summary of key points

In this chapter we have highlighted the four common traps to managing change. Many executives I work with fall prey to them because they find it exceedingly hard to let go of what has made them successful so far. Change will always threaten our identity, creating the spectre of possible failure and potentially diminishing – at least temporarily – our hard-earned knowledge and power.

Yet as we saw with Twyla Tharp, if we don't have a big enough 'stage' to play on today we must invent a new metaphorical rooftop to showcase our abilities. If we are suddenly being challenged by new players we must get ready to 'give up what we love' in order to reinvent ourselves, like Miles Davis. If we are threatened with disruption, we can still 'have a plan without having a plan' like Fred Prysquel. We can also avoid the transition traps by trusting our capabilities and dreaming without barriers to embrace new technologies as Lord Mitchell did in the fledgling computing world of the 1970s, to creating new business models like Arthur Bastings, and to launch ambitious portfolio careers like Stacey Cartwright.

The key point is that we need to become better at recognizing these traps to avoid the associated paralysis they cause in the face of transitional change. This means framing our dreams more ambitiously, being more open to creating or exploring options, no matter how unconventional they may initially appear, thinking more highly of our own ideas and judgments and applying our intuition free from self-limiting beliefs.

In the next chapter I will explore in more detail how we can counter these transition traps and build our Change Mindset further using what I call the transition triggers.

CHAPTER SIX

The SPARK practices: Transition triggers and how to use them

Success is stumbling from failure to failure with no loss of enthusiasm. WINSTON CHURCHILL

I was reminded of this quote, loosely attributed to Winston Churchill (Elberse, 2013), during my interviews about what had helped leaders get beyond the FAIL factors in the last chapter and what they had learned in the process.

The answers, which I will discuss in this chapter, are a set of additional practices that can accelerate change and act as a complement to the underlying traits of courage and empathy from Chapter 4. These also map back to the transitional life stages as we move from our early experiences of imitation and differentiation through to our more mature stages of activation and integration. I will tie all these concepts together in the next chapter by way of a Change Mindset masterclass.

To prepare for this, let us examine the five practices that emerged as the most common and effective accelerators of change, and which counter the FAIL traps. There are five transition triggers forming the acronym SPARK.

- Spirit: finding our essential self
- Partnership: using the power of other people
- Alternatives: the pursuit of possibilities

- **Reason:** evaluating and making sense of our choices
- **Knowledge:** using purpose to guide action.

When mastered, these triggers become an important set of behavioural tools and principles for individuals, groups, and organizations facing change.

Transition trigger 1: Spirit – finding our essential self

Always remember that you are absolutely unique.
Just like everyone else. MARGARET MEAD

This quote attributed to Mead may seem flippant but it accurately reflects her strong belief in the importance of our collective human identity as the key to living successfully in groups. Equally, it reminds us how our own individual uniqueness will always stand us apart from the ocean of others alongside whom we live and work. Our own personalities, preferences, choices, values and beliefs differ from those of others. We can think of these unique differences as constituting our 'spirit'.

The importance of knowing what sets us apart from others is part of our early life stage transition from imitation (who) to differentiation (what). Yet spirit takes us a step beyond this notion as a deeper exploration of who we are in the context of change and life's journey. It forms the basis of our most important choices and decisions beyond the initial question of who I am being in this change situation (Chapter 4). It moves us into the territory of the later life stages of activation (how) and integration (why). Spirit can therefore be seen coming into play when we are faced with bigger life questions and more important choices during change. Spirit becomes the foundation for our judgments and decision-making in these moments, leading to more meaningful actions and ultimately a truer expression of ourselves.

Those I spoke to described this search for their spirit variously as finding what mattered to them most; identifying their personal values; clarifying their deeper beliefs; or finding some 'energizing principle'. Clarity about our deeper identity was also felt to be a prerequisite for effective decision-making and leadership in key moments of change and transition. This seemed particularly important in mid-life. At this stage of our development many of us move away from our earlier technical expertise into a more integrative space. We begin to take into consideration the wider environment as we make choices, and we begin to use our networks to create capability and build the conditions for growth. We also start to apply our whole life's experiences and make our judgments with more care, in order to create a sense of 'flourishing', be this for ourselves or for those we lead.

If we are searching for 'change management' tools in the context of our busy professional lives and action-oriented businesses, existential language about spirit may seem questionable or even jarring. But the theme of our spirit appeared consistently throughout my research as leaders looked to shape bigger and more impactful changes for themselves and others. Management expert Charles Handy described the value of 'finding your soul' and 'staying close to it' throughout life's endeavours as did Peter Hogarth, who was very clear about how important it is to 'follow your soul'. Similarly, Annmarie Lewis of Rainmakers explained the enlightening discovery of her 'calling' as the mission to elevate others through greater justice in society.

How does spirit manifest in the context of business and change? Arthur Bastings elevates the notion of spirit as an energizing principle for organizations to another level. As a former MD at Discovery and now founder of Arthur Bastings Collective, he shared with me his vision of how leaders can foster change and transition through greater spirit at the organizational level. 'At the corporate level and in the organizational context you can't really separate the personal from the professional. So if you're an integrated being, your leadership presence has to be part of that. You can't show up differently at work than how you are in the rest of your life.' Bastings believes this philosophy is the key to attracting and retaining the best talent in a VUCA world. He explains, 'The younger generations, the Millennials and Gen-Z, are looking for careers and organizations that deploy them in settings that are more balanced, emotionally and spiritually. The spiritual in an organizational sense is therefore about having a sense of mission, a sense of a journey, and a sense of values. It's about having a sense of growth as a person, and feeling that the organization is committed to facilitating that growth.' How many organizations successfully achieve this? Bastings is of the opinion that very few companies in the last decade had accomplished this, with most legacy organisations finding it even harder to adapt. This, he believes, is the reason so many companies find it challenging to successfully 'go digital' – another common ambition in the current corporate *zeitgeist*.

But he sees light at the end of the tunnel. As younger generations enter the workforce, organizations must change. 'It's a shift in the cultural mindset to create an environment where younger generations are motivated and interested in staying. Too often, instead of a more 'spiritually aware' organization, you get the 'diversity' programme or the 'talent' programme, but in the end it's all window dressing.' Bastings actively expresses his spirit every day as a leader 'at the apex of the energy pyramid' as he puts it. And in his sector, which deals with creative talent and young entrepreneurs, injecting this sense of spirit into the organizational culture is proving an essential competitive advantage.

But this journey to find our spirit is not simple. Many leaders told me it had taken the best part of their careers to discover it. Many were still on the journey as they lived through successive personal and professional transitions that tested them in new and unexpected ways. But all of them agreed that discovering a sense of our true self facilitated this and was key to effectively tackling the bigger transitions that occur later in life. Finding our True North is the point from which we can 'Push the boundaries of where we can be taken seriously' as the executive coach Peter Hogarth puts it. Or as the poet David Whyte expresses it, 'Reality is invitational. Every day we are invited to be bigger than ourselves.' This captures the intangible but essential search for our spirit as leaders of change (Whyte, 1990).

We can also look outside the business world to find some inspiring examples of spirit in practice.

In the 2018 documentary *Free Solo,* the 34-year-old pioneer free climber Alex Honnold demonstrates his unique skills in heart-stopping footage taken by suspended camera crews. They capture live his bid to become the first free climber to conquer the 900-meter sheer granite face of El Capitan in Yosemite National Park, California (Chin et al, 2018). Using only his fingers and feet to hold his body on the vertical rock face, Honnold climbs without the assistance of ropes, pins or support. He feels for only the tiniest bumps and cracks in the glacier-smoothed granite before making his next move, inching upwards on the rock face. His extraordinary achievement garnered both an Academy and BAFTA award for Best Documentary in 2019 for the film producers at *National Geographic.*

Honnold's unique accomplishments in *Free Solo* are the result of discipline, detailed planning and an unrelenting focus in this highly dangerous and technical profession. Despite his young age, Honnold is also a powerful illustration of finding one's spirit and then using it to extraordinary effect in situations of risk and uncertainty. In the film he speaks with great clarity about why he chose this path: 'I had a purpose: to be the best climber I could be. And I didn't need many material possessions. The less stuff you have the more focused you can be on the things that matter. I was also happier than most people, because I was doing exactly what I loved, and doing it at the highest level.' The spirit of Alex Honnold is this: a burning desire to be the best climber he can be through unrelenting discipline, meticulous planning and laser sharp focus. It is his precise, minutely planned and rehearsed movements that allow him to safely rise 900 meters into the blue California sky utterly unaided.

We can see a more down to earth illustration of spirit in sports legend Sir Alex Ferguson, long-time Manager of the UK football team Manchester United. Some of the star players who rose to fame under his guiding hand include footballer turned entrepreneur David Beckham, controversial but gifted Frenchman Eric Cantona, and the serial record-breaking Cristiano Ronaldo. Famous for his unforgiving feedback meted out on unsuspecting players who failed to live up to his high standards, Ferguson nonetheless instilled deep loyalty that enabled exceptional performance from those under his leadership. He has been profiled extensively in books and films on leadership for his winning ways. But in the 2021 Netflix documentary *Never Give In* we witness a different Ferguson, as he reflects on his recovery from a life-threatening brain haemorrhage that almost killed him in May 2018, age 76 (Ferguson, 2021). Ferguson's quest for his spirit shines through the film as he describes his humble beginnings in the shadows of the rough Glasgow shipyards, and how he decided to choose the one thing that he believed would provide meaning for him and an escape from those industrial surroundings: football. His passion and commitment to the game over the next four decades, initially as a successful player, resulted in him becoming one of the greatest football managers of all time.

But despite having found his calling, his journey was not all glory and accolades. Early in his managerial career he was frequently criticized by the press and many doubted him as he took on various leadership roles and provoked change. Yet he persisted with his unique management style, eventually disproving the naysayers and achieving his legendary success streak with Manchester United. Part of his spirit appears clearly in the film when he says, 'You have to treat losing as a part of winning. Losing is part of life. But when it happens, you find yourself.' In other words, failure can also be an important part of finding yourself and your spirit. Among other things, his ability to learn from failures, leverage the diversity of each player and nurture their unique talents set him apart as a leader. He was also never afraid to change things, often rebuilding his football team even in times of success. In fact, Ferguson's management approach was developed as a Harvard Business School case study in 2012, just before his retirement, resulting in 'Ferguson's Formula'. Ferguson found his spirit in the game of football and used it to guide him though four decades of change, challenge and doubt.

Thus, knowing deeply who we are and what drives us plays a key role in how effectively we deal with change. Leaders who are self-aware in this way, and who stay open and curious, will naturally have better intuition and insight than those who aren't. They will instinctively recognize key transition points as they occur and will be better able to understand what these changes mean for them and those around them. Honnold's spirit, with its unique focus and unrelenting discipline, helps him out of trouble when he is faced with an unexpected facet on a rock face. And Ferguson's spirit and conviction helped him through a quarter century career at United, where despite the world of football having changed dramatically, he never stopped adapting.

All the leaders I spoke with told me about a similar level of focus and discipline as they worked through these types of questions for themselves. However long it takes, discovering and then applying our spirit to navigate transitions will be a powerful tool for anyone seeking to more effectively lead change.

Transition trigger 2: Partnership – the power of other people

Alone we can do so little, together we can do so much.   HELEN KELLER

The 17th Century poet John Donne reminded us in Chapter 4 that 'No man is an island'. We used this as the basis for exploring why empathy is an essential skill when leading change. The second transition trigger builds on this as we explore the importance of not only empathizing with others in moments of change, but of actively seeking their advice and tapping into their experiences too. The power of other people can be the key to improving the quality of our analyses, assessments and decision-making during change. As the American author and disability rights advocate Helen Keller reminds us in the above quote, it is other people who are often most critical to our own successes in life.

Making decisions in uncertain times can feel like a lonely undertaking, and you might think it should therefore trigger an instinct to seek other views. Yet inviting feedback and help from others is not the natural habitat of powerful leaders. My observation of many executives in these situations is a distinct tendency to remain stubbornly on their 'islands'. They valiantly try and solve complex problems alone at their desks or work-from-home offices, believing it is their job to work things out. Many of the leaders I spoke to admitted they had spent years with this fruitless and solitary approach, trying and often failing before finally seeking partnerships in change. This was especially true for more complex or novel change challenges, where a combination of ego and expectations kept them toiling away in isolation.

But those who became more curious about why things weren't working found that when they changed their approach and began reaching out to their networks for input, suddenly their perspectives opened up and options multiplied. The diversity of views that come with dialogue and debate inject new energy that naturally creates broader options and more ideas for handling change. It turns out that using the all-important power of others during uncertainty unlocks our own personal power to navigate change. Even the most highly qualified experts can benefit from such additional perspectives. Professor Khaw illustrates this wonderfully in his story about his relationship with the young and little-known Dennis Hassabis at DeepMind, leading to significant innovation in the British national health system.

'Networking' has by now unfortunately become an overused buzzword. But the leveraging of relationships that I am talking about here, when managed with discernment, takes us well beyond the management-speak. Unlocking the real power of other people to ensure better outcomes in high stakes situations means actively seeking, building on and then deliberately applying their ideas in an authentic and purposeful way. The stories I heard from the leaders who do this well were not about exploiting their networks or contacts to negotiate resources away from them or access more information. Nor was it to simply copy their methods, as benchmarking is the domain of traditional change management. The level of connection and relationship required here is much more about the vital sharing of ideas and the wider exploration of potential outcomes through collaboration. It involves working from a level playing field and sparring together through dialogue and a generosity of spirit to tackle important issues. These kinds of exchanges require us to be fully open to others in a non-judgmental and non-competitive way. They require humility, rather than competing for, or appropriating, all the best ideas.

An example of this appears in *Free Solo*. Alex Honnold does not at first glance come across as a gregarious networker, focused as he is on the intense training and preparation needed for his extraordinary ascents. Yet in a profile by the Harvard Business Review, he talks about the power of others in helping his own success (Harrell, 2021). The fact is that he collaborates widely, despite his solitary vocation. When asked about the process of collaboration and the role of diversity in learning, he admitted, 'The more eyes you have on a problem, the more likely you are to find unique solutions.' His willingness to tap into the power of other people is clear in his story about inviting a fellow climber to bolt new routes on a cliff edge near Las Vegas. In the process of climbing together, he realized that working with the complementary differences between them resulted in a higher level of achievement. 'My friend is probably the strongest professional sport climber in America. I'm taller, but he's stronger, so I have to be more creative about how I'm using my body to figure out the best way to climb with somebody who's so different.' Honnold's biggest solo climbs still involve the intensely single-minded task of scaling sheer rock faces alone and without ropes or safety material. But even as a world expert in his field, like Professor Khaw, he still relies on the power of others to spar, test, and achieve better outcomes. This is especially true in new or unexpected situations involving life threatening risks. 'In climbing,' he says, 'your partner is literally holding your life in their hands.' He therefore chooses people he can trust implicitly for their judgment in uncertainty.

Another vital aspect of harnessing the power of relationships when navigating change is the art of accepting criticism. The quality of our decisions appears to be directly proportional to the degree of challenge we invite from others. And while this is one of the most uncomfortable and naturally unwelcome experiences, I heard many stories of how the best outcomes occurred following the most personally challenging conversations. And when I asked these leaders where they turned to seek out such challengers, the response was also unanimous. The most helpful challenges occurred very close to home, with the people they trusted the most, who knew them best, and who could really challenge their thinking even if the result contradicted their own conclusions.

Fred Prysquel. of Vilebrequin Fashion unquestionably cites his wife Yvette as his most trusted advisor and sparring partner in situations of change. As we spoke on his terrace in St. Tropez, he described to me how she was always the first one to challenge him in any important business matter. As they built the company together over the years, she would routinely provoke debate, challenge his assumptions, and encourage change and innovation until, from their humble beginnings in the basement of a shop in 1971, this positive friction was part of what created a brand that became worth nearly $100m by the time of its eventual sale.

Similarly, art critic Martin Gayford also shared with me the value of 'tough love', saying, 'You can't exempt yourself from criticism.' Gayford experienced this first-hand when he shared the first 20,000 words he had written for his biography *Michelangelo: His Epic Life* with his wife (Gayford, 2017). She promptly dismissed it as 'just not good enough yet', adding, 'You can do much better than this.' And, he told me, 'She was quite right.' The point is that having witnessed him craft his other best-selling art books, she knew his capabilities so well that she could recognize instantly where he was not at his best. Likewise, Charles Handy always credits his late wife Liz with the most productive edits to his own work.

Stacey Cartwright also agreed with the idea of seeking out challenging feedback, citing a close friend who challenged her to think more seriously through her career options. The provocation eventually lead to her biggest professional transition, ultimately opening the door to her non-executive directorship portfolio.

What surprised me in these conversations was the fact that most of these sparring partners were not managers, boards or even executive coaches. We often assume that our best learning will come from structured interventions by our superiors, training companies, or HR professionals. But the leaders I spoke to assured me that it was from the closer and more intimate ties of friends, family and only the occasional peer or colleague, that true insights and real constructive criticism emanated. It was their ability to challenge, push the boundaries, and truth-tell that gave these conversations such power. A pat on the back at work or some other vague gesture of approval seemed to have very little meaningful impact in moments of real uncertainty where the stakes are higher. We need to be suitably challenged.

Constructive criticism, therefore, is often more valuable than enthusiastic agreement. In the language of coaching, our most useful critics act as sandpaper: highly abrasive but ultimately creating a smoother surface on which to improve ideas and uncover fresh insights. Tough love is what will help us navigate uncertainty by compelling us to change, because it is during these challenging conversations that we learn, reflect and ultimately improve our decision-making. As Gayford says, 'These moments are a staging post on the way to success.'

In my own case, it was certainly the power of other people and the process of asking for feedback that tipped this research project from possibility into reality. I had been considering how to investigate the question of transitional change after feeling disillusioned when observing our reactions to the global Covid-19 pandemic in early 2020. I had begun to write down my thoughts about it but soon found that asking others for feedback on the idea and offering to explore their own experiences of transitional change was far more powerful than simply gathering my own thoughts or researching existing change theories. By getting in touch with other people, and by showcasing their own lessons learned, the material suddenly came to life. It was these new insights about more powerful ways to lead change that led to what I now call the Change Mindset.

So while not all of us will be scaling El Capitan like Honnold, the practice of harnessing relationships for advice and feedback more purposefully to unlock new insights will enhance our power to scale our own heights during change. As Honnold does with fellow climbers when figuring out his new routes on dangerous terrain, the practice is about becoming a thinking partner with others to solve complex problems in high stakes and unpredictable scenarios.

Transition trigger 3: Alternatives – the pursuit of possibilities

It's a world of increasing pressure, but it's also a world of expanding opportunity. JOHN HAGEL

For many people, the prospect of change often instils fear and paralysis. Unfortunately, fear is also a common tool used by CEOs trying to implement change. This blunt instrument, according to Hagel in his book *The Journey Beyond Fear*, 'Implies that everything is going to collapse if we don't do something' yet is mostly ineffectual. Similarly, Professor Constantinos Markides of London Business School, in his own book *Organising for the New Normal*, says, 'Nothing is further from the truth' when referring to whether this fear tactic works (Markides, 2021). He emphasizes instead how leaders can engage their employees in change much more effectively with some surprisingly simple tactics. Making the rationale for change personally relevant, engaging with people's emotions as to why the change is important for the firm and its customers, and drilling down into what the change actually means for each employee are just a few of his refreshing recommendations. The essence of his advice is to open up possibilities for people.

Both these authors reinforce what I have heard from other leaders about the value of exploring alternatives during change, even when we feel confronted with dead ends.

But why is this transition trigger – seeking alternatives – so hard to pull? We will all face major choices or crossroads at least a few times in our lives. These moments can be personal, professional, financial, spiritual, or relational – and can often open up important new chapters in our lives. Yet the leaders I interviewed about these unchartered moments all recalled the fear of failure.

The first reason this happens is that, as adults, we naturally want to feel in charge of our lives. Not knowing what will happen next makes us feel threatened and magnifies the potential negative consequences of our actions in our mind, often leading to inaction, which of course means we do not embark on the change.

The second reason is that because we want to look 'smart', we tend to isolate ourselves during change and try to figure things out on our own, away from potential judgment or criticism. But again this tends to be counterproductive, as it obstructs our ability to explore options more freely, and we end up with analysis paralysis.

The third scenario involves power and status, when leaders become overly self-focused and incapable of questioning themselves because of their position in their organizations or the dominant culture. Such leaders come to truly believe that they alone have the competence and intelligence to work through these challenging issues, but of course fail to widen their options. Sometimes, this is even reinforced by those around them who imitate them by agreeing, or hold back their own views through fear. In either case, the change effort likely fails due to a lack of diversity in the process. At best, the result will be a mediocre middle ground that merely reflects current biases or previous solutions, without generating new insights.

So, involving others during change seems like an obvious thing to do, but is harder in practice than it seems. However, it can be done if we reframe the threat (change) as an opportunity (possibilities) and then actively seek a diversity of opinions and options.

I witnessed one powerful example of seeking alternatives when I worked at advertising agency Saatchi & Saatchi. In the early 2000s we were suddenly faced with the threat of disruption from the advent of digital advertising so we had to find new ways of crafting communications and promotional messages for our clients. We knew the core strength of the agency was in creative thinking, and so together with the European Creative Director John Pallant we instigated a series of ideas exchanges through what we labelled our 'ideas academy'. We drew together the most diverse groups of people possible from the regional agencies and held weekend workshops at our Madrid agency for over a year, where we used a wide variety of stimuli to help us think about the future. We brought in actors and storytellers, we visited museums, we explored the city using treasure hunts, and together with Pallant we invented new creative processes called 'tribes' that aimed to unlock the group's most creative ideas without judgement, evaluation or constraints. The approach paid off and the agency was able to continue generating revenue using new structures such as digital campaigns, hybrid solutions and greater co-creation with clients. This was an active use of the third transition trigger: always seeking wider alternatives and more options.

Pallant went on to win a series of awards and has since founded BLITZWORKS, a strategic and creative consultancy offering a much faster, more collaborative, transparent and productive way of working with clients. Their unique positioning builds on the work at Saatchi & Saatchi and offers a fast track to create platforms in days rather than months, offering 'creative development at speed'.

The key lesson here for leaders faced with transitional change is to deliberately step outside our comfort zone, beyond our personal analyses, prior experiences, and the groupthink of like-minded people. We must reframe threats as opportunities and consult widely before making important decisions. The effort needed to seek honest and challenging external views is of course greater than repeating what we know already. But as leaders like Pallant can attest, being able to lower one's ego long enough to seriously welcome ideas and challenges from others, and then being open to exploring these different avenues is key to being resilient, reliable and relevant when navigating uncertainty.

The academic and management literature corroborates these conclusions about the pursuit of possibilities. The theory of appreciative inquiry originally developed by David Cooperrider and Suresh Srivastva in 1985 while working at The Cleveland Clinic first illustrated the so-called 'observer effect' (Cooperrider and Srivastva, 1987). They found that rather than advocating or exchanging opinions, which is the usual approach to managing change, the act of inquiry can more powerfully generate actual solutions. Questions aimed at what has worked in the past, what might be possible in the future, or what might 'give life' to a situation will psychologically shift the weight of the conversation towards more positive options. This technique can then pivot a conversation or even an organization into more of a 'growth mindset', where positive framing for change becomes the dominant narrative, as opposed to resistance or competing opinions. Such collaborative and dialogic methods are a marked departure from the more common 'deficit mentality' most teams and organizations gravitate towards in uncertainty, where we obsess over what went wrong, what needs fixing, and who is to blame for our lack of clarity. Appreciative inquiry and similar methods for positive change management work by promoting debate, exploring alternatives, and building on each other's ideas to generate more options.

Organizational psychologist Ed Schein provides another example for the pursuit of possibilities, having coined the notion of 'humble inquiry' in his early work (Schein, 2013). After years of advocating change as a consultant to organizations, he describes the moment in which he discovered the power of a 'soft' approach using powerful, open questions to generate possibilities rather than prescribe answers in difficult moments of change. He found that this exposed the underlying patterns that were getting in the way of progress, which in turn would begin to generate broader dialogue, thus bringing people together around shared common ground and exploring new avenues through 'inquiry' rather than staying locked into individually-focused agendas. When simple but authentically curious questions are asked in a group setting, we can 'play back' what is in the room and unlock the potential of leaders who are otherwise unable to get over their ingrained patterns of behaviour, personal assumptions, or competing views. In most leadership settings, especially during change and uncertainty, defensiveness and egos will still drive the agenda. Yet with a more generative approach that keeps everyone open to alternatives, and without judgment, inquiry and options become core tools for change.

As leaders during change – individually and collectively – we all owe it to ourselves and those we lead to step into this unknown space with a deliberate learning stance and an openness to new possibilities.

Transition trigger 4: Reason – evaluating and making sense of our choices

When we are no longer able to change a situation, we are challenged to change ourselves. Between stimulus and response there is a space. In that space is our power to choose our response. In our response lies our growth and our freedom. VICTOR FRANKL

The Viennese psychiatrist, Viktor Frankl, wrote wisely and eloquently on the subject of our human reactions in times of stress and uncertainty. He described of the choices that exist, even in the face of despair, in his book *Man's Search for Meaning* (Frankl, 1946). During the Second World War Frankl was uniquely able to observe how humans coped with the tragedies of wartime, including during his internment in a Nazi prison camp. What he noticed there was counter-intuitive. He describes how the prisoners who survived the longest were the ones who comforted others or gave away their last piece of bread, not those who tried to protect themselves by defending their limited territory or fighting over scraps of food. As a scientist, the behavioural theories he later constructed as a result of this traumatic period led him to believe in the power of choice in any circumstances, even when there appeared to be literally no escape. His message of hope and responsibility highlights our inner freedom and how we can still choose our actions, reactions or attitudes under even the most extreme stress. His experiences led him to believe that, as humans, our deepest desire and need is to search for meaning and purpose.

Frankl survived the war, published his work in 1946, and went on to develop a suite of therapeutic techniques to help victims cope with various kinds of trauma. His method of 'logotherapy' had patients reframe their experiences to emphasize their ability to choose more constructive attitudes rather than feelings of hopelessness. Though Frankl's science was not universally accepted at the time, his essential insight about our innate need for making sense of life, and our ability to choose how we react in moments of change, seems clear. Since his death in 1997 at the age of 92, his ideas about seeking meaning, purpose, identity and fulfilment have been widely adopted by academics and behaviouralists, and increasingly appear in the management literature as methods for leading change.

Thus, realizing we have choices, and then weighing them up and making sense of them, is a critical skill to build a Change Mindset. Seeking greater clarity about the choices we make can build confidence for our present and future transitions. The leaders I spoke to about this question of meaning spoke of it as the essential work of crafting our own story and building a narrative for how we act in different moments of change.

Sometimes this can involve an entire redefinition of ourselves as the result of change. Author Charles Handy told me how he did this midway through his career. He used to dread cocktail parties and public events because people would ask him what to write on his name badge. 'Having been a business school professor, the Royal Warden at Windsor Castle, a broadcaster and a writer I was often stumped by this question,' he told me. His wife Liz, not known for beating around the bush, suggested he simply call himself Charles Handy, 'and see what happens'. This seemed to work well until one evening when at an event a person came up to him (he was not wearing the name badge) and commented, 'I understand Charles Handy is here this evening.' To which Handy replied, 'Yes he is, and I am he.' The other person looked at him, paused, and asked, 'Are you sure?'. Apart from a slight blow to his ego, this exchange made Handy realize that he could in fact define himself however he liked, preferably using a term that would have the most meaning for him. This led him to coin the phrase 'social philosopher' which didn't exist at the time but which has been on his name badge ever since. He told me he was very satisfied when, sometime later, he saw a publication list him as such. Yet the ability to label oneself so clearly with meaning can elude many of us. We typically remain defined by our job title, our employer, our degree, or whatever happens to be written on our name badge at a conference.

In Chapter 4 we quoted Wittgenstein who said, 'The limits of my language mean the limits of my world.' The importance of finding our own language for who we are and the choices we make when navigating change was a consistent theme among the leaders I spoke to. It enabled them to create consistency in their actions in times of change and transition with the idea that we always have choices to reinvent ourselves. This possibility can be as challenging as it is liberating, but every one of us should attempt at least once in our lives to redefine ourselves during moments of change, creating a new 'name badge' that widens our horizons and guides our choices.

What would it feel like to determine how we want to be seen in the world and be clear on what it really means, be it doctor, lawyer, mother, carer, explorer or social philosopher?

Transition trigger 5: Knowledge – using purpose to guide action

'The cave you fear to enter holds the treasure you seek.'
JOSEPH CAMPBELL

In *The Hero with a Thousand Faces* the American Professor of Literature, Joseph Campbell, was one of the first to study the field of comparative mythology. In so doing, he uncovered surprisingly common patterns and themes throughout literature, art, poetry and myth over the centuries (Campbell, 1949). He found similar archetypal heroes across continents and cultures as he studied the world of myths – from ancient Egypt to Greece, India, Persia and the European Middle Ages. This research led him to propose the theory of a 'monomyth', which describes a common 'hero's journey' as a metaphor for the arc of our human experience. The points along the hero's journey include a call to action, a burning platform and apotheosis, as the protagonist gains enlightenment, eventually returning to the 'village' from where the journey began, bringing new insights or powers to the community. The hero's journey has proved so relatable that it has become the basis for storytelling, movies and even management theories, appearing across many aspects of our everyday lives. Hollywood adopted the idea as a now-standard format that never fails to capture our emotions and keep us on the edge of our seats. We follow heroes such as George Lucas' Star Wars characters, Steven Spielberg's Indiana Jones, or Pixar's Woody in the Toy Story franchise, empathizing with their quests and adventures. The essential attraction of the archetypal hero is the courage and determination they will show in confronting danger and the unknown. We probably all aspire to living adventures like Indy or Woody in some way, helped along by a cast of characters who confront and comfort us in equal measure.

The fifth transition trigger of knowledge and finding purpose during change is in a sense a call to action to create our own 'hero's journey'. We spoke in Chapter 4 about the importance of self-determination as an aspect of courageous leadership and building a Change Mindset. The first transition trigger in this chapter also explored how to find our spirit by tapping into our underlying values and beliefs as a kind of internal compass.

But here we are looking at purpose to be a compass in our lives in a more forward looking way, exploring what further impact we might create by living with more focus and vision. Self-knowledge in this context is about our ability to actively define our evolving identity and therefore our purpose as a lever for change throughout our lives. The leaders I spoke to all recognized the imperative to find a purpose in their own life journeys, and this especially so in mid-life. Campbell's reference to the 'treasure we seek' refers to the inner purpose we all have within us but are often afraid to explore or define. It is the next step after differentiation, and a further anchor to our confidence and sense of self as we deal with change and uncertainty over the longer journey of our lives.

Psychologists and academics have long studied why we are compelled as human beings to create meaning and find purpose in what we see and experience in the world around us. Whether through our laws, religions, societal rituals or mythology, we seek structures to guide our actions and look for patterns to understand how the world around us works. The comparative mythology of Joseph Campbell illustrates how these primal human needs extend as far back as the early Buddhist and Persian civilisations before 1,000 BC.

But our search for meaning as a species can be seen even further back in the Neanderthal caves of Lascaux and Chauvet in Southwest France. In *Cave of Forgotten Dreams*, German Director Werner Hertzog guides us through a mesmeric sequence of images of prehistoric cave paintings at Chauvet that appear to ask questions about time, space, our place in the world, and the existence of natural and 'magical' phenomena (Hertzog, 2010). Carbon dating of these drawings estimates they were etched into the cave walls by its inhabitants an incredible 30,000 years ago, far preceding most earlier known cave paintings. The artists used charcoal from their fires and pigments from plants and the earth to replicate their surroundings in vivid and often surreal imagery. In the narration, Hertzog hypothesizes that, even as Neanderthals, when we most likely still lacked any shared language or writing, we were still compelled to make meaning of the world around us using art. Some of the animal figures appear to be moving, being drawn in successive positions over the same area of rock in a technique reminiscent of a Disney cartoonist sketching out a storyboard for a Mickey Mouse sequence. Anthropologists at Chauvet believe these early humans were interpretating their surroundings and capturing their 'understanding' of the world as a way to find meaning and purpose for things they couldn't comprehend (seasons, stars, sunrises). I visited Chauvet after seeing the Hertzog film, and indeed there is a sense of spiritual power in those images, some of them drawn thousands of years apart yet close together or even overlapping on the same hunting scene, as successive generations continued to build their own stories and impressions. Most rock carvings and primitive art I have seen around the world, from Southern Africa to the Atacama Desert, exhibit similar patterns: nature, animals, gods, humans, often following rituals, stories, and dances. These heroes were also on their respective journeys and attempting to understand their place in the changing world among animals, trees, rivers, storms, day and night, the seasons and the phases of the moon.

Yet acquiring knowledge and finding purpose during change has always been a challenge. In prehistory, our ancestors drew on cave walls in an attempt to explain the frightening and unpredictable world. In the Middle Ages, historians and writers also mourned the unpredictability of the human condition and the world. Scottish philosopher Thomas Hobbes famously opined in his 1621 tome *Leviathan: Or the Matter, Forme and Power of a Commonwealth, Ecclesiasticall and Civil* that life for most people in his time was 'solitary, poor, nasty, brutish and short' (Hobbes, 1651). This was certainly the case in Hobbes' 17th century Europe where war, disease and poverty were more common than heroic deeds or enlightened accomplishments. Yet we, as humans, have always been compelled to seek solutions and improve our odds in uncertainty. Perhaps the artists of Chauvet were also trying to control or predict unexpected change events through their art and rituals. For Hobbes, he envisioned a better world in response to change and the vulnerability of the individual by imagining social and public structures that would support the population, ensuring the best possible outcomes for the greatest number of people. In our modern VUCA world our human reaction to change still lies somewhere in between the mysteries of Chauvet, the gloomy view of humanity proposed by Hobbes, and the hope offered by the mythical hero's journey.

Many of us may still fear entering the cave that holds the treasures we seek to find our purpose. But taking a first step into an unknown future is an essential skill for life today. And doing so with greater purpose will inevitably increase our chances of success. This and the other SPARK practices in this chapter help us do this by triggering purposeful action in uncertainty, whether it be to launch a new project, change jobs, start a company, move house, switch professions or re-label ourselves entirely.

Summary of key points

In this chapter I have highlighted the five common transition triggers that leaders can use to accelerate change. When applied alongside an awareness of the transition traps from Chapter 5, and the attributes of courage and empathy from Chapter 4, we become significantly more effective in navigating transitions. The successful ingredients for the Change Mindset therefore become:

- Acting consistently during any change situation with courage and empathy
- Maintaining vigilance over the FAIL transition traps
- More actively practicing the SPARK transition triggers.

In Chapter 7 I will combine these frameworks into a set of change archetypes that provide further insights into how we can face the external challenges of our VUCA world, irrespective of where we find ourselves on our life stages journey.

CHAPTER SEVEN

The transitions masterclass: Dreamers, drivers, shapers and sherpas

*Life is not a problem to be solved, but a reality
to be experienced.*   SØREN KIERKEGAARD

The 19th Century Danish philosopher Kierkegaard was also a theologian, poet, and social critic. He is widely considered to be the first existentialist philosopher and this quote attributed to him encapsulates one of the keys to successful change that emerged during my interviews for this book: Seeing life and transitions as *possibilities*, not *problems*.

Why a masterclass?

Our journey so far started in Chapter 1 by defining 'transitional change' as: 'A compelling external threat or opportunity that requires a bold and specific response from us as leaders'. I subsequently explored the multiple reasons why these transitional changes are so hard to navigate successfully. Building on developmental psychology, I identified four natural life stages we all experience: *imitation, differentiation, activation, integration* – and the lessons we can learn from each one about change. This gave us four tenets of powerful change leadership: *person (who)*, *passion (what)*, *permission (how)* and *purpose (why)*, with four related questions we need to ask ourselves in any moment of change:

· Who am I being in this change situation?
· What can I specifically bring to it?
· How can I move to action faster?
· Do my actions fit the Why of my purpose and values?

We also looked at *courage* and *empathy* as two further core building blocks of a Change Mindset. These skills augment our change capability, while the FAIL and SPARK conditions can either slow us down or speed us up respectively as we navigate transitions.

But having built these frameworks and tools, what is the next level of change mastery when it comes to bigger, more complex and more risky transitions where our decisions have longer term and wider impact? This is the question I explore in this chapter.

Why we need change mastery

We know that in a VUCA world, transitional changes are being thrust upon us with increasing regularity. Moreover, these disruptions are raising new, fundamental questions about our most important life choices. How we spend our time, where we live and work, the role of our families, our health and our relationships are all being re-prioritized due to these tectonic shifts. I talked earlier about the 'Great Resignation' which is now continuing as a globally recognized phenomenon, raising questions for employers as they lose talent, governments as the lose tax revenues, and cities as they lose population density.

How we respond individually and collectively to these large-scale disruptions will determine the future health of our global ecosystem in the coming decades as we seek a sustainable future for ourselves, our communities, our organizations, and the environment.

You might say this is nothing new, and that the need for bold decisions in the face of uncertainty has always been with us. Dr. Jules Goddard of London Business School reminded me that decisiveness has been a preoccupation of leaders for some time. He quotes British advertising legend Sir

John Hegarty, as being fond of saying, 'Often, our lives are made up of only three or four moments that shape us.' But if we believe that to be true, the decisions we make in those moments truly do determine our future, and if we miss them we are doomed to be victims of change rather than architects of our future.

So as we face more frequent change and disruption, the question becomes: Can we – both individually and collectively – more powerfully master change?

In my interviews for this book, I did meet some true 'change masters' who seemed to possess a deeper level of confidence and proficiency when navigating transitions. Through these conversations four profiles, or what I call 'change archetypes' emerged. I found that each of these archetypes sourced their change mastery primarily from one particular life stage that had taught them especially valuable lessons about change. This may have been during their experience of imitation (who), differentiation (what), activation (how) or integration (why). And while most of these leaders had experienced each of the four life stages to some degree, the key point was they had paid particular attention to the moments that mattered most, and had then brought the lessons learned with them into adult life.

So to master change at this higher level our task begins with this self-insight.

As you read through the archetypes below, you may feel that you possess the characteristics of several but typically I find that leaders will identify more strongly with one particular archetype. If you do, it would indicate that you discovered your natural change orientation at a particular time during a specific life stage. The opportunity to develop change mastery now comes as we learn to mine the power and insights from this time in our lives.

I have called the four change archetypes 'dreamers', 'drivers', 'shapers' and 'sherpas'. Dr. Goddard kindly helped me craft our definition for each one.

The dreamer

An actor, imitating and often pretending from childhood to be someone they are not, but also a player and explorer, still consumed with curiosity and inquisitiveness. Dreamers are experimentalists, refusing to settle down or conform to standard notions of a 'job' or being a 'mature' individual in society. They push boundaries and use creativity to drive change while bringing others with them through empathy. The fundamental driving question for them is: 'Who am I being in this change?'

The driver

An achiever, through differentiation, drivers endlessly pursue their goals and ambitions, wanting to be acclaimed as winners. Sometimes self-promoting but always self-directed, they enrol others in their plans, stretch their notions of success and are boiling over with the desire to succeed. They are strivers who can't, and won't, relinquish the role of entrepreneur – doing things, inventing things and pursuing new objectives. They drive change using their natural courage, strengths and innate attributes. The fundamental driving question for them is 'What can I achieve through this change?'

The shaper

A master who has found full permission to activate their ideas and expertise, amalgamating their network to create wider impact. Shapers express and display their hard-won skills in a focused pursuit, knowing the 10,000 hour rule and knowing themselves. They are comfortable with their mastery having achieved their wider ambitions and live out their vision using all the tools and resources available. Courage and empathy marry to create to drive change across complex ecosystems. The fundamental driving question for them: is 'How can I cause a wider change to happen?'

The sherpa

A sage, an old soul, or a prophet of sorts. Shapers have made peace with the world, with their ambitions, and with opposing viewpoints, values, perspectives and the other tensions of leading a fulfilled and examined life. They have come to terms with the pluralism of moral values and intellectual positions. They are self-actualized through reconciliation, synthesis, and being the 'most complete expression of themselves.' They share themselves and their purpose generously and with empathy across their networks and ecosystems to support wider change and transformation, 'paying it forward' and guiding others to more courageously confront their own transitions.

The 'change masters' I interviewed, no matter what archetype they *primarily* inhabited, had learned to draw something from *all* these archetypal skills to navigated change over the long term and in ways that created impact and even paradigm shifts. They had reformatted business models, changed the landscape of entire industries, and helped evolve the attitudes of large groups through teaching, writing, influence and activism. The fundamental driving question for them is 'Why am I creating this change?'

In the next chapter we will provide some practical tools you can use to enhance your change mastery around these archetypes, but first let us meet some of the archetypal change masters and see what we can learn from their experiences.

Dreamers: Exploring our world

You wander from room to room, hunting for the diamond necklace that is already around your neck.

RUMI

Why we need dreamers

This metaphor for life penned by Persian poet Rumi seven centuries ago still reminds us that channelling our identity (who) and looking within ourselves and is often where the answers to complex problems lie (Helminski, 1999). In our chapter on empathy we spoke about Michel de Montaigne and his humble inquiry: 'What do I know?' Montaigne and Rumi, though centuries apart, both epitomize the dreamer archetype. These are leaders who master change through child-like curiosity, unbounded open-mindedness, self-reflection, non-judgment and appreciating 'what is.' Curiosity with humility is the hallmark of the dreamers.

We need these dreamers because their unquenchable curiosity creates new opportunities for change when others feel blocked. They make an impact by revealing new ways of thinking. They ask the right questions, thinking out of the box when faced with complexity. They dream big and believe that nothing is impossible. Dreamers wake up every day asking 'What if...?' They source their power from the most valuable attributes of the first stage of life – imitation. They learn this from observing others, exploring the environment, taking in the best of what is on offer, and creating possibilities using their natural creativity, curiosity and humanity. Let us meet some of the dreamers, both past and present.

An elemental force

Poet Pablo Neruda was an archetypal dreamer, shaped by a childhood curiosity about the vast forces of nature surrounding him in his native Chile. In his autobiography, *Confieso Que He Vivido,* we first meet him as a young boy living in a cabin with his father who worked on a railway hauling timber from the rainforest to the sawmills hundreds of miles away. Neruda would wander beneath the towering canopy of trees all day, discovering plants and animals in the mossy undergrowth of the jungle. He managed to keep hold of this child-like curiosity as he later explored the more complex world of social conflict and labour unrest in mid-20th-Century Chile (Neruda, 1974). His constant search for the truth, his curiosity about the human condition in his country, and his ability to transpose these experiences into the realm of poetry garnered him the 1971 Nobel Prize for Literature. Described as 'Poetry with an elemental force that brings alive a continent's destiny and dreams' (Giewrow, 1971), his words would profoundly influence his country and the world. Neruda's homes in Santiago and Valparaiso still reflect this power, artistry, and humour. Visiting his eccentric 'ship' house in Valparaiso some years ago, I stood in his upper storey writing studio. From there the ramshackle port that has been home to traders, explorers, pirates and prostitutes for centuries can be glimpsed through the round porthole windows. Approaching his writing desk, I could still see traces of colour in the small inkpot. He always wrote in green, calling it 'The colour of hope.' Neruda was indeed a dreamer, and he used the power of his poetry and his humanity to change the societies of his time.

Is reality up for grabs?

Consultant and behavioral scientist Barry Oshry is another dreamer I have come to know in recent years. He is best known as the inventor of the Power Lab, a revealing behavioral simulation that creates artificial power gaps across groups in order to expose the human fragility and dysfunctions that occur in the absence of structure (Oshry, 2007). In our interview for this book Oshry told me from his home in Boston, 'In organization after organization I found the same self-limiting patterns of behaviour: misunderstandings across organizational lines, destructive conflict, disengagement, and customer dissatisfaction. But the vast majority of these issues are not deliberate or personal; they are invisible and systemic.' Oshry created this unique experience as part of his Seeing Systems academic work about how we deal with 'the other' ie people who are not like us and therefore see the world differently, which often leads to divergence and conflict. As he told me, his techniques are about creating a new awareness of what is inevitable in human interaction. 'Change is about illuminating other people. It's about turning the lights on when you thought they were already on.'

Oshry's curiosity and insights began forming early as child in Boston. His creative spark had him toying with art, theatre, writing, and even publishing in the form of a school newspaper. Growing up in the 1940s he also learned about the Holocaust from newsreels, magazines and newspapers, and even as a young boy aged just 13 he wanted to understand what could drive entire nations towards such extreme levels of conflict. Later, as a young academic, he was an eyewitness to much of the social and racial turmoil of 1960's America, rubbing shoulders with characters like Abby Hoffman of the Chicago Seven. He found himself on the front line of these momentous changes in American society and politics yet, like Neruda, he stayed curious and non-judgmental as he observed these human behaviours and social dynamics. His dreamer attributes allowed him to distil these experiences into powerful management tools that would help thousands of executives understand the sources of conflict in their organizations.

I asked Oshry about his ultimate goal as a dreamer: 'I want to create a global social movement, improving humanity's ability to understand the Other'. He dreams that his insights and his tools will reduce conflict, combat inequality, and help leaders at all levels navigate complex change on the global stage. But it won't be easy, as he warns, 'In our increasingly polarized society, rationality is up for grabs. Groups are closing down to protect themselves and shut out others. It is a bad sign for democracy and stability everywhere. As humans, in a crisis we must either navigate or disintegrate.'

Oshry has just celebrated his 90th birthday yet with his child-like curiosity he continues to conjure fresh ways to expose our human frailties and offer new insights to lessen the distances between us. I am confident his work will steadily gain a wider audience as we all seek new tools to face increasing polarisation, disagreement and conflict in virtual and physical world and his drive and his dream remain undiminished: 'It's the passion of a guy who's angry at what he sees.'

The power of randomness

Robert Greene is another dreamer who has navigated change and transitions by drawing on his early life experiences. In one of his popular TED talks the American author describes how it was the '50 jobs in 36 years' during his 20's and 30's that unconsciously equipped him to become what he is today: a recognized authority on power. He tells how this 'slow accumulation of knowledge' gave him all the material he needed to write his bestselling works: *The 48 Laws of Power, The Art of Seduction, The 33*

Strategies of War, and *The 50th Law* with rapper 50 Cent. Greene is an archetypal dreamer, like Neruda, using his creativity, curiosity and a life of trial and error to inspire his audiences and readers to also reimagine their own lives (Greene, 2021).

But the quintessential dreamer may have been Steve Jobs, the pioneer of personal computing who, with Steve Wozniak, co-founded Apple Inc. Jobs was not the electronics engineer or computer expert. That was Wozniak, whose Apple I computer went on sale in 1976. But what Wozniak didn't have was Jobs' ability to dream like few others. Jobs started off life as an outsider and was unconventional in being a hippie, dropping out of College, experimenting with drugs and working on an apple farm which inspired the naming of his company. Despite experiencing setbacks that included being forced out of Apple in the 1980s, he never stopped dreaming and challenging boundaries. During his time away from Apple, Jobs played an instrumental role in the visual effects industry by funding Pixar, which on to produce the first 3D computer animated feature and much-loved film, Toy Story. Jobs, as a dreamer, was renowned for his 'reality distortion field', his ability to convince himself and others around him through a mix of charm, bravado, and hyperbole that whatever impossible task at hand was possible. This modus operandi was instrumental in developing the Apple ecosystem (iMac, iPod, iTunes, iPhone, App Store) with industry - transforming ramifications that have made Apple the first company to reach a $3 trillion valuation in 2022. Jobs rarely displayed the empathy that is also characteristic of the dreamer archetype, but his relentlessly exploratory nature, captured in the company advertising campaign, qualifies him in all other respects: think different.

How to become a dreamer

Dreamers may sound like impractical idealists in a world of harsh realities, but the ones I met are not just passive observers of human nature. Neruda, Oshry, Greene and Jobs all took bold steps and confronted risk to create change around issues they passionately believed in. They responded willingly to the 'call to action' described by Joseph Campbell in his comparative mythology work where he also describes a common dreamer characteristic: our desire to explore beyond our own 'safe limits'. The power of the dreamer as a leader of change lies in accessing the primal drives for curiosity, creativity and humanity. Their key skill is to willingly embark on a journey of exploration without fear of failure.

Many innovations have resulted from dreamer attributes, from Tim Berners Lee's original internet code (written in just 9,555 lines of code) to the scientists behind the breakthroughs mRNA vaccines (creatively derived from cancer treatments) and the Alfafold technology from DeepMind that predicts the behaviors of protein molecules (derived from the original AlphaGo gaming AI by Demis Hassabis).

You may recognize some of the other dreamers we have already met in this book who also built their change mastery in this way. They include Fred Prysquel. of Vilebrequin, Annemarie Lewis of Rainmakers, and Arthur Bastings of Arthur Bastings Collective.

If you are lucky enough to work with dreamers you can harness their power by involving them in any situation which requires big picture or blue-sky thinking. Dreamers are relentlessly optimistic, so include them when the going is tough or you feel at a dead end, as they will inevitably lift the mood and inject new energy. Also expose them to people or ideas outside their immediate area, as they will naturally spark off this new stimulus and bring insights back into your work. Finally, include them in new teams or project configurations that require connection and empathy, as they naturally build bridges and find common ground.

Drivers: Know thyself

Whether you think you can or can't, you're probably right.   HENRY FORD

Why we need drivers

With this pithy observation attributed to Ford, he reminds us of the importance of acting when faced with change, even if we don't know what the outcomes will be. Drivers are adept at 'believing they can' because they know themselves inside out – what they are good at, what they are capable of, and how they can use those natural strengths to activate and invigorate others in times of change.

We need these drivers because they apply their core strengths with passion (what) to a wide range of complex problems. They volunteer their expertise and insight because they have spent extended periods – often years – learning their craft and perfecting their skills. They are motivated by complexity, undaunted by obstacles and are willing to share their resulting knowledge with others. They source their inner power from the second stage of life, differentiation, where they find their strengths, their passion, and strive to apply them. Let us meet some drivers and see how they use their passion.

Finding our inner core

Anyone who, like me, was fascinated as a child by the story of Vikings and their adventurous navigation across vast oceans in small wooden ships will be captivated by Roskilde. A small coastal town in Denmark, it has been faithfully reconstructed in its original form as a settlement of shipbuilders from the 10th century. But the main attraction is not the village with its low slung timber dwellings and half completed ships lying in the work yards; it is the large structure on the shore nearby that is built to face the horizon over which the Vikings launched their invasions to the northeast coast of England in 793 AD.

This museum houses the nearly intact remains of five Viking *Skuldelev* ships. They are almost 1,000 years old, built between 1030 AD and 1042 AD and later sunk with stones beneath the waves of the shallow fjord in order to block the sea channel from future invaders.

Research shows that the shipbuilders of the time were able to discern the lines of greatest strength within each timber beam they worked with, judging with their hands and eyes the length, girth and grain of each trunk. The Viking ships' exceptional seaworthiness is partly the result of each master carpenter's passion for finding and then maximizing the natural inner strength of each beam that made up the vessel.

Similarly, drivers are adept at finding the 'grain' of their strengths and using this inner passion to be the strongest timbers of the metaphorical ships they sail across the seas of change. Let us meet some of these drivers and see how they put their passion to work.

Navigating the world of professional services

Barrister, consultant, adviser and author Calvin Jackson decided to undertake a PhD in executive pay regulation well into his sixties as a 'prelude' to his book to be published in 2022, *The Professional Standards Of Executive Remuneration Consultants*. I have known Jackson for over two decades from when we were colleagues in the world of executive pay at consultancy Watson Wyatt (now Willis Towers Watson). Throughout, he has been a consummate driver, building and leveraging his deep expertise as a lawyer and consultant to serve his business clients, the UK criminal justice system, and now examining aspects of executive remuneration, which are much in need of reform. Across these endeavours he actively promotes the cause of responsible capitalism.

Age is certainly not slowing Jackson down, and his energy and drive was triggered early when he discovered his strengths and decided exactly how he wanted to deploy them. 'At 14 I wrote to the Institute of Chartered Accountants and the Law Society about their entry requirements,' he told me, 'so I was already thinking about being a professional advisor of some sort.' This early choice was remarkable given his parents were an RAF bomber pilot and an antiques dealer. The first in the family to go to university and study law, he pursued a successful 25-year career in this chosen field advising remuneration committees, often working alongside his colleague Martin Lutyens, who we met earlier, to advise boards and industry bodies on executive pay.

Jackson's driver mindset led to considerable success by his mid-career, and today he is using his expertise in a more integrative way to influence what he calls responsible capitalism. 'I began to feel a duty to pull others up the ladder who may have been less fortunate, because the capitalist system simply isn't doing it for them.' In a deliberate move to hone his skills for this next transition to reshape the entire capitalist system, Jackson returned to practicing at the Bar, undertaking UK Legal Aid work to defend suspects who can't afford their own lawyer. 'In court under Legal Aid, it sometimes seems the prosecutor hates you, the judge hates you, the jury hates you, and the defendant probably hates you as well. But you have to do your absolute best for them. And that makes you quite persuasive.' Having refreshed his courtroom skills he felt prepared take on a new paradigm shift, saying, 'The idea of responsible capitalism very much captures my imagination.'

I asked him how he developed his passion to become such a driver of change. 'I realized pretty early on that to be successful in business you've got to work really hard, be tenacious, dedicated and honourable. Hard work is simply a given for credibility, whereas tenacity comes from failing a few times. At the highest level you must also completely lose any fear of speaking out. If you don't, you're not doing right by your client.'

As for creating impact on a bigger stage as a driver, Jackson is clear about his passion. 'In responsible capitalism I'm probably more driven than when I was 14. It's about trying to be useful and do something that moves the debate forward.'

His advice for others wishing to become drivers? 'Ask yourself: what are the particular skills that you represent the very, very best of, and what can you do with those to make a difference?'

I have no doubt that Jackson's drive to leverage his deep expertise on the bigger stage will indeed move the Capitalism 2.0 debate forward.

Cross cultural drivers

Most of the drivers I know are operating in Anglo-Saxon or Western cultures, where self-reliance and individual achievement are the cultural norm. I wanted to test the driver hypothesis in a more international context, so approached film producer Masao Takiyama, a Sony Executive who had spent much of his career opening new markets for Sony in Thailand, Taiwan, Korea, and Hong Kong as well as across Europe and America.

Takiyama grew up during the post-war reconstruction of Japan of the 1950s, where poverty and hardship persisted well beyond the end of the war. Yet modernization was also fast approaching. The *Atlantic Magazine* vividly described this era in its March 2014 edition with a photo spread of baseball games, bikinis and kimonoed women hula-hooping (Taylor, 2014).

Perhaps it was this environment of change and novelty that prompted the young Takiyama to find his personal drive for success despite the collective and hierarchical culture of his country. Certainly he was inspired by a new magical device that was suddenly bringing the world of storytelling into Japanese living rooms: television. Hooked on the new Japanese TV series such as *The Newspaper Reporters,* he resolved at age 14 to become a journalist and live in this world of stories and adventure. Knowing about his teenage dream, a friend from a film magazine offered him an assignment through which he gradually learned the trade, being paid by the page, until age 24 when his driver spirit helped him again, this time to get hired by the domestic and international distribution arm of Fuji TV Networks. The new CEO there had ambitions for a global Fuji TV business and was asking for volunteers to open new distribution markets. Takiyama immediately raised his hand and became one of the first young international Japanese executives at the forefront of the fledgling global TV industry. He again taught himself how to perform this new job, learning resilience, tenacity and creativity over the next five years as he secured some of Fuji's early non-Japanese clients.

In time, Takiyama's passion for stories opened the door to a new entertainment medium called anime, and he became an early architect of the new format, doing the first global distribution deals in Europe and America. He would later produce many of the most iconic anime series and films of the 1990s and 2000s, reinventing Sony Pictures Entertainment's children's programming model in the process.

My conversations with Takiyama and other Japanese and APAC-based executives suggest that being a successful driver is possible in any context, even in countries like Japan with its predominantly conservative ethos and collective social norms. Takiyama used his driver attributes to open new markets, produce innovative entertainment formats, and globalize Japanese entertainment. Finding his personal drive early on shaped his subsequent actions and when I asked him what advice he would offer other Asian leaders aspiring to be drivers in their own contexts, he replied simply: 'Raise your hand.'

How to become a driver

Jackson and Takiyama operate in very different cultural and industry contexts but both epitomize the driver archetype. The essence of the driver is to discover one's strengths early and then fearlessly activate them, seeking new ways to create maximum impact through focus and expertise. You may recognize some of the other drivers we have already met, who also source their change mastery by differentiating themselves through their unique skills and then leveraging this deep expertise to provoke change. They include Peter Hogarth of the Change Partnership, Stacy Cartwright of Burberry, and Parry Mitchell of the British House of Lords.

If you have access to drivers, these are the people who will create action and take the initiative, so deploy them when bold moves are needed in uncertainty or when you need to raise the game to a new level. Drivers will deploy their strengths effectively in the face of such challenges, and can energize others to do the same.

Shapers: The art of permission

It is improvisation that lets you defy the impossible.   PHILIPPE PETIT

Why we need shapers

We saw in Chapter 3 how permission (how) is a powerful skill to 'unstick' our natural threat response to change, and in Chapter 5 we explored how to avoid the FAIL behaviors by activating our strengths more deliberately. The shapers take these skills one step further.

They craft new stories by integrating multiple views they have gathered. They analyze wider data sets to explore what may be possible by making connections. And they expand the world for others by creating new paradigms and vocabularies, following Wittgenstein's dictum: 'The limits of my language mean the limits of my world.' The language of shapers expands the repertoire of what others see as possible. Shapers source their inner power from the third stage of life – activation – and give themselves full permission to apply their skills and expertise across a wider ecosystems.

We need shapers because they activate change through others and create a sense of permission and what is possible for themselves and others. They carry out courageous acts that challenge conventions, and bring together disparate groups of brilliant people with an inspiring vision to tackle their biggest change challenges.

In his recent book *Social Physics,* Alex Pentland reinforces this idea of connecting and shaping. In his research he found that it was not the 'brightest' who had the best ideas, but those who were best at harvesting ideas from others. Similarly, it was not the 'most determined' who drove the greatest change, but those who most fully engaged with others. Pentland's macro view is that, 'Social phenomena are made up of billions of small transactions between individuals, with value created by the flow of ideas in a human generative process.' To achieve this, he identifies the leadership skills of 'exploring' (seeking *different* rather than *best* ideas), 'social learning' (collective intelligence that emerges from pooled ideas) and 'diverse networking' (where contrarian views are welcomed) (Pentland, 2014). This focus on changing the connections between people through permission rather than the people themselves is an excellent metaphor for the shaper archetype.

Let us meet some of these shapers.

Down to the wire

French artist and acrobat Philippe Petit is a very unique shaper. In perhaps his most daring expression of permission he famously stole into the World Trade Centre during the night of August 6, 1974. He and his small team climbed the fire escape stairs to reach the rooftop of the 107th floor undetected. They then proceeded to set a 200kg steel cable between the Twin Towers over the next few hours. At dawn, Petit placed his slippered foot on the wire, 400 meters above Manhattan's streets, and holding an 8-meter balancing pole commenced his traverse. In total he made eight crossings and spent 45 minutes on the wire before being arrested by police when he stepped back onto the roof. In the 2008 documentary *Man On Wire* and a subsequent TED talk, Petit talks about his skills as a shaper. His craft requires the ultimate permission to do seemingly impossible things as a tight rope walker, magician, and actor. He describes this permission as a clear set of elements: 'Passion is the motor of my actions. I need tenacity to be perfect in my execution. Intuition helps me make the right choices in uncertainty. And improvisation lets me defy the impossible: faith replaces doubt.' Petit has been a shaper for decades, challenging our views about change, transformation and what is humanly possible. For him as a shaper, permission remains paramount. 'I would never take the first step onto the wire unless I convince myself I can get to the other side.' (Petit, 2012).

VCs for PPE

Petit's permission is of an intensely personal nature, but he is still a consummate change agent in challenging the impossible to make change possible. For other shapers it is more about the external rather than the inner game. Dame Kate Bingham came to the fore in May 2020 during the Covid-19 pandemic as she was appointed, controversially, as Chair to the UK government's Vaccine Task Force, whose role it was to procure adequate and timely supplies of vaccine and then ensure strategic deployment. There had been a disastrous initial attempt by the UK government to secure personal protective equipment (PPE) and other vital medical supplies including ventilators. Bingham reshaped the role, bringing a venture capitalist mindset to the table and creating fresh permission to think differently about setting up the infrastructure for vaccine clinical trials, manufacturing and distribution. In an FT interview at the time of her appointment she explained how she applied the principles of collaboration, partnership and risk management to shape different outcomes. 'The first thing was to be partners, not adversaries. That is very unlike normal government procurement, which is all about the cheapest price. Expecting failure is also very different. In VCs and in my funds I expect a proportion of failures, whereas in government you have one failure and the press is all over you.' Her shaper approach paid off and her team went on to secure 350m doses of six different vaccines, ensuring the UK would be at the forefront of the global vaccination effort (Cookson, 2020). Bingham has since been commended for her approach and accomplishments by scientists and the international media.

Thinking rather than doing

Another shaper, Sir Andrew Likierman, has held senior and influential academic positions as a shaper at London Business School and other institutions for over four decades.

I interviewed him at his home in London about how he had developed his shaper skills. Likierman's ability to transition smoothly between ideas and environments was learned early. As the son of immigrants in the North of England, he told me, 'The world of my parents, Central Europe, was very different from our small town in Lancashire, and that was also different from the world of the British boarding school system that I went to later. So in a sense I had to be adaptable quite early. My family had already made a big transition.' In addition to this early cultural and social adaptability, Likierman learned through the family textile business the essential skills of good execution, thoroughness and the importance of reputation.

This set him up to carve his own path as a young graduate, choosing a different road from the family enterprise, one that was centered on 'thinking rather than doing' as he puts it. His natural gifts for thinking, numeracy, and logic drew him towards the world of finance where he qualified as an Accountant. But it was his innate curiosity about complex problems that led to an invitation to join the UK government think tank, the Central Policy Review Staff. This early experience allowed him to apply his innate shaper skills with 'freedom to think independently around a complex issue, thoroughly research the question, and then produce clear and concise advice to Ministers.' Assignments like these provided Likierman with a platform for further Shaping as he moved between academia and government, first advising Parliamentary Select Committees and then in the Treasury as Head of the UK government Accountancy Service. His clear thinking and contributions across a wide range of issues as a shaper led to a knighthood in 2001 for his work prompting the UK government to radically change its planning, control and reporting systems.

While his early achievements showcased a breadth of intellectual skills, it has been Likierman's shaper mindset that helped him develop the powerful networks and relationships that drove change in government, as a Professor of Management, and then as dean of London Business School. There, he orchestrated several successful rounds of fundraising while enhancing the School's reputation through research, while reaching hundreds of students and leaders every year with his teaching.

Today, not content to retire in his 70's, he continues to be a shaper and is heading steadily towards being a sherpa. He has further leveraged his networks and global reputation to launch intriguing new research into the role of judgement in management. Having already been published in the HBR in 2020 on this topic, and appearing on numerous other platforms since, Likierman continues to influence the world of business and leadership with this new work.

Intrigued by his seemingly inexhaustible curiosity and undiminished passion for working with new people and testing new ideas, I asked him how he would advise other leaders seeking to build their own shaper skills: 'Find your natural gifts and then apply them on as wide a stage as possible. Connect people and ideas. Welcome opportunities as soon as they arise and then figure out the 'how'.' When I asked what his ultimate goal was for his work, he responded with classic British understatement, 'It's the idea of getting people excited and interested in the new ideas on judgement in management that I'm developing.'

I have no doubt that Likierman is on track to get many more people excited and reshape our understanding of judgement at a global level.

Shaping across cultures

I was again curious to test my shaper hypothesis in a more international context, so put a call into Ken Munekata, another Sony executive and former colleague. During his time at Sony, Munekata built significant parts of the global entertainment business as Head of Strategy. He also held a pivotal shaper role straddling cultures between the Japanese headquarters and the Los Angeles entertainment business where I worked. Today Munekata continues his Shaping skills as an entrepreneur and philanthropist, and he spoke to me from his home in Tokyo about being a shaper in the Asian context.

The results were again illuminating. Despite what we know about Japan as a conservative and compliant culture, Munekata found many ways to overcome this cultural reticence as he widened his network and connected diverse groups to create new business ventures in both Japan and America for Sony.

Again, as with many other change masters, early life played a key role. Munekata had followed a traditional upbringing in Japan, but as an adolescent he found he was already curious about the world outside. Even geography lessons fascinated him as he went to sleep wondering how it could possibly be daylight in America. At 16 he persuaded his parents to send him to the US where, outside Japan for the first time, he had to learn to interact with foreigners, make connections, and find his 'voice'. 'In Japan,' he told me, 'the right answers are largely predetermined, but in America I had learned to read the room and trust my intuition.' This shaper mindset and the permission it created freed him to experiment. 'I thought, if I don't succeed so be it, I can start over again.' His personal mantra became: 'Always take a small step beyond what you have been doing already.'

This mental agility differentiated him in Japan, but he was able to be a shaper there nonetheless. 'In Japan you're supposed to do what you've been told to do,' whereas for Munekata, 'life is about how you deal with new people and new situations'. As a shaper building his networks, he always made a point to share his lessons and views with younger Japanese employees, helping them to also widen their own horizons as a new generation of leaders.

I asked Munekata how to be a shaper in the Asian context. 'Try to build self-determination and find who you are, even if it goes against the predominant culture. Avoid the trap of your position becoming your identity – still a common scenario in Japan.' In talking about networks, his advice was also clear. 'Cultivate relationships. Today I realize the friendships I built across borders and boundaries during those years are the source of my happiness.' Like Takahashi, Munekata's experience suggests that overcoming our own cultural limits to tackle change in new ways is possible in any context if you are clear and committed. As he puts it, 'Find something meaningful to you and pursue that with courage.'

How to become a Shaper

Shapers complement their technical expertise with building social capital, creating networks, and activating multiple resources to solve complex problems. They spot new talent and build diverse and multi-skilled teams. They are excellent cross-functional leaders, entrepreneurs and innovators. They create permission for themselves and others to live lives 'true to themselves'. And their skills move them into positions of influence where they can further shape the future with new solutions in a wider context.

Other shapers we have already met, who also source their Change Mastery by creating permission to break boundaries (How) include Laura McKeaveney of Novartis, Professor Peng Khaw of Moorfields, and of course Gillian Tett of the Financial Times.

Use the shapers around you when you need to build coalitions or create networks beyond your immediate area. Deploy them on larger scale projects where integration and pulling multiple resources together are required. Shapers naturally seek a bigger stage and greater impact through networks, so look to them as leaders in any large-scale change or transformation scenario where relationships are key.

Sherpas: Leading change through purpose and meaning

That is no country for old men.   WILLIAM BUTLER YEATS

Why we need sherpas

It was Charlie Miller who introduced me to the poem *Sailing to Byzantium* by William Butler Yeats, which opens with the above line (Butler Yeats, 1928). Perhaps more widely remembered as the title of a Hollywood film about oil prospecting in early 20th Century America, the poem charts the life of the writer as he is drawn away from the country of his youth, with its emphasis on vitality and achievements, and into a longer journey to find meaning.

Yet with this maturity and the acceptance of a journey towards old age, we are confronting our 'shadow side' in Jungian terms, and as Yeats reminds us, we are all 'sailing to Byzantium'. This journey is an elegant analogy for the deeper and more thoughtful role of sherpas as change masters. For these leaders reflection, wisdom and meaning are the levers they pull to ignite and sustain significant and purposeful change.

In my interviews with sherpas they, too, were all 'sailing to Byzantium'. In the process they were extracting deeper meaning and finding greater purpose in their change efforts and experiences. The kinds of questions that emerged during these conversations were no longer to do with achievements or expertise. Rather, they took the form of 'What do you want to be remembered for?'; 'What do you believe to be the most complete expression of yourself?'; or even, 'If you were to achieve your full potential, how would that impact the world?'

We need sherpas because, ultimately, we all seek meaning and purpose in what we do. Sherpas source their inner power from the fourth stage of life – Integration – where we find meaning and purpose in our actions, bring our entire life experience together, and use our insights and achievements to 'pay it forward' and help others. Sherpas are masters at shaping beliefs, challenging assumptions, and reshaping the wider context for change. They can influence and inspire whole organizations, public bodies and even societies to take on transformational change, offering a frame, a path or a dream of what the future might be.

Let us meet some of the sherpas and explore how they do it.

Stripping away identity

Miller once told me a story about finding purpose over a drink at the Union Oyster House which, in addition to serving extremely good oysters at its weather-worn sloping counter, lays claim to being America's oldest restaurant, serving food from the Pre-Revolutionary days of 1826. As the story goes, a senior Japanese executive (not from Sony) had approached the restaurant and asked if he could try shucking oysters for a while. Somehow he stayed on doing it for an entire year. The question that arose as we imagined this experience in the context of change and purpose was: 'What would happen if you dispensed with all the symbols of your personal and professional life? The house, car, job title, and office?' This stripping away of status would normally trigger alarm bells from loss of psychological safety and threats to our *raison d'être*. Yet it seems this particular executive wanted to clean the slate and create an open space to examine his past life and its purpose. Who was he beneath the corporate uniform he had been wearing for years, how could he make sense of his past life, find meaning and purpose and, we imagined, use that to start a new phase of life? Miller didn't know where the executive eventually went next but the story provided a vivid example of what it takes to deliberately search for meaning and purpose on the journey to becoming an integrated person and perhaps a sherpa who can lead others. In other words, fearlessly testing our core motives while consciously sailing to Byzantium in the second half of our lives.

Many leaders in mid-life will take time off to reflect on how to make sense of their experience, hoping to come back with a renewed purpose or an idea to create impact around some change that they see as important in the world. The pilgrimage to Santiago de Compostela or climbing Mount Everest are some of the more visible examples of such a journey, often undertaken by people somewhat older than one might imagine for such physical challenges. But whether through a physical journey for a reflective one, this final life stage transition is not a simple exercise. Becoming a sherpa requires entirely lowering our ego, questioning our deepest motives and choices, being open to serious challenges from others, and making sometimes difficult trade-offs between our comfortable position as adults and the risks of playing on a new and different stage as a sherpa.

But those who do make this commitment can find themselves re-energized with the belief that their impact and legacy will be significant as agents of real and lasting change.

Navigating a dangerous age

If you don't know him well, the standard CV of Jules Goddard feels rather business-like. It includes a Wharton MBA and Professorship at London Business School, but belies the wider and deeper aspect of his work as a sherpa. The small print in his biography reveals a range of creative, philosophical and experimental interests.

Among them: Goddard has spent time in the creative world of advertising with David Ogilvy of O&M in New York. He emigrated to France to restore chateaux in the Dordogne. He is a founding member of The Management Lab (MLab), that pursues radically different ways of organizing work in business. He has reinvented senior-level, enterprise-wide leadership programmes by teaching creativity, innovation, and leadership in new ways at a number of business schools. And he has captured these ideas and philosophies in a broad collection of books and papers on novel models of management. Reflecting his continuous thirst for knowledge, he was recently appointed to the council of the Royal Institute of Philosophy.

I spoke to Goddard at his summer home in Provence about being a sherpa and another of his favorite topics: teaching executives how to think completely differently about their work and their lives. His vast experience with organizations has allowed him to galvanize his thoughts about the current dominant mode of thinking for leaders, as 'looking backwards (last quarter's results), inside (organizational focus) and separately (usually in silos).' To counter this and lead change in a VUCA world, he advocates instead a bolder view of life and business that, 'looks forwards, outside and together.' He also speaks about the 'dangerous decade' for many leaders, often between 40 and 50, when their current success as drivers or shapers can disguise a hidden deficit. In theory, he says, at this stage we should be at the height of our powers. We have honed our expertise through differentiation and achieved our most important career objectives through the activation of our strengths.

Yet Goddard works with many leaders in this age and experience bracket who, when faced with pressure or major uncertainty, suddenly find they lack the confidence or certitude to act. Sometimes the imposter syndrome suddenly kicks in, paralysing action. Sometimes the expectations to perform under pressure lead to poor or rushed decisions. And in other cases the new complexity might reveal a hitherto undetected lack of judgment and insight. Goddard finds these situations surprisingly common among these otherwise 'successful' leaders. Who among us has not found ourselves suddenly out of our depth or bewildered by an unexpected turn of events? Abruptly our confidence evaporates, what we thought we knew seems questionable, and our reputation and status suddenly look vulnerable. Worse, Goddard says, far from recognizing and supporting leaders through these difficult scenarios, most organizations fail to provide the tools or training needed to counter this mid-career blind spot. What is needed at this stage is deeper reflection and self-awareness, and the ability to question our old assumptions, replacing them with new mindsets. But practicing these integrative change skills are rarely part of our corporate KPIs, and the performance cultures of most organizations still value action over reflection. It is troubling to think of the number of prominent leaders who are making the most important decisions in today's world (and in the midst of a global pandemic) who are also exactly in this dangerous age bracket and organizational context.

Goddard emphasizes how our self-awareness in these critical years will either enable or disable our potential as change leaders. I asked him how leaders might better prepare themselves for change and uncertainty at these times. 'We must define a more challenging periphery for ourselves,' he says, 'This requires us to define the size and shape of the stage we want to play on. Then we must occupy that space with confidence and clarity.' With this focus, he believes leaders at any stage can create something 'greater than ourselves'. Failing to pass this test, however, can result in an increasing spiral of personal and professional failures: risk avoidance, inaction, defensiveness, poor judgment, blame and eventually some big career mistakes.

Sherpas like Goddard dedicate their efforts to helping leaders and organisations break out of these dangerous patterns. As he says, 'Self-reinvention is key. Otherwise we are all losing confidence as a society and as humans.'

The second curve

We have already met Charles Handy in this book, clearly also a sherpa. His writings, consulting and lectures have challenged leaders for decades about how to widen the lens of their decision-making, gain maturity and perspective as leaders, and take bolder action in the face of change and transition.

My favourite book by Handy, which encapsulates his sherpa spirit, is *The Second Curve*. In it he clearly and lucidly lays out the biggest questions for leadership, business and society as we march towards an uncertain future (Handy, 2015). I have shared some of Handy's insights already in this book, so suffice it to say that both he and Goddard exemplify the skills of the sherpa. We can also turn to their many books, papers, online talks and lectures to learn about also becoming sherpas.

Your voice will be heard

Sherpas like Handy and Goddard have made it their profession to guide others towards more courageous choices. But sometimes sherpas change lives with just a phrase or in a moment. Lisa Robinson-Davis did so in the moment we had a coffee break during a conference when she said simply, 'Andy, I believe when the time is right your voice will be heard.' This was one of those three or four life moments referred by Bob Hagerty, and it triggered a series of reflections and events that led to a significant transition in my own life: becoming an author.

How to become a sherpa

Sherpas exercise their change mastery by seeking meaning and purpose in the wider context of their whole life experience. Handy and Goddard have already inhabited this territory for some years. Other sherpas we have met in this book include Professors Amy Edmondson at Harvard, Niro Sivanathan of LBS and Dr. Mee Yan Judge Cheung of NTL, all sherpas by definition in their vocation as teachers.

If you are lucky enough to have sherpas in your ecosystem, they are invaluable anchors in times of turbulent change and transition. They will naturally offer perspective, step back and put things into context, and defuse the anxiety and complexity others experience in the face of risk and uncertainty. Sherpas are best deployed at the highest level of strategy and thought leadership, yet they are not always the most senior leaders in organizations, so look for opportunities to deploy them deliberately irrespective of their role or status.

Having seen how the archetypal change masters develop their skills and use them to navigate transitions, we can now map their journey onto the Change Mindset.

FIGURE 7.1 Life stages and the change archetypes

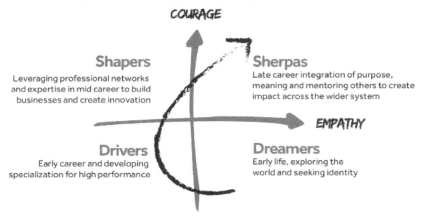

The Change Mindset and the arc of human development

We have seen how our psychological life stages provide the basis for us to learn about change and transition. Our early life consists of exploring the world and seeking our identity – learning from our role models, experimenting with new ideas, and gradually forming our own persona. The mindset and attitude of this early stage is characterized by curiosity, creativity, and a desire to explore the world. As we move into adolescence and early adulthood, we differentiate ourselves and begin to make important life and career choices – creating the platform for our future specialization and expertise. We then leverage these choices further by finding the permission to activate our ideas and insights, expanding our footprint in our mid-careers to achieve higher performance and impact. As we mature further, we broaden our views, work across disciplines, and lead larger groups or projects in our work. We develop others as well as ourselves and build change capabilities by sharing our expertise, building networks and enabling innovation. Finally, late career change masters develop a more integrative view of leadership, seeking purpose and meaning in transitions and 'paying it forward' in a more deliberate way to create the widest possible impact in organizations, ecosystems, and society.

It is important to note that the sherpa archetype will not necessarily be the end goal for every leader, nor are its associated skills the right approach for every change situation. From the perspective of a fully integrated life, the sherpa archetype does represent the ultimate pulling together of our life's work. However, in the context of change leadership, many executives I work with are highly effective operating in one or other of the archetype categories. The key to change mastery is first to unlock the power of our own change archetype. With this in hand, we can then enhance our skills by learning and practicing the attributes from the other archetypes through reflection and further life stage experience. This range of skills and knowledge will then allow us to deploy the most appropriate skills and mindsets in the face of any particular change challenge.

Thus, how far any of us choose to develop our change capabilities will be a matter of choice and personal orientation. However, my conclusion from meeting change masters is that we all have the potential to unlock the power of the change archetype to achieve mastery if we choose to. It is possible, with self-awareness, focus and discipline, to become more integrative and powerful catalysts for change as we build our Change Mindset.

I also believe that such mastery is fast becoming an essential leadership requirement for us as we tackle change, transitions and uncertainty in an increasingly VUCA world.

Summary of key points

In this chapter I have explored the links between the change lessons learned from our life stages and becoming change masters by leveraging these, practicing courage and empathy, and building a powerful Change Mindset.

The change archetypes that now provide a further method to access the potential of our own experience about change and transitions, providing a vocabulary for us to more powerfully lead change as dreamers, drivers, shapers or sherpas.

The links between these elements can be illustrated as follows:

TABLE 7.1   Change archetypes and the life stages

LIFE STAGE QUADRANT	PRIME MOTIVATING BEHAVIORS	PERSONAL DEVELOPMENT FOCUS	LEADERSHIP QUESTIONS TO NAVIGATE CHANGE	CHANGE MASTER ARCHETYPE
1 - Early Life & Identity	Imitation	Person	Who?	Dreamer
2 - Early Career	Differentiation	Passion	What?	Driver
3 - Midlife	Activation	Permission	How?	Shaper
4 - Late Career & Maturity	Integration	Purpose	Why?	Sherpa

In Chapter 8 I offer a practical change toolkit and a set of simple diagnostic tools to help you identify your own change archetype, further build your Change Mindset, and identify actions to achieve a higher level of mastery.

In Chapter 9 we will end by re-introducing the change leaders I interviewed for this book, distilling their key lessons learned and sharing their key advice for others seeking to build their own Change Mindset.

CHAPTER EIGHT

The Change Mindset toolkit: How to improve decision-making in uncertainty

Life can only be understood backwards; but it must be lived forwards. SØREN KIERKEGAARD

Our journey so far

Our journey started by examining transitional change, which I defined as: 'a compelling external threat or opportunity that requires a bold and specific response from us as leaders.'

We then explored why such transitions are hard to navigate successfully and how cognitive and emotional paralysis can hijack us in these situations. The answer was to build a more effective Change Mindset in the face of this psychological reality. I hypothesized that our personal life stages could illuminate a path to this by mining our earlier life experiences. We translated these life stages into four tenets of change leadership with the questions: who, what, how and why; or person, passion, permission, and purpose. Answering these questions allows us to develop new power, or 'agency', to unlock action during times of uncertainty.

Research with other leaders uncovered the two fundamental attributes of a successful Change Mindset: courage and empathy. Courage gives us the internal power to move forward in uncertainty, while empathy provides the insight to do this in ways that integrate our external context and the needs of others. Layering these attributes into our decision-making during transitions increases our likelihood of success. But despite these skills there are traps and triggers than can help or hinder us so we use the FAIL and SPARK practices to strengthen our Change Mindset.

In the last chapter I brought together these ideas into a framework to master change and transitions using the change archetypes of dreamers, drivers, shapers and sherpas. In this chapter we conclude with a practical set of diagnostic tools to analyse your own change readiness and further build your Change Mindset. Finally, in Chapter 9 we will re-introduce you to the leaders interviewed for this book, distilling their key lessons learned and advice for others leading change in a VUCA world.

Armed with a Change Mindset, the question for us as leaders now becomes: 'Where am I in my journey towards change mastery and how can I reach the next level?'.

What follows is a series of tools for personal and professional development to help answer this question.

These tools can support anyone seeking new insights about their power to navigate change – as a leader, a professional, a parent, a partner or friend. They can also apply to individuals, teams, groups or entire organizations as a set of principles to accelerate change.

The toolkit includes:

1 The change lifeline
2 The courage and empathy pyramid
3 The change readiness index
4 The archetype finder
5 The life stage ladder

Before you start, here are some suggestions to get the most out of using these tools:

- Think carefully through each step, make notes and be honest about your capabilities.
- If you are working on a shared or group challenge, involve others as you work.
- Take time to apply each tool: up to an hour if working alone, up to a day for group work.
- Revisit these exercises often; it takes time and practice to build a Change Mindset.
- Stay positive and curious about what this all means for you or your team and organization: change is about curiosity, seizing opportunities and becoming more confident in taking action and trusting your intuition as change occurs.

FIGURE 8.1 The change lifeline

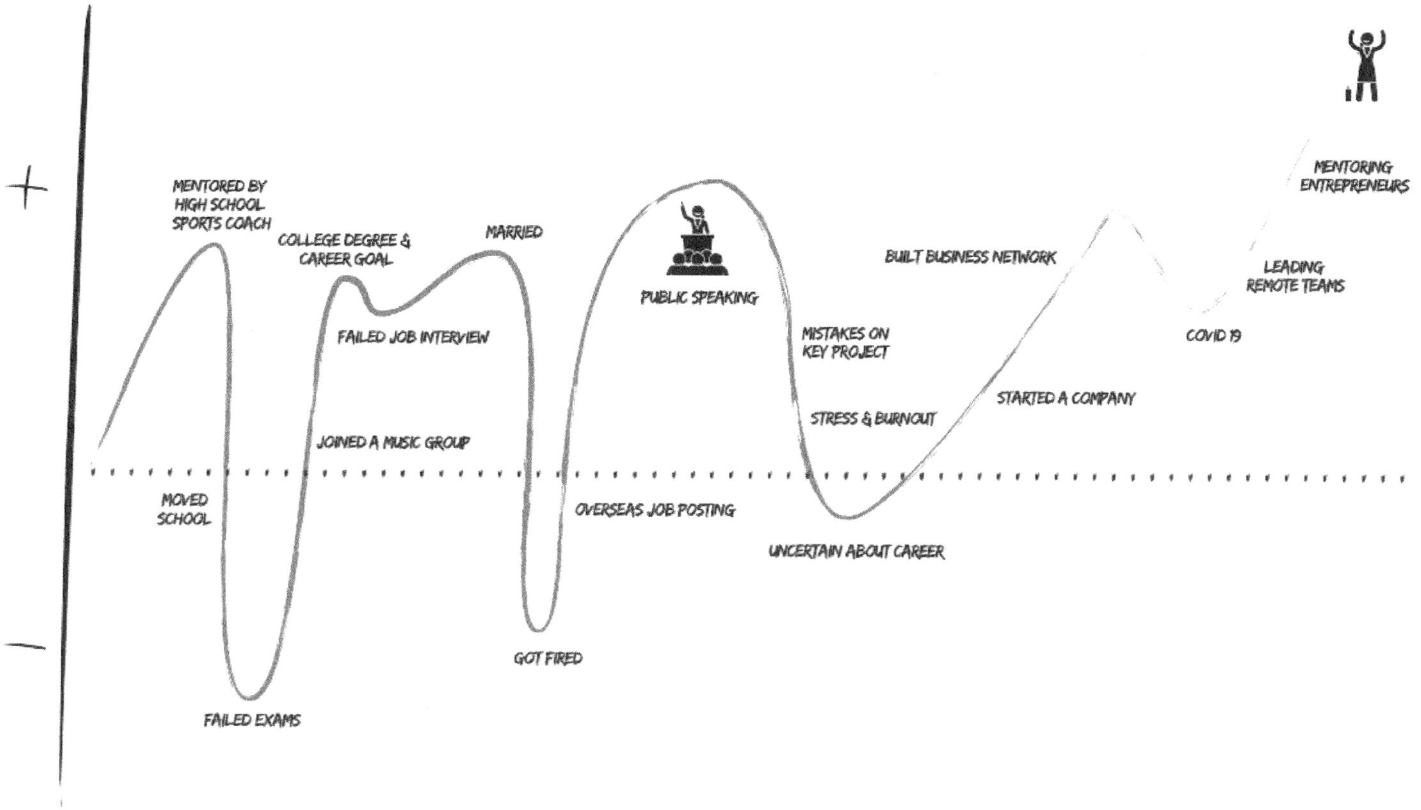

Labels on the lifeline (in order):

MENTORED BY HIGH SCHOOL SPORTS COACH

COLLEGE DEGREE & CAREER GOAL

MARRIED

FAILED JOB INTERVIEW

JOINED A MUSIC GROUP

MOVED SCHOOL

FAILED EXAMS

PUBLIC SPEAKING

BUILT BUSINESS NETWORK

MISTAKES ON KEY PROJECT

STRESS & BURNOUT

OVERSEAS JOB POSTING

UNCERTAIN ABOUT CAREER

GOT FIRED

STARTED A COMPANY

COVID 19

BUILT BUSINESS NETWORK

LEADING REMOTE TEAMS

MENTORING ENTREPRENEURS

+

−

Tool 1: The change lifeline

What this is

A tool to reflect on your previous experience of change and the key lessons learned.

How to use it

Step 1: Draw a horizontal line in the middle of a page representing your life (personal, as a team, or for the organization) from your earliest memories to today.

Step 2: Think about specific situations when you were confronted with transitional change, i.e. a significant new context or challenge that was outside your control but that required an active response from you.

Step 3: Plot these moments on the lifeline as either positive (above the line situations where you succeeded with the change, creating new ideas and finding more effective actions), or negative (below the line situations where you failed to make the change happen, which led to further problems, or where your efforts were simply inconclusive). The height and depth of your peaks and valleys should represent the relative magnitude of each significant success or failure. Add a word or symbol next to each peak or trough to remind you of the situation and bring them to life in your memory.

Interpretation

Proceed in two stages, one for moments above the line and one for moments below. In each case ask yourself these questions:

1 What was happening at this particular moment?
2 What do you believe caused the good or bad outcome – was it your mindset, attitude, relationships, resources, judgment, or some external factor?
3 Looking back now, ask yourself what lessons you could learn from this experience – personally if you are working alone or collectively if you are working in a team.
4 Now describe how you might apply these lessons to greater effect in the future.

  • From moments above the line, how can you replicate those conditions more often?

- For moments below the line, how can you avoid or mitigate those conditions and outcomes?

Here are some common examples of learning from success and failure during change:

- **A job interview**: You may have failed an important interview that required a different way of working or a new leadership style. This may have taught you a lesson about being less authoritative, more collaborative, more open to diversity or simply asking better questions.
- **A new career assignment**: You may have taken on a new job in a different region or country and failed to fit in with the local team. This may have taught you a lesson about cultural differences and the need to adapt your style, for example becoming more communicative (required in France), more focused on relationships (common in Latin America), less of a risk-taker (important in Japan), more respectful of hierarchy (expected in Germany), less impatient (a common blind spot for Americans), or more consensus driven (expected in Denmark or Holland).
- **A professional challenge**: You may have been put in charge of a new innovation team or transformation project and failed to deliver results under a tight time schedule. This may have taught you that you had to be less of a perfectionist in your analysis, delegate more, accept other points of view, increase your risk tolerance, and embrace failure or unexpected outcomes as you quickly tested new ideas.
- **An unexpected promotion**: You may have been promoted into a role where are you felt anxious about your abilities and had imposter syndrome, but found that people warmed quickly to you and were eager to follow your lead. Particularly if you had previously been in more technical roles, this could have revealed that you were much more of a natural leader than you imagined, or that you could powerfully galvanize people during change.
- **Getting fired**: It is safe to say that everyone will get fired at least once in their career, often through no fault of their own. Such an event may have caused you to reflect on your career choices, and you could have discovered that you were entirely in the wrong profession, leading you to reinvent yourself into a new space such as teaching, volunteer work, a creative enterprise, or applying your skills in a different industry sector.

Actions you can take

Once you complete your individual or collective life line and reflect on what happened in each change event, make notes in the space below about your top three lessons learned and what you can now do differently when next faced with a change or transition.

1 _____
_____
_____

2 _____
_____
_____

3 _____
_____
_____
_____

Tool 2: The courage and empathy pyramid

FIGURE 8.2   The courage and empathy pyramid

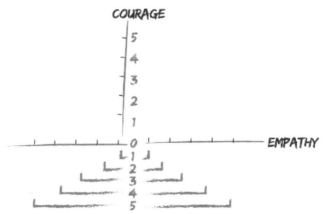

What this is

An assessment to measure your ability to display courage and empathy during transitions.

How to use it

Step 1: Rate your current ability to deploy courage and empathy in situations of change using the following scale:

0: Low skill level or not used at all

1: Rarely used and only when pushed by others or by circumstances

2: Used occasionally during change but not consistently and not always with a strong impact

3: Used regularly and with skill to improve outcomes, bring others with you and obtain results

4: Always applied with deliberate focus, clearly communicated, and with proven impact

5: This attribute is part of your DNA which you apply consistently to powerfully drive change

Step 2: Use the following chart to plot your results and connect the dots to form a pyramid. Notice the overall size, width and height of the pyramid within the chart area.

Interpretation

Courage and empathy develop naturally over time for most leaders – with courage steadily increasing with experience, and empathy often starting high in our early years, taking a dip in mid-career and then building up again later in life. This pattern is not universal and I have coached many young leaders who display exceptional courage alongside natural empathy early in their careers. Equally, I have worked with late career leaders who have yet to find the courage in themselves to take on real change despite years of accumulated experience. However, the general pattern holds true.

The larger our pyramid, the stronger our attributes are. The more symmetrical the pyramid, the more balanced our use of courage and empathy is. The key as change leaders is to develop our skills so that we 'own' a large, even pyramid of skills.

FIGURE 8.3 The balanced courage and empathy pyramid

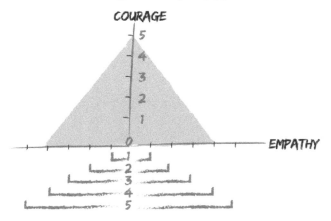

But whatever stage we are at, these two attributes remain key predictors of successful change, so measuring them allows us to understand how effective we are at navigating transitions. Increasing awareness is the first step to improvement, and more deliberately applying these skills over time helps us achieve a Change Mindset. This assessment can be used as an individual, team or as a measure of organizational change readiness.

Actions you can take

IF YOU HAVE A TALL PYRAMID – COURAGE EXCEEDS EMPATHY

FIGURE 8.4 The tall courage and empathy pyramid

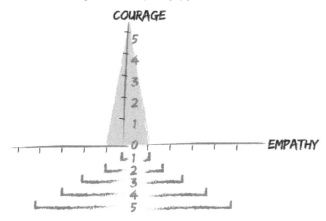

This indicates confidence when facing change and a bias towards deliberate action. Our courage enables us to confront challenges, take risks, and try out new ideas even if their impact is unknown. Courage is clearly an important skill in tackling uncertainty, but there are also risks of an 'empathy gap' that creates a potential blind spot for leaders with this profile.

- You may ignore or not understand the wider context and the consequences of your actions.
- You may not engage or bring others with you because you fail to take their needs into account.
- You may alienate key stakeholders or customers as you pursue your single-minded idea.

To be a successful change leader or group, you will need to bring deeper empathy into your courageous change acts. Use these practices to develop your empathy as a counterbalance to courage during change.

1 Empathy tends to occur naturally in early life stages, so reflect back on this period in your life.
2 Remember times when you needed to integrate other people in your plans, and how you did it.
3 Ask yourself how to do this now by seeking and understanding the perspectives of others.
4 Include other people in your decision-making, seek common ground and create shared context.
5 Always consider the bigger picture and how your actions might create wider social benefits.

IF YOU HAVE A FLAT PYRAMID – EMPATHY EXCEEDS COURAGE

FIGURE 8.5 The flat courage and empathy pyramid

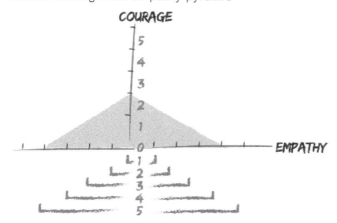

This indicates a strong ability to use intuition, understand the bigger picture and engage others during change. Your empathy skills naturally create alignment between people and ensure relevance as you ask good questions, consider alternatives, and think about the wider consequences of your actions. But here too there are risks in relying too much on empathy to navigate change, and a 'courage gap' can block your progress.

- You may waste critical time as you seek too many opinions, options, or strive for consensus.
- You may avoid commitment, feeling you can't meet others' needs in more complex scenarios.
- You may alienate key stakeholders as you pursue balance or a higher order social agenda.

To be a successful change leader or group, you will need to develop more action-orientation and decisiveness. Use these practices to counterbalance your empathy.

1 Courage tends to build from success, so reflect back on previous moments of decisive action.
2 Ask yourself the consequences of inaction and use that to accelerate your decisions.
3 Bring a sense of urgency into your thinking and your actions for the change you face today.
4 Seek others with strong action orientation and include them in your thinking process.
5 Consider the bigger picture to make better trade-offs between social and strategic choices.

Tool 3: The change readiness index

What this is

A measure of your change readiness, as the ratio between your SPARK and FAIL orientation.

How to use it

Step 1: As an individual, team or organization, review the definitions of the SPARK and FAIL practices in the table below and rate your current level of skill under each attribute, using the following scale:

0: Low skill level or not used at all
1: Rarely used and only when pushed by others or by circumstances
2: Used occasionally during change but not consistently and not always with strong impact
3: Used often and skillfully to improve outcomes, bring others with you and achieve results
4: Always applied with deliberate focus, clearly communicated, and with proven impact
5: This attribute is part of your DNA which you apply consistently to powerfully drive change

Step 2: Next, add up your values for each line and use the following two charts to plot your results. Connect the dots to form a star. Now add up your total score for 'S' and divide by 5. Similarly, add up your total score for 'F' and divide by 4. This weighted result will yield either 'S>F' or 'S<F'.

TABLE 8.1   SPARK boosters

SPARK BOOSTERS	DEFINITION	SKILL 0-5
Spirit	Finding our essential self	
Partnership	Using the power of other people	
Alternatives	The pursuit of possibilities	
Reason	Evaluating & making sense of our choices	
Knowledge	Using purpose to guide change	
	TOTAL SCORE	0-25

TABLE 8.2   FAIL blockers

FAIL BLOCKERS	DEFINITION	SKILL 0-5
Framing	Failure to dream big enough	
Asking	Failure to explore options	
Imitation	The danger of mimicry and pleasing others	
Limitation	Imposter syndrome and the inner critic	
	TOTAL SCORE	0-20

FIGURE 8.6   SPARK boosters

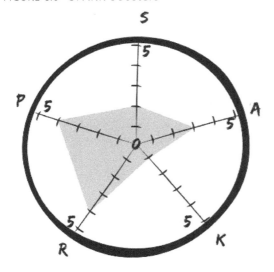

	SKILL
S	2
P	4
A	3
R	4
K	1
	14

FIGURE 8.7 FAIL blockers

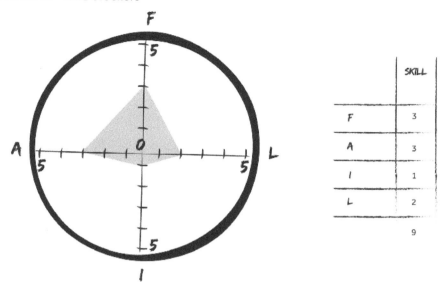

Interpretation

Once complete, notice the overall size and shape of your stars. The larger your star, the stronger your attributes are. In terms of the ratio, the goal is to build your skills to achieve 'S>F' in any change scenario, maximizing your 'S' value and minimizing your 'F' value. In this illustration the overall weighted result is positive (S>F), though of course any individual factor score below 5 means there is room for improvement in your Change Mindset:

$$F = 9/4 = 2.25$$

$$S = 14/5 = 2.80$$

$$S > F$$

The key is to become more consistent in your use of SPARK and FAIL behavioural practices, which will help close the gap between intention and outcomes as you navigate change, in turn increasing your individual factor scores and your overall S:F score. This assessment can be used to create a snapshot in time about your current mindset and attitude towards change, or as a way to measure and track progress as you undertake specific actions in any change situation – individually or collectively.

Actions you can take

If you have low SPARK scores

This indicates that in times of change and under stress you are likely to operate alone, limit your options, and focus on immediate outcomes and details rather than longer term or more purposeful impact. This action orientation at the expense of a wider, more reflective and inclusive approach can also compromise longer-term goals and your ability to bring others with you for the change in question.

To be more deliberate in using the SPARK practices, try the following actions.

Spirit:

- Reconnect with your values and essential self – who are you, what is important to you?
- Connect these values and your identity to the change so it acts as a compass for action.
- Bring others with you by asking them the same questions about their own values and beliefs.

Partnership:

- Share your beliefs and goals with others and enrol them in your cause for change.
- Use your networks to widen your perspective and consider others' ideas for the change.
- Listen for feedback and take the advice of others to build on your own views.

Alternatives:

- Don't think something is good just because it's yours, keep seeking out new ideas.
- Use creative techniques such as brainstorming or crowdsourcing to maximize options.
- Seek new possibilities in unexpected places: stories, movies, history or adjacent industries.

Reason:

- Write down, map out, and thoroughly review your analysis and the logic you are using.
- Seek input and support from others to assess, evaluate and make sense of your choices.
- Park your emotions and force yourself to take more objective, measured decisions.

Knowledge:

- Define a purpose or higher-order goal related to the change situation.
- Use this as a guide in more difficult situation to balance trade-offs or take risks.
- Pay special attention to how stress can block reason in moments of change.

If you have high FAIL scores

This indicates that in times of significant change and under stress you tend to get easily blocked by uncertainty or perceived risk. You may also feel insecure about your decisions and over-weight the opinions or expectations of others. You may default to repeating what has already been tried, or fall back on case studies from other people or situations that may not be relevant to the current context.

To be more deliberate in avoiding the FAIL traps, try the following actions:

Framing:

- Define the widest frame you can for the change: what might be possible?
- Enroll others in blue-sky thinking to push your own thinking and imagination.
- Ask empowering questions: what would you do if you had no fear about this change?

Asking:

- Make a plan to methodically explore as many options as possible and track progress.
- Deliberately take time to reflect on this wide array of choices and avoid dismissing them too early.
- Don't let constraints, resources, or technology limit your exploration – you can narrow down realistic options later.

Imitation:

- Be aware of anyone you might be trying to please or gain approval from.
- Avoid repeating what has already been tried by others, especially those you may admire.
- Check the originality of your thinking: are you imitating somebody else's approach?

Limitation:

- Quieten your inner critic and remember that all change involves uncertainty and a psychological threat.
- Be aware of those in power or people too close to who may overly influence your choices.
- Speak and think in the first person about the change: 'I want', 'I believe', 'I recommend'.

Tool 4: The archetype finder

What this is

A map to identify and unlock the full power of your change archetype.

How to Use it

FIGURE 8.8 The archetype finder

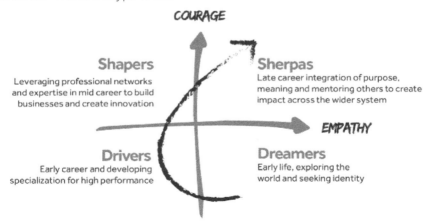

Step 1: Consider the definitions of the four change archetypes discussed in Chapter 7 and select which one you most closely identify with. Most leaders feel they have skills in several of the archetypes, but there will be one that you will likely gravitate towards more strongly, reflecting your core change orientation. This orientation can be individual or collective when working in a group.

Step 2: Our change archetype is a source of power to drive change actions more successfully. Ask yourself what behaviours, mindset and attitudes form your archetype and how these give you greater power to act in uncertainty. Use the table below to capture these ideas. Leave the other archetypes and the right column blank for now.

TABLE 8.3   The archetype builder

WHAT IS YOUR PRIMARY CHANGE ARCHETYPE?	WHAT KEY SKILLS & ATTRIBUTES ARE YOU USING TODAY?	WHAT ARE POTENTIAL SKILLS TO DEVELOP TOMORROW?
Dreamer	1. 2. 3.	1. 2. 3.
Driver	1. 2. 3.	1. 2. 3.
Shaper	1. 2. 3.	1. 2. 3.
Sherpa	1. 2. 3.	1. 2. 3.

Interpretation

Each of us has a change archetype that emerges from a period in our life when we learn the most significant lessons about adaptability and navigating transitions. Dreamers, drivers, shapers and sherpas each possess unique skills that give them power to navigate change. When we become aware of our primary archetype, we can use its power to rekindle experiences from our former life stages and apply them in our adult life to better navigate the change challenges we face today. Groups and organizations can also have a collective change archetype, for example a 'driver' team or a 'shaper' organization.

Mastering the dreamer archetype

We all experience a stage of imitation early in life, generally between our childhood and our teens. We are driven to copy our parents, teachers, friends and others we admire. The motivation at this stage is to gain acceptance into social groups. We see these as desirable and want to belong in environments that we believe are 'right' for us. As a result, we imitate the behaviours, attitudes, beliefs and rituals of these role models and mentors. As adults, many of us may still have a primary change archetype that focuses on fitting in, aligning with those we feel affinity with, and striving for harmony across a wider group.

There is great power in this archetype as the dreamer:

- Connecting easily to others and building rapport among potentially divergent views
- Showing natural empathy in change situations by acknowledging stakeholder needs
- Incorporating expertise and insights from others through curiosity and a growth mindset.

However, the limitations of deploying only the skills of a dreamer are:

- Potentially lacking a clear sense of self and having a powerful 'voice'
- Lacking the force to act independently, and needing to seek permission from others
- Avoiding the necessary conflict or disagreement needed for change, triggering a 'courage gap'.

Actions you can take

To unlock the full power of your dreamer archetype try these practices:

1 Remind yourself of your natural strengths as a dreamer: curiosity, empathy and imagination.
2 Put these attributes to use with greater conviction, and avoid seeking approval.

3 Question the relevance of people or groups you normally seek guidance from.
4 Practice accepting difference, disagreement or conflict as a natural part of the change process.
5 Develop a set of 'operating principles' to use these natural strengths more deliberately to close the 'courage gap'.

Mastering the driver archetype

Once we have mastered the art of imitation and what it brings us by way of connection and empathy, we move towards the experience of defining our perimeter more clearly. We seek to find out who we are and to build psychologically towards a state of differentiation. We define our profession, career choices, and ambitions as we discover and express ourselves. This process is often nudged by feedback as we try on different identities, and through guidance and mentoring from friends, managers or colleagues as we mature. Discovering our strengths in a more differentiated way increases the clarity of our personal and professional goals, and how we might become 'known for something'. Differentiation as adults opens the door to more deliberate choices in the context of change.

The power of the driver archetype therefore comes from:

- Clarity about our strengths and how to deploy them deliberately to achieve our goals
- Energizing others towards greater achievement through conviction and vision
- Triggering action during change and uncertainty to help others where they may feel blocked or unsure.

However, the limitations of deploying only the skills of a driver are:

- Leaving others behind as we push ahead with our own convictions, even if we may be right
- Causing conflict or disagreement as we drive our vision, triggering the 'empathy gap'
- Ignoring cultural nuances, protocols or even rules as we strive for our own desired results.

Actions you can take

To unlock the full power of your driver archetype try these practices:

1 Start with your gifts as a driver: energy, ambition, conviction and clarity.
2 As you put these attributes to use, involve and engage others in feedback about your plans.
3 Widen your lens to find new voices you may gain insights from: avoid the 'usual suspects'.
4 Communicate clearly and often to engage, but always use dialogue to hear others' views.
5 Develop 'operating principles' to check understanding, ask open questions, consider alternatives, take time to reflect, and be curious about diversity of views to close the 'empathy gap'.

Mastering the shaper archetype

The psychological step between drivers and shapers is essentially the move from a personal Change Mindset to a collective Change Mindset. As drivers, we achieve success by focusing on specialization. We often have yet to discover the value of integration through sharing our knowledge and tapping into wider networks to drive change. Many professionals operate successfully as experts with only a passing interest in the wider context or how they might create impact beyond the 'silo' of their own work. However, when pushed by unexpected change or disruption, even these successful drivers will need to tap into the wider system to source new ideas and partnerships that address these new unknowns.

Often, the trigger for this will be a perceived opportunity to play on a bigger stage while at the same time realizing we lack the networks, resources, or sponsors to make things happen at this bigger scale.

The power of the shaper archetype therefore comes from:

- Widening our aperture to identify networks or partners to address bigger change challenges
- Using our maturity and intuition to enrol others in this broader change journey
- Subjugating our own agenda to create a broader and more collaborative vision that inspires and engages others.

However, even though shapers are powerful change agents, there are still limitations in only using these skills:

- Shapers excel at mobilizing diverse resources, but they may still fail to see the bigger picture.
- Achievement remains the focus of a shaper's efforts, rather than meaning or purpose.
- Shapers can also be dangerous if they become too narcissistic and fail to value wider integration during change.

Actions you can take

To unlock the full power of your shaper archetype, use these practices:

1 As you mobilize networks for change, always remain aware of others' interests and needs.
2 Explore the emotional engagement required as well as the technicalities of your change plan.
3 Always ask yourself: 'What is the bigger picture and how else can I impact this change situation?'
4 Communicate this clearly to help other people take the necessary risks to 'get on board'.
5 Develop 'operating principles' to pay attention to signals around you, see the bigger picture, and consider the views of others in your network to ensure collective action for change.

Mastering the sherpa archetype

Not everyone I interviewed had experienced this final stage of heightened empathy coupled with great courage. But in the context of the global pandemic, climate change, resource scarcity and other VUCA factors, most leaders I speak to admit to feeling they must now ramp up their change skills. To do this, many are trying to learn from other powerful change agents. These benchmarks are the sherpas, those who seek meaning, purpose and bring a powerful sense of integration to all their change work. They navigate complexity with courage, empathy, and meaning, seeking systemic change far beyond just short term or situational outcomes that solve an immediate problem.

The power of the sherpa archetype therefore comes from:

- Widening our world view to encompass truly transformational change
- Working across multiple systems and levels in business or society for greater impact
- Shifting paradigms and entering the conversations that 'make or break the planet'.

There are no real weaknesses in the Change Mindset skills of true sherpas. Our only weakness is that we currently do not to have enough of them. In today's VUCA world, more sherpas are needed in leadership roles everywhere, from business to education, science, academia, government and beyond.

Actions you can take

To become a sherpa, or to further unlock the power of this archetype if you already have some of these skills, use these practices:

1. Set aside time to reflect seriously about your values, purpose and higher ambitions.
2. Always seek meaning in your efforts and actions – be thoughtful and deliberate.
3. Ask yourself how you can make the biggest impact in a transition – humanly, socially, and morally.
4. Actively seek contrarian views that challenge your own thinking about what might be possible.
5. Develop 'operating principles' to identify and continually evolve your purpose, share your life experience with others, teach and guide them, and make your work and life choices such that they combine a sense of meaning and a higher ambition that might impact the world.

Mastering the journey through the archetypes

The best change masters I have met are intimately familiar with their change archetype and know how to unlock its power.

But they also go beyond their core driver, striving to enhance their Change Mindset by exploring the other archetypal attributes as well. They will develop their change skills by travelling across the whole change archetype map, constantly, learning and applying wider insights during a lifelong journey that accumulates the lessons of each life stage as they evolve from dreamer to driver, shaper and sherpa.

The opportunity for us as change leaders is therefore to continually develop and broaden our self-awareness to more fully develop our Change Mindset, practicing *all four archetypal skill sets* as we continually strive to achieve the next level of the Change Mindset.

To start this process, you can go back to the table above and populate it with potential developmental behaviours and actions in any of the secondary archetypes you feel ready to explore. Use the right-hand column to note down these specific ideas and actions personally or as a group.

Tool 5: The life stage ladder

What this is

A tool to determine your current life stage as a change leader, and how to integrate your wider change journey through a Change Mindset.

How to use it

Step 1: Use the following questions to explore your overall life experiences so far:

1 Who or what did you want to be like when you were a child, and why?

2 How and when did you transition from imitating others to developing your sense of self?

3 When and how did you identify the unique gifts that differentiate you from others?

4 How did you find permission to activate these deeper ambitions for your own achievements?

5 How do your work and life choices today integrate a sense of purpose and meaning?

6 How much of your life experience have you shared with others as a teacher or guide?

7 What do you hope to be remembered for, and how might your work impact the world?

Step 2: Given your answers above, choose a point that reflects your current life stage. This point may also correlate to your core change archetype. This result can now help you build further skills and awareness to move around the Change Mindset map, learning to draw on the attributes of your secondary archetypes in your journey towards more integrative change leadership.

FIGURE 8.9 The life stage ladder

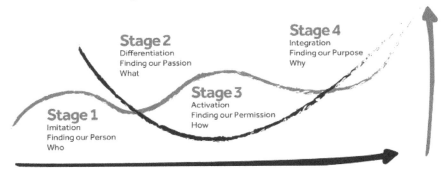

Interpretation

Relatively few adults achieve Stage 4 'integration' during their working careers, and most mid-career professionals will operate successfully at either Stage 2 with clear differentiation or in some cases at Stage 3 using activation to drive more significant change. It is also possible to be a successful professional or leader even at Stage 1 if we are adept at noticing things around us, integrating the views of others, and applying creativity to explore alternatives – all of which are attributes of the imitation stage. The life stage ladder exercise is therefore not an assessment in the sense of achieving a score. Rather, it aims to help us understand who and where we are as agents of change, and invites us to reflect on how evolve to the next level. The key is to use this diagnostic as a way to widen your perspective and challenge your own assumptions about how you behave when faced with uncertainty, individually or collectively.

Actions you can take

There are three transition points where we 'cross the line' between life stages and can use this experience to build our Change Mindset. Here is how you can more deliberately step across these lines from where you are today.

IF YOU ARE AT STAGE 1

The psychological transition you need to make is from imitation to differentiation. When successful, you will experience a feeling of having 'found your voice'. Try these practices to move across the line:

1 Stop imitating other people's ideas, actions or ways of thinking.
2 Seek your essential self by questioning your values and what is important to you.

3 Start to differentiate your views, opinions, and actions from those around you.

4 Create a more unique personal and professional identity by re-labelling yourself.

5 Share this often with others in situations of leadership and change to embed your identity.

IF YOU ARE AT STAGE 2

The psychological transition you need to make is from differentiation to activation. When successful, this will naturally 'manifest' greater permission for you to act on your deeper ambitions. Try these practices to move across the line:

1 Be clear about your differentiated sense of self – who are you, what do you stand for and what are you passionate about?

2 Define and test your strengths – feedback, psychometrics and 360s can be helpful for this.

3 Use these strengths to define how and where you want to drive change more powerfully.

4 Share these goals and ambitions with other people and start to build an 'activation network' for change.

5 Look for practical, measurable ways to raise the bar and be more confident in leading change.

IF YOU ARE AT STAGE 3

The psychological transition you need to make is from activation to integration. When successful, you will find your words and actions impacting a wider context including people, your organization and perhaps even society in important moments of change. Try these practices to move across the line:

1 Begin to reflect on your purpose as it relates to activation – do you have a higher order goal for yourself and others?

2 Find ways to activate this by consolidating your life's experiences towards this vision.

3 Begin to engage others in this sense purpose to help them also make meaning during change.

4 Seek out more courageous change pathways that can also change the way others think.

5 Move beyond the self to 'we' through advocacy, purpose and sharing your vision with others.

Conclusion

Mastering change powerfully is not an easy task, but my hope for you is that the frameworks and stories in this book, and the tools in this chapter, will equip you and those around you to build your own more powerful Change Mindset.

As we have seen, change masters can be of any age (a teenager like Greta Thunberg or the writer Charles Handy at well over 80), any profession (data expert Demis Hassabis or medical surgeon Sir Peng Khaw), and any culture (Afro-Caribbean social entrepreneur Annmarie Lewis or Japanese media executive Ken Munekata).

But irrespective of their particular age and background, change masters will always use their Change Mindset to provoke and influence change in their own unique way (Martin Gayford and Gillian Tett are both writers but influence their respective audiences in very different ways).

The key point is that we all have the power to be change masters if we choose to remain open, curious, courageous and empathetic while building our Change Mindset.

And in our VUCA world, a Change Mindset to navigate transitions is becoming more than just a choice.

As Sir Andrew Likierman reminds us: 'Transitions used to be voluntary acts of change, today they are a necessary part of our existence. Life must be a series of changes and transitions.'

Taking the time to build your Change Mindset

If transitions and change today are a necessary part of our existence, how can we also make the time to build these essential skills for our own Change Mindset? Just reacting to the daily demands of work, life, family and well-being can take up most of our available hours, leaving little time for practicing change skills.

Once again, the ancient Greeks come to our aid. We all know *kronos*, which is defined as time governed by the chronological flow of hours. But the Greeks also have another word for time, *kairos*, which is 'time governed by quality and flow.' This intriguing notion suggests there is a different way to consider time and how we spend it. Switching from *kronos* to *kairos* can offer us a powerful first step towards practicing change skills and using the time we have in more purposeful ways.

So let us thoughtfully embrace our individual and collective transitions with *kairos* and build our Change Mindset skills through open eyes, deliberate practice and conscious choice, always asking:

- Who am I being in this change situation?
- What unique value can I bring to it?
- How can I move faster into action?
- Do my actions fit my purpose and values and answer the question, 'Why?'

By posing these simple questions the next time you are faced with a major transitional challenge, you will have just taken your first step to building a more powerful Change Mindset.

I wish you success!

CHAPTER NINE

Dramatis personae: Lessons from powerful leaders on navigating change

In order to build the theories, frameworks and toolkits in this book I spoke to over two dozen senior leaders from a range of disciplines including business, science, journalism, academia, politics, conservation, media, design and the arts. Their own experiences of transitional change greatly helped in building and validating the Change Mindset model, the role of courage and empathy in navigating transitions, and the FAIL and SPARK practices.

These generous and exceptional people all volunteered their time and insights to contribute to this project, and I am indebted to them for their honesty and candour. Here they share their key lessons learned about navigating complex change, and one piece of advice for others seeking to build their own Change Mindset.

Management and leadership

Gillian Tett – anthropologist, author and Chair of the Editorial Board and US editor-at-large, the Financial Times, *New York, USA*

TOP THREE CHANGE LESSONS LEARNED

1 Find a passion in life and pursue it with an inner obsession.

2 Kick back against expectations to find what is hidden within you.
3 Don't avoid plan B or C – setbacks are gifts that hold learning.

ONE PIECE OF ADVICE FOR OTHERS
'Give yourself permission to roam and collide with the unexpected.'

Charles Handy CBE – social philosopher, management writer and founding Professor, London Business School, London, UK

TOP THREE CHANGE LESSONS LEARNED

1 Have the courage and imagination to define what you want to be.
2 Every setback is an opportunity to create something new.
3 Stay close to your soul.

ONE PIECE OF ADVICE FOR OTHERS
'Move house.'

Dr Mee-Yan Cheung Judge – founder, Quality and Equality Ltd and Academic OD Practitioner, Oxford, UK

TOP THREE CHANGE LESSONS LEARNED

1 Start with your gifts.
2 Use yourself as an instrument of change.
3 Always have compassion.

ONE PIECE OF ADVICE FOR OTHERS
'Be the change you want to see.'

Barry Oshry – founder of Power+Systems, writer and consultant, Boston, USA

TOP THREE CHANGE LESSONS LEARNED

1 Creativity is at the heart of change and transition.
2 The ultimate act of change is to create a social transformation.
3 Always seek to understand *'the other'*.

ONE PIECE OF ADVICE FOR OTHERS
'Change is about illuminating other people – turning the lights on when they thought they already were.'

Academia and education

Jules Goddard – Fellow at London Business School and member of the council of The Royal Institute of Philosophy, London, UK

TOP THREE CHANGE LESSONS LEARNED

1 Make it a practice to be a contrarian.
2 Self-reinvention is the key to avoid losing confidence in society and in ourselves.
3 Don't ignore what history and philosophy can teach us about leadership and change.

ONE PIECE OF ADVICE FOR OTHERS
'Keep defining a more challenging periphery for yourself.'

Sir Andrew Likierman – former dean and Professor of Management at London Business School, London, UK

TOP THREE CHANGE LESSONS LEARNED

1 Find and then use your natural gifts.
2 Welcome opportunities, and then figure out the 'how'.
3 Don't commit to deliver anything that is not thoroughly researched.

ONE PIECE OF ADVICE FOR OTHERS
'Transitions used to be voluntary acts of change, today they are a necessary part of our existence. Life today must be a series of changes and transitions.'

Professor Amy Edmondson – Novartis Professor of Leadership and Management at Harvard Business School, Boston, USA

TOP THREE CHANGE LESSONS LEARNED

1 Say we live in a VUCA world but we go about our lives as if it weren't.

2 Human nature makes the right behaviors really hard.
3 Remember that enquiry is a rare beast.

ONE PIECE OF ADVICE FOR OTHERS
'Psychological safety is key to navigating change with confidence.'

Professor Niro Sivanathan – Associate Professor of Organizational Behaviour at London Business School, London, UK

TOP THREE CHANGE LESSONS LEARNED

1 Unconscious bias plays a key role in our ability to navigate change.
2 Always check your assumptions – are you just protecting the status quo?
3 You have to take the risk of being wrong in order to succeed at change.

ONE PIECE OF ADVICE FOR OTHERS
'Don't be afraid to drop your tools.'

Health and life sciences

Professor Sir Peng Tee Khaw – director, National Institute for Health Research Biomedical Research Centre at Moorfields Eye Hospital and UCL Institute of Ophthalmology, London, UK

TOP THREE CHANGE LESSONS LEARNED

1 Always balance passion with compassion.
2 Align your actions to your strongest true purpose.
3 Listen and be curious to find out about other people.

ONE PIECE OF ADVICE FOR OTHERS
'Get yourself into the conversations that can change the lives of people on the planet.'

Laura McKeaveney – former Global Head of Patient Engagement and Global Head of Human Resources at Novartis Pharmaceuticals, Basel, Switzerland

TOP THREE CHANGE LESSONS LEARNED

1 Be the person who breaks the spell to get others moving.

2 Practice self-empathy – where are you, what have your learned, what's next?

3 It can be very satisfying to be right but it can be even more satisfying to be kind.

ONE PIECE OF ADVICE FOR OTHERS
'When there is an opportunity, just give it a shot.'

Business and technology

Arthur Bastings – founder and CEO, Arthur Bastings Collective and former president and MD at Discovery Communications, Singapore

TOP THREE CHANGE LESSONS LEARNED

1 Learn to seek and accept feedback.
2 Move towards the friction and use it to make things happen.
3 Take your own development seriously because you can't delegate it.

ONE PIECE OF ADVICE FOR OTHERS
'Our teachers can be many things, so be open to them.'

Lisa Robinson Davis – Vice President Quality and Compliance at PetSmart, Phoenix, USA

TOP THREE CHANGE LESSONS LEARNED

1 Learn how to be quiet so you can hear others.
2 Always challenge your own leadership style and your preconceptions.
3 When change occurs, get out of your comfort zone and step into new spaces.

ONE PIECE OF ADVICE FOR OTHERS
'When the time is right, your voice will be heard.'

Ken Munekata – former MD of Sony Pictures Japan and entrepreneur, Tokyo, Japan

TOP THREE CHANGE LESSONS LEARNED

1 Avoid the trap of your position becoming your identity.

2 Always take one small step beyond what you are already doing.
3 There is always more than one correct answer.

ONE PIECE OF ADVICE FOR OTHERS
'Go and see for yourself.'

Masao Takiyama – film producer and media executive, Tokyo, Japan

TOP THREE CHANGE LESSONS LEARNED

1 Find your passion early in life.
2 Be confident about your intuition and act on it with courage.
3 Always remain adaptable and open-minded, because things move fast.

ONE PIECE OF ADVICE FOR OTHERS
'Raise your hand.'

Stacey Cartwright – former CEO of Harvey Nichols, CFO of Burberry and non-executive director, Dubai, UAE

TOP THREE CHANGE LESSONS LEARNED

1 Don't be afraid to move from safety to risk – this is often when we learn the most.
2 Finding passion and excitement in what you do is what will give you the courage to lead.
3 When feeling trapped, do three things: recognize what is happening, seek advice from people you trust, and really listen so you hear what they are telling you.

ONE PIECE OF ADVICE FOR OTHERS
'Define what you really want your life to look like, and then work backwards.'

Banking, finance and professional services

Peter Hogarth – founder of The Change Partnership and executive coach, London, UK

TOP THREE CHANGE LESSONS LEARNED

1 Always push the boundaries of where you can be taken seriously.
2 Ask yourself what you would do if you had absolutely no fear.
3 Eliminate your self-limiting beliefs.

ONE PIECE OF ADVICE FOR OTHERS
'The most important thing is to follow your soul.'

Calvin Jackson – barrister-at-law, executive pay advisor and author on executive remuneration, London, UK

TOP THREE CHANGE LESSONS LEARNED

1 Be intellectually curious and always try new things.
2 Work hard, be tenacious, dedicated and honourable.
3 Make sure you have a point of view and lose any fear of speaking it out.

ONE PIECE OF ADVICE FOR OTHERS
'Our higher duty is to do whatever you can to move the debate forward.'

Social enterprise, conservation and NGOs

Annmarie Lewis OBE – Head of Culture and Leadership, Youth Custody Service and founder of Rainmakers Worldwide, London, UK

TOP THREE CHANGE LESSONS LEARNED

1 Recognize and learn from the pivotal markers in your early life.
2 Stay close to those trusted people who remind you who you are, both the good and bad.
3 Find your calling and use its focus and passion to create the opportunities that will shape your destiny.

ONE PIECE OF ADVICE FOR OTHERS
'When you surrender to your calling, the doors fly open. As soon as you put yourself first, they will slam shut again'

Martin Lutyens – chairman of the UK and US Lutyens Trusts and former trustee at Glyndebourne, Gloucestershire, UK

TOP THREE CHANGE LESSONS LEARNED

1 Keep your mind open by having broad outside interests.
2 If you ever ask 'Is there more to life?' move on immediately.
3 Look after your people because it frees them up to do their best.

ONE PIECE OF ADVICE FOR OTHERS
'Throw away the cue cards.'

Charles Miller – founder of The Children's Initiative, educator and accidental entrepreneur, Portland, USA

TOP THREE CHANGE LESSONS LEARNED

1 Embrace change at every stage of life, because we are all 'sailing to Byzantium'.
2 We are all imposters but the trick is to follow opportunities regardless.
3 Discard the uniform and allow yourself to be who you really are.

ONE PIECE OF ADVICE FOR OTHERS
'Focus on the experience, not the outcome.'

Government and politics

Lord Parry Mitchell – Member of the House of Lords and technology entrepreneur, London, UK

TOP THREE CHANGE LESSONS LEARNED

1 Work hard to be a contender.
2 Don't assume everyone else is like you.
3 Be prepared for failures and make sure you learn from them.

ONE PIECE OF ADVICE FOR OTHERS
'There is a different *you* in there if you look for it.'

Fashion, art and design

Martin Gayford – art historian and author, Cambridge, UK

TOP THREE CHANGE LESSONS LEARNED

1 Find what you are shaped to do, and then have the courage to walk away from what isn't you.
2 Don't think something is good just because it's yours.
3 Failure is a staging post on the way to success.

ONE PIECE OF ADVICE FOR OTHERS
'You have to sacrifice something in order to make things happen.'

Fred Prysquel. – designer and creator of Vilebrequin Fashion, Saint Tropez, France

TOP THREE CHANGE LESSONS LEARNED

1 Always follow your instincts.
2 Be prepared to be a contrarian.
3 When you see an opportunity or a gap in the market, move fast to own it.

ONE PIECE OF ADVICE FOR OTHERS
'*Il faut toujours avoir un plan, mais sans avoir un plan.*' 'You must always have a plan, but without having a plan.'

Siobhan Stanley – executive coach and artist, Hastings, UK

TOP THREE CHANGE LESSONS LEARNED

1 Listen for the moments when you might shed your skin.
2 Be clear on what to say yes to and what to decline.
3 Tune the radio back onto your station.

ONE PIECE OF ADVICE FOR OTHERS
'Life is a series of delicious accidents.'

Conclusion

This book is built on three pillars that create the framework to build a Change Mindset.

- Behavioural psychology and neuroscience
- Consulting and coaching experience
- Personal life experience.

In this last category, I have drawn heavily on my own change journey to create this book. I reflected on how and why I may have succeeded or failed when facing changes that were mostly beyond my control at various stages of life.

What lessons have I learned? I grew up in an international family with a French mother and South African father and so was faced early on with the questions of who, what, how and why. Living in South Africa, Canada, Switzerland, France, the US and the UK over the years has posed the question repeatedly of where my cultural roots are, my values, priorities, and my sense of belonging.

In the 1970s global travel was the exception for young people like me, and so leaving friends behind as I moved through a series of schools in new countries were fairly definitive experiences, and many people I had known faded quickly into the background. Today, Facebook, LinkedIn and Easyjet keep our global networks close by our side and in view, but before the internet and cheap travel life was very different. As a result, I had to learn how to make new friends after each move, adopt the culture, and often become conversant in a new language. I learned early on to let go of people and places without judgment, to join new groups fast and with an open mind, and to be observant and malleable enough to pick up cultural and behavioural signals quickly in order to fit in. I had to accept new rituals, norms and attitudes without prejudice. Sometimes this was easy – like when I joined an international school in Switzerland full of kids with similar experiences. Other moves were more difficult, including a family move to Apartheid-era South Africa as a teenager, after a liberal upbringing in Europe and North America. Even as a relatively privileged white male at university in Johannesburg, I found the frequent presence of riot police on campus unnerving. The routine arrests and 'banning' of student friends deemed a 'danger to the State' for their statements or demonstrations against racism or social issues was shocking to me. My previous school in Switzerland comprised dozens of nationalities and ethnic backgrounds and even had its own Student United Nations, the S.U.N., that routinely debated international issues and the politics of the day.

My reaction as a 20-year-old student – more naive at that age than seriously political – was to form a musical group that quickly became multiracial and included players like Jack Lerole who later featured on Paul Simon's multi-million selling *Graceland* album. Even indirect protest was frowned upon by the authorities and the police often broke up our concerts with dogs and in combat gear as we played in clubs and festivals around the country. We were routinely stopped and questioned when we drove our bandmates home at night to the outskirts of Soweto and while I was probably never in real danger, the experience was still unnerving.

I eventually left South Africa after graduation while the band, christened *Mango Groove*, went on to garner international success combining swing, jazz and the township *kwela* style we had begun with. But I was heading for New York. I was 25, had a one-way plane ticket in one pocket, $500 in American Express traveller's cheques in the other and my 1970 Fender Stratocaster along with my suitcase. But I wasn't planning on furthering my musical career in America. Rather, I had written a personal letter to each of the *Fortune* top 50 CEOs announcing my imminent arrival on their shores and asking for a job in 'business'. I had copied their names and the addresses of their corporate headquarters from the university library copies of *Fortune*, and had cajoled my mother with her electric typewriter into typing up the letters for me.

Needless to say, no one wrote back offering me a job. I did receive two polite rejection letters (Merrill Lynch and Marsh McLennan) and one from Dow Jones, who said that I could contact them again 'if you ever happened to be in New York' which they were clearly not expecting. After much badgering from my temporary lodgings in the Bronx I did land an interview there, during which I embarrassed myself by not knowing that the company published *The Wall Street Journal*. This didn't deter me from suggesting that I would make a good journalist, after which the hiring manager patiently explained that only the top few graduates from Columbia Journalism School ever made it into the company each year, and with an unknown degree from a school in Africa that nobody had heard of, I did not qualify. Having been politely shown the door, I further badgered the personnel manager (every day for a month) until she relented and found an opening in 'international personnel' on the flimsy basis that I spoke French and therefore might be useful as the company launched its European edition of *The Wall Street Journal* in Belgium (which was 'Europe, where they speak French, right?').

So having convinced myself the streets were paved with gold in America (mainly from movies, popular music and books as a teenager) I, of course, found the reality quite different. I made countless faux pas in those early years socially and professionally as I tried to find my feet in that complex and contradictory culture, and did so again as I moved to other roles in Boston, Paris, San Francisco, Los Angeles and now London.

But as I look back on these experiences with the benefit of hindsight, I realize they were fundamental to building my own Change Mindset. Letting go, dreaming big, saying yes, realizing when you've failed and always, always asking for advice were key skills without which I would not have survived. Being able to laugh at myself and never assuming I had the answer also proved useful, particularly after two decades residing among the British who will never let you get away with any pretence whatsoever. Now, as a coach and consultant accompanying leaders on their own journeys of change, these lessons and stories are often useful to provoke thinking and challenge assumptions.

But I have by no means arrived. Today I am still building my own Change Mindset and have come to believe that the journey of self-definition continues throughout life, as Charles Handy says. I still have doubts about my origin story and my least favourite question at a cocktail party remains 'Where are you from?' But working through these reflections and undertaking new research on the question of change has helped me compile what I hope will be a helpful roadmap and working toolkit for others facing similar questions.

You can probably guess by now that my own change archetype is a dreamer. I am still energized by curiosity about the world and what is possibile, about other people and what makes them tick, and about how as human beings our complex psychology creates magic and chaos in equal measure.

Aristotle speaks of humans as 'empty vessels' when we are born. It is up to us, then, to fill ourselves with the right attributes and take actions that shape our lives with purpose. In the realm of leading change and transitions, I believe that with courage, empathy and a Change Mindset we can successfully navigate change as dreamers, drivers, shapers and sherpas.

If, in some small way, this book can contribute to what we know already about change and human behaviour, I will have achieved my aim. My wish now is that you too will grasp the opportunities for change that present themselves every day, and manage your own transitions with greater determination and confidence. I hope this will also help you make the difference you seek in the world.

A powerful Change Mindset will be key for all of us to successfully inhabit our VUCA world – personally, professionally, organizationally, financially, socially and even spiritually.

The road from Shigatse

Our change journey in this book started on the road to Shigatse 20 years ago. When I returned to Los Angeles after that trip, I scanned through my proof sheets of Kodak Tri-X film and chose about 30 images that seemed to capture the essence of that remote and thoughtful place: peaks, rivers, pilgrims, temples, monasteries, children, and creeping modernization.

Those large sepia-toned prints went on their own journey from Los Angeles to London, Tuscany, and Paris as I organized shows to share some of the impressions I had experienced. I hoped they might contribute to other efforts to preserve Tibet and its ancient culture of prayer, reflection and compassion. I don't know whether these small gathering achieved this, but when I heard some years later that the Dalai Lama was on his way to Edinburgh for a lecture on Tibetan Buddhism, I decided to donate them. I rolled each print into a long cardboard tube, paid the extra baggage fee, and duly arrived at the conference centre. After the lecture, a saffron-robed monk appeared and ushered me down a hallway, indicating a small side room where I was told to leave the tubes propped against a wall. That was the last I saw or heard of them.

But that particular letting go was easy: I retained the vivid memories of the road to Shigatse and harboured an optimistic hope that those pictures might some day adorn the wall of a Tibetan house in Dharamshala, bringing to its owner a reminder of the space and light of their homeland.

In retrospect, those amateur forays into exploring the wider world of human experience probably seeded the ground for my subsequent vocation to become a kind of organizational anthropologist, accompanying leaders in exploring what change means for them and their people in the world of business and entrepreneurship.

References

Introduction

Tett, G (2009) *Fool's Gold: How Unrestrained Greed Corrupted a Dream, Shattered Global Markets and Unleashed a Catastrophe*, Little Brown, London

Tett, G (2015) *The Silo Effect: Why Every Organisation Needs to Disrupt Itself to Survive*, Little Brown, London

Tett, G (2021) *Anthro-Vision: How Anthropology Can Explain Business and Life*, Random House Business, New York

Chapter 1

Birkinshaw, J (2017) *Fast/Forward: Making Your Company Fit for the Future*, Stanford University Press, Palo Alto

Brower, T (2020) Successful Change Management: 6 Surprising Reasons People Resist Change And How To Motivate Them To Embrace It Instead, *Forbes*, 16 February, available from: https://www.forbes.com/sites/tracybrower/2020/02/16/successful-change-management-6-surprising-reasons-people-resist-change-and-how-to-motivate-them-to-embrace-it-instead/?sh=1ee67c441562 (archived at https://perma.cc/UT9K-THMY) [Last accessed: 3 January 2022]

Codrington, G (2010) TIDES of Change: the five trends disrupting business in the next 5 years, *Tomorrow Today Global*, available from: https://www.tomorrowtodayglobal.com/2009/12/03/after-shock-the-five-trends-disrupting-business-in-the-next-5-years/ (archived at https://perma.cc/Z3XV-GCWA) [Last accessed: 28 October 2021]

Criado Perez, C (2020) *Invisible Women: Data bias in a world designed for men*, Vintage, London

De Smet A, Dowling B, Mysore M, Reich A (2021) It's Time for Leaders to Get Real About Hybrid, *McKinsey Quarterly Report* (online) McKinsey & Company, available from: https://www.mckinsey.com/business-functions/people-and-organizational-performance/our-insights/its-time-for-leaders-to-get-real-about-hybrid (archived at https://perma.cc/T6JB-GAWB) [Last accessed 1 November 2021]

Edmondson, A (1999) Psychological Safety and Learning Behavior in Work Teams, *Administrative Science Quarterly* [44] (2), pp 350–383

Edmondson, A (2018) *The Fearless Organization: Creating Psychological Safety in the Workplace for Learning, Innovation, and Growth*, Wiley, New York

Edmondson, A (2021) Interview with the author, A Craggs, 20 May 2021

Ferguson, N (2021) *Doom: The Politics of Catastrophe*, Penguin Press, New York

Gratton, L & Scott A (2017) *The 100-Year Life: Living and Working in an Age of Longevity,* Bloomsbury Business, London

Heffernan, M (2011) *Wilful Blindness: Why we Ignore the Obvious at our Peril*, Simon & Schuster, New York

Heffernan, M (2017) Fear of losing a top spot at work will hinder you, *Financial Times*, 20 February, available from: https://www.ft.com/content/1e997d4e-f43b-11e6-8758-6876151821a6 (archived at https://perma.cc/47JN-4BRW) [Last accessed: 3 January 2022]

Leher, J (2011) The Value of Simulation, *Wired*, 29 June, available from: https://www.wired.com/2011/06/the-value-of-simulation (archived at https://perma.cc/J8BG-NXXE) [Last accessed: 3 January 2022]

Nicolaou, E (2020) Kitty O'Meara, Author of 'And the People Stayed Home', Opens Up About Writing That Viral Poem, *Oprah Daily*, 19 March, available from: www.oprahdaily.com/entertainment/a31747557/and-the-people-stayed-home-poem-kitty-omeara-interview (archived at https://perma.cc/37M3-GQVR) [Last accessed: 3 January 2022]

Rozovsky, J (2015) The 5 Keys to a Successful Google Team, *Re:work*, 17 November, available from: https://rework.withgoogle.com/blog/five-keys-to-a-successful-google-team (archived at https://perma.cc/LMK4-83FB) [Last accessed: 1 November 2021]

Taleb, N (2007) *The Black Swan: The impact of the highly improbable*, Random House, New York

Turkle, S (1984) *The Second Self: computers and the human spirit*, The MIT Press, New York

Turkle, S (2021) *The Empathy Diaries: A memoir*, Penguin Press, New York

Weick, K (1996) Drop Your Tools: An Allegory for Organizational Studies, *Administrative Science Quarterly*, [**41**](2), pp 301–313

Chapter 2

Bridges, W (1991) *Managing Transitions: Making the most of change*, Addison Wesley, Boston

Erikson, E (1950) *Growth and Crises of the Healthy Personality,* Josiah Macy, Jr. Foundation, New York

Frost, R (1916) The Road Not Taken, *Mountain Interval*, Henry Holt & Company, New York

Gratton, L and Scott, A (2016) *The 100-Year Life: Living and working in an age of longevity*, Bloomsbury, London

Jacques, E (1965) Death and the Midlife Crisis, *International Journal of Psychoanalysis* [**46**](4), pp 502–14

Jung, C (1960) *Synchronicity – An Acausal Connecting Principle,* Princeton University Press, Princetown

Jung, C (1969) *Collected Works of C.G. Jung, Volume 9 (Part 2): Aion: Researches Into the Phenomenology of the Self,* Princeton University Press, Princeton

Jung, C (1970) *Collected Works of C.G. Jung, Volume 8: Structure and Dynamics of the Psyche*, Princeton University Press, Princeton

Tett, G (2015) *The Silo Effect: Why Every Organisation Needs to Disrupt Itself to Survive*, Little Brown, London

Yunus, M (1999) *Banker to the Poor: Micro-lending and the battle against world poverty*, PublicAffairs, New York

Chapter 3

Argyris, C (1999) *On Organizational Learning,* Wiley-Blackwell, Oxford

Docter, P (2021) 'Soul' Creators On Passion, Purpose And Realizing You're Enough, *NPR Radio Fresh Air with Terri Gross,* 23 April, available from: https://www.capra dio.org/news/npr/story?storyid=990140919&__cf_chl_jschl_tk__=3GdgCIXim3WS SDU6xKXNJI7XpPwrXnf65d2y3EXUlEM-1639324842-0-gaNycGzNCNE (archived at https://perma.cc/7BLX-N6TK) [Last accessed 4 January 2022]

Gayford, M (2010) *Man With a Blue Scarf: On Sitting for a Portrait by Lucian Freud*, Thames & Hudson, London

Gayford, M (2021) *Spring Cannot be Cancelled: David Hockney in Normandy*, Thames & Hudson, London

Goleman, D (2021) The Purpose Driven Boss, *Korn Ferry*, available from: https://www. kornferry.com/insights/this-week-in-leadership/the-purpose-driven-boss (archived at https://perma.cc/55FG-HKKE) [Last accessed: 3 November 2021]

Gormley, A & Gayford, M (2020) *Shaping the World: Sculpture from Prehistory to Now*, Thames & Hudson, London

Kazantzakis, N (1952) *Zorba the Greek* (translated by Carl Wildman), John Lehmann, London

Kazantzakis, N (1960) *The Last Temptation* (translated by Peter Bien), Simon & Schuster, New York

Markides, C (2021) *Leading in a Disruptive and Disrupted World*, Lecture Series at London Business School

Plato, Apology 38a5-6 (1966) *Plato in Twelve Volumes, Vol. 1* (translated by Harold North Fowler) Harvard University Press, Cambridge, MA or William Heinemann Ltd London

Reyburn, S (2019) A Great Wealth Transfer Is Coming, *New York Times*, 18 December, available from: https://www.nytimes.com/2019/12/18/arts/design/great-wealth-transfer-art.html (archived at https://perma.cc/DEG7-254T) [Last accessed: 3 November 2021]

Tett, G (2021) *Anthro-Vision: How Anthropology can Explain Business and Life*, Random House Business, New York

Chapter 4

Balinbin, A (2021) Empathy is the Skill of the Future, GoogleSays, *BusinessWorld*, 4 February, available from: https://www.bworldonline.com/empathy-is-the-skill-of-the-future-google-says/ (archived at https://perma.cc/F3VW-CAL5) [Last accessed: 24 November 2021]

Bateson, M (2010) *Willing to Learn: Passages of Personal Discovery*, Steerforth Press, Penguin Random House, New York

Brown, B (2012) *Daring Greatly: How the Courage to Be Vulnerable Transforms the Way We Live, Love, Parent, and Lead*, Gotham Books, Sheridan WY

Brown, V (2021) Digital Nomads: The Reality of Running a Business from Anywhere, *Financial Times*, 30 June, available from: https://www.ft.com/content/d54b6064-397d-4fea-ad61-2d24c0e00c32 (archived at https://perma.cc/57K5-YYBC) [Last accessed: 24 November 2021]

Churchill, W (1937) *Great Contemporaries*, Alfonso XIII, Thornton Butterworth, London

Cook, T (2018) The David Rubinstein Show, 13 June [YouTube], available from: https://www.youtube.com/watch?v=2ZfGBGmEpRQ (archived at https://perma.cc/4JBE-E53D) [Last accessed 4 January 2022]

Cundy, A (2021) How to Shine as a Digital Transformation Leader, Financial Times, 10 January, available from: https://www.ft.com/content/e057ed7b-2b4c-44b9-92b2-cbd07522cfe2 (archived at https://perma.cc/93HW-9RHM) [Last accessed: 24 November 2021]

Dewar, C, Keller, S, Sneader, K, Strovink, K (2020) The CEO Moment: Leadership for a New Era, *McKinsey & Company*, 21 July, available from: https://www.mckinsey.com/featured-insights/leadership/the-ceo-moment-leadership-for-a-new-era (archived at https://perma.cc/ZA48-EXAT) [Last accessed: 24 November 2021]

Donne, J (1624) *No Man is an Island*, Devotions upon Emergent Occasions, UK

Duckworth, A (2017) *Grit: Why Passion and Resilience are the Secrets to Success*, Vermillion, London

Durant, W (1926) *The Story of Philosophy*, Simon & Schuster, New York

Fauci, A (2021) On Vaccinations And Biden's Refreshing Approach To COVID-19, *Fresh Air NPR*, 4 February, available from: https://www.npr.org/sections/health-shots/2021/02/04/963943156/fauci-on-vaccinations-and-bidens-refreshing-approach-to-covid-19 (archived at https://perma.cc/62RN-QLTF) [Last accessed: 4 January 2022]

Fink, L (2021) Larry Fink's Letter to CEOs, *BlackRock*, available from: https://www.blackrock.com/corporate/investor-relations/larry-fink-ceo-letter (archived at https://perma.cc/4NLY-JREW) [Last accessed: 24 November 2021]

Foroohar, R (2021) Sherry Turkle: Why was I asked to make Steve Jobs dinner? *Financial Times*, 26 March, available from: https://www.ft.com/content/7a9471e6-434f-4ae0-9ce6-ff3f6e4c597d (archived at https://perma.cc/35TU-GST7) [Last accessed: 24 November 2021]

Gallo, C (2014), The Maya Angelou quote that will radically improve your business, *Forbes*, 31 May, available from: https://www.forbes.com/sites/carminegallo/2014/05/31/the-maya-angelou-quote-that-will-radically-improve-your-business/?sh=6005068c118b (archived at https://perma.cc/JC3U-7SBF) [Last accessed: 4 January 2022]> Note: although attributed to Angelou, according to *Richard Evans' Quote Book*, 1971 (Publisher's Press, ASIN: B000TV5WBW) it is a close paraphrase of an earlier quotation attributed to Carl Buehner: 'They may forget what you said but they will never forget how you made them feel.'

Goodhart, D (2020) *Head, Hand, Heart: Why Intelligence Is Over-Rewarded, Manual Workers Matter, and Caregivers Deserve More Respect*, Allen Lane, London

Jenkins, S (2021) Geoff Crowther, Guidebook Writer, 1944–2021 (d. 13 April 2021), *Financial Times*, 14 May, available from: https://www.ft.com/content/5227b4bd-8df8-4372-8483-c2686e485602 (archived at https://perma.cc/738F-TC6E) [Last accessed: 4 January 2022]

Mathuros, F (2017) Restoring the Compact Between Business and Society, *World Economic Forum*, 18 January, available from: https://www.weforum.org/press/2017/01/restoring-the-compact-between-business-and-society/ (archived at https://perma.cc/PDB7-G594) [Last accessed: 24 November 2021]

Meade, M in Keys, D (1982) *Earth at Omega: Passage to Planetization*, Branden Press, Boston

Montaigne, M (1993) *The complete essays* (M. A. Screech, Ed. and Trans.), Penguin Books, New York

O'Hagan, S (2021 Jane Campion: 'Film-making set me free... it was as if I had found myself', *The Guardian*, 7 November, available from: https://www.theguardian.com/film/2021/nov/07/jane-campion-the-power-of-the-dog-interview (archived at https://perma.cc/252K-24UU) [Last accessed: 4 January 2022]

Rattan, A & Ibarra, H (2021) How mindsets can make all the difference, *Think@LBS Online Magazine*, 9 April, available from: https://www.london.edu/think/how-mindsets-can-make-all-the-difference (archived at https://perma.cc/Y77S-87UK) [Last accessed 3 November 2021]

Rogers, C (1951) *Client-centered Therapy: Its Current Practice, Implications and Theory*, Houghton-Mifflin, Boston

Sneader, K (2020), The Future of Business: 2021 and Beyond, *McKinsey & Company*, 9 December, available from: https://www.mckinsey.com/about-us/covid-response-center/mckinsey-live/webinars/the-future-of-business-2021-and-beyond (archived at https://perma.cc/94HF-65JZ) [Last accessed: 24 November 2021]

Tett, G (2021) *Anthro-Vision: How Anthropology can Explain Business and Life*, Random House Business, New York

Thoreau, H (1854) *Walden or Life in the Woods*, Ticknor & Fields, Boston

Wittgenstein, L (1922) *Tractatus Logico-Philosophicus*, Routledge Kegan Paul, Milton Park

Whyte, D (2012) *Pilgrim*, Many Rivers Press, Langley WA

Chapter 5

Bonham Carter, H, *Financial Times Weekend Festival*, September 2020

Cantor, S (2021) PBS American Masters (2021) *Twyla Moves*, available from: https://www.pbs.org/wnet/americanmasters/twyla-tharp-documentary/16724/ (archived at https://perma.cc/UN2W-T79G) [Last accessed 24 November 2021]

Clance, P, and Imes, S (1978) Impostor Phenomenon in High Achieving Women: Dynamics and Therapeutic Intervention, Psychotherapy: Theory, *Research & Practice Journal*, [15](3), pp 241–247

Grant, A (2021) *Think Again: The Power of Knowing What you Don't Know*, WH Allen, London

Homegardner, T. What Is The Great Resignation And How Will This Affect Job Seekers? *Forbes*, 2 August 2021 https://www.forbes.com/sites/forbescoachescouncil/2021/08/02/what-is-the-great-resignation-and-how-will-this-affect-job-seekers/?sh=1099c99f39c6 (archived at https://perma.cc/7TFG-5KYP) (accessed 25 November 2021)

Johnson, S (1750–52) *The Rambler,* Jones & Company, London

Kennedy, RF. (1966) *Day of Affirmation Address*, University of Cape Town, South Africa

Lawrence, T (1935) *The Seven Pillars of Wisdom*, Alden Press, Oxford

Lythcott-Haims, J (2021) *Your Turn: How to be an Adult*, Henry Holt and Co., New York

Marie, M (2021) 4 Tech Startups Jumping On The Upcycling Trend, *Floww,* 22 June, available from: https://www.floww.io/feed/4-tech-startups-jumping-on-the-upcycling-trend (archived at https://perma.cc/JZY8-4ZNG) [Last accessed: 4 January 2022]

Nelson, S (2019) *Miles Davis: The Birth of Cool*, Netflix, Eagle Rock Entertainment & Firelight Pictures, available from: https://www.netflix.com/gb/title/80227122 (archived at https://perma.cc/75SW-YPWK) [Last accessed: 4 January 2022]

Rock, D (2008) SCARF: A Brain-Based Model for Collaborating With and Influencing Others, *NeuroLeadership Journal*, [1](1), pp 44–52. Available from: http://dcntp.org/wp-content/uploads/2015/03/Readiness_for_change.pdf (archived at https://perma.cc/RSJ7-H7PV) [Last accessed: 4 January 2022]

Ware, B (2012) *The Top 5 Regrets of the Dying: A Life Transformed by the Dearly Departing*, Hay House UK, London

Chapter 6

Chin, J and Chai Vasarhelyi, E with Honnold, A (2018) *Free Solo,* National Geographic Documentary Films

Campbell, J (1949) *The Hero with a Thousand Faces*, Pantheon Books, New York

Cooperrider, D, and Srivastva, S (1987) *Appreciative Inquiry in Organizational Life* in Woodman, R. W. & Pasmore, W.A. (eds.). *Research in Organizational Change And Development., Vol. 1.*, JAI Press, Stamford, CT pp 129–169

Elberse, A (2013) Ferguson's Formula, *Harvard Business Review*, available from: https://hbr.org/2013/10/fergusons-formula (archived at https://perma.cc/4G3J-P346) [Last accessed: 23 December 2021]

Ferguson, J (2021) *Sir Alex Ferguson: Never Give In*, Amazon Prime, DNA Films and Passion Pictures

Frankl, V (1946) *Man's Search for Meaning,* Jugend & Volk, Vienna

Gayford, M (2017) *Michelangelo: His Epic Life*, Penguin UK, London

Hagel, J III (2021) *The Journey Beyond Fear: Leverage the Three Pillars of Positivity to Build your Success*, McGraw-Hill Education, New York

Harrell, E (2021) Life's Work: An Interview with Alex Honnold, *Harvard Business Review*, available from: https://hbr.org/2021/05/lifes-work-an-interview-with-alex-honnold (archived at https://perma.cc/L8HM-X4TD) [Last accessed: 24 November 2021]

Hertzog, W (2010) *Cave of Forgotten Dreams,* IFC Films, Sundance Selects

Hobbes, T (1651) *Leviathan: Or the Matter, Forme and Power of a Commonwealth, Ecclesiasticall and Civil*, Andrew Crooke, London

Lash, J (1981) *Helen and Teacher: The story of Helen Keller and Anne Sullivan Macy*, American Foundation for the Blind Press, New York

Markides, C (2021) *Organizing for the New Normal: Prepare your Company for the Journey of Continuous Disruption*, Kogan Page, London

Peers, J (1980) *1,001 Logical Laws, Accurate Axioms, Profound Principles, Trusty Truisms, Homey Homilies, Colorful Corollaries, Quotable Quotes, and Rambunctious Ruminations*, Fawcett Books Greenwich, CT. Note: designated 'Meade's maxim' but not linked directly to her.

Schein, E (2013) *Humble Inquiry: The Gentle Art of Asking Instead of Telling*, Berrett-Koehler Publishers, Oakland

Whyte, D (1990) *Where Many Rivers Meet: Poems*, Many Rivers Press, Langley WA

Chapter 7

Butler Yeats, W (1928) *Sailing to Byzantium,* Simon & Schuster, London

Cookson, C (2020) Scientists Defend Controversial Head of UK Vaccine Task Force, *Financial Times*, 13 November, available from: https://www.ft.com/content/9f08cd41-c895-4138-ba37-6f9c36fcef31 (archived at https://perma.cc/DC37-BXRM) [Last accessed 25 November 2021]

Ford, H, attributed but not proven to be a direct quote Campbell, J (1949) *The Hero with a Thousand Faces*, Princeton University Press, Princeton

Gierow, K (1971) Nobel Prize for Literature, Ceremony Speech, available from: https://www.nobelprize.org/prizes/literature/1971/ceremony-speech/ (archived at https://perma.cc/9VZR-BRHC) [Last accessed: 4 January 2022]

Greene, R (2021) The Key to Transforming Yourself, TEDxBrixton, [YouTube], available from: https://www.youtube.com/watch?v=gLt_yDvdeLQ (archived at https://perma.cc/XA5X-U9P3) [Last accessed 25 November 2021]

Handy, C (2015) *The Second Curve: Thoughts on Reinventing Society*, Random House, London

Helminski, K (1999) *Rumi Daylight: A Daybook of Spiritual Guidance,* Shambhala Publications, Boulder

Neruda, P (1974) *Confieso Que He Vivido*, Editorial Seix Barral, Barcelona

Oshry, B (2007) *Seeing Systems: Unlocking the Mysteries of Organizational Life*, Berrett Kohler Oakland, CA 2007

Pentland, A (2014) *Social Physics: How Good Ideas Spread – The Lessons from a New Science*, Penguin Press, London

Petit, P (2012) The Journey Across the High Wire, *TED*, available from: https://www.ted.com/talks/philippe_petit_the_journey_across_the_high_wire?language=en (archived at https://perma.cc/5NR2-NZCM) [Last accessed 25 November 2021]

Taylor, A (2014) Japan in the 1950s, *Atlantic Monthly*, available from: https://www.theatlantic.com/photo/2014/03/japan-in-the-1950s/100697/ (archived at https://perma.cc/2NF9-MUJW) [Last accessed: 25 November 2021]

Van Der Leeuw, J (1928) *The Conquest of Illusion*, Alfred A. Knopf, New York. Note: often attributed to Kierkegaard as a slightly altered version of the quote 'The mystery of life is not a problem to be solved; it is a reality to be experienced.'

Chapter 8

Kierkergaard, S (1849) *Kierkegaard's Journals and Notebooks, Volume 4: Journals NB-NB5*, Princeton University Press, Princeton NJ (2011)

Index